# BOOTS ON THE LINE

## WALKING 1000 MILES OF BRITAIN'S DISMANTLED RAILWAYS

### STEPHEN LEWIS

First published 2007 by True To The Line Publications

**ISBN 978-0-9557236-0-5**

Printed and bound by CPI Antony Rowe, Eastbourne

*Broomielaw Station (above), Leaderfoot Viaduct (front cover), Trackbed on The Cairn Valley Railway (back cover)*

# CONTENTS

# CONTENTS

# CONTENTS

# CONTENTS

## SECTION 3 - FURTHER READING AND REFERENCES

# ACKNOWLEDGEMENTS

My first thanks must be to my wife, Ruth, who has uncomplainingly watched me disappear many times to explore 'some old railway line' over the last six years or so. She has also shown great patience, and has been a pillar of support in my efforts in writing this book.

Secondly, I must thank Dave Nolan for dreaming up 'NEDRAT', and walking with me on the first seventeen walks.

Lastly, I must thank my best friend Chris Harrison, for the being with me for every mile of every walk in this book. Without him walking 1000 miles of dismantled railway would not have been possible.

---

*This book is dedicated to all the men of vision and muscle who engineered and built our railways.*

*"One does not sell the earth upon which the people walk"*
**Tashanka Witko (Crazy Horse), Chief, Oglala Sioux (c.1849 – 1877)**

# SECTION 1

# WALKING THE LINE: AN OVERVIEW

# Introduction

This book is about *walking* dismantled railway lines in England and Scotland. It is not a book about driving from one point of interest of an old line, taking a photograph, and then driving to the next point of interest; although I do not dispute the validity of such an approach. The old lines detailed herein have actually been walked, either wholly or as close as possible to the trackbed of the former Permanent Way, with any deviations described in the text. Having walked 1000 miles of dismantled railways, and having accumulated a lot of information and photographs from these explorations, it seemed a fitting landmark to write this account.

All of the routes walked in this book were former standard gauge passenger lines. The primary purpose of this book is to tell the story of our 1000 mile exploration, and subsequently to be a practical route guide to the dismantled railway lines described. This book is aimed at those with a curious nature and a spirit of adventure. The walk descriptions included, should however be read with caution, as our network of dismantled railway lines is in a constant state of change with all manner of influences affecting the state of the old lines. These influences range from the full blown obliteration, right through to re-instatement as a railway or re-use cycle/walkway with a myriad of scenarios in between. In an attempt to humanise the walk descriptions to a degree, I have also included a few anecdotes from our walks, which originally involved three and latterly two friends. Hopefully the atmosphere of, and our approach to walking the old lines is accurately conveyed.

In our early days we employed a somewhat lackadaisical approach to our walks that became steadily more organised over time as our interest (fanaticism?) grew. We also have tried to enjoy ourselves 'après-line' along the way, and indeed we have had many amusing experiences in some obscure 'one-horse' towns across our small, but incredibly diverse country.

I have not attempted to cover the history of our dismantled railways in any detail, as this area is more than adequately covered in many excellent books written by rail historians, some of which are detailed in the recommended further reading list. Many railway features from the walks are described in detail, with some being illustrated by the photographs at the end of each walk description. This book, however, is not an attempt at a 'nice' picture book, although I do hope that the accompanying photographs inspire and inform the reader, whilst helping to capture the essence of dismantled railways and their subsequent on-foot exploration. A few walks have no accompanying photographs due to camera malfunction or the poor quality of the prints.

For those interested, the vast majority of photographs included in this book, have been scanned using a Nikon Coolscan V ED digital scanner, from both black and white and colour 35mm transparancies and negatives. Subsequent manipulation was done using Adobe Photoshop Elements 5.0. A few direct digital images have been included. All photographs are from the author's collection unless otherwise stated.

# The Creation of Britain's Dismantled Railway Network: A Polemic

No one would have believed, in the last years of the nineteenth century that our comprehensive railway network, at that time still undergoing expansion, would be dismantled on an unimaginable scale in less than seventy years.

Railways have been closed almost from the time of their invention, with closures gaining pace post-1900, with early railway closures usually caused by local or regional economic problems, with a steady drip of ad-hoc closures happening across the country almost unnoticed until the 1950s.

It is well documented that the most significant and organised decline of our rail network coincided with the politically encouraged, and inexorable growth of private road transport through the 1950s and 60s. It was, however, not until the early 1960s that rail closures became intensely political, and I dare say that most people have heard of 'The Beeching Axe', if only as a distant memory from a school history lesson. In an alleged attempt to 'save' our ailing railways, the prescribed remedy from Dr. Richard Beeching, the then Chairman of The British Transport Commission, was amputations i.e. close 'non-profitable' parts of the rail system. Dr. Beeching published a report entitled 'The Reshaping of British Railways' on 27th March 1963; a title that even the most devious of today's spin doctors would have been proud of. An alternative, if less snappy, title might have been: 'Using dubious statistics to close large parts of the rail network, to encourage people to buy and use cars'.

Beeching's 'Reshaping' report originally proposed the closing of around 5,000 miles of railway to passengers, and 2,363 stations. These closures, totalling approximately one third of the rail network, were all carefully listed in Appendix 2 of the 'Reshaping Report'. Whenever I look at this list it never ceases to amaze me that it was ever actually compiled and published. Surely, such a sinister list; a pre-determined mass destruction of our rail network should have been 'Classified', 'Confidential', 'Top Secret' or something? The 1960s must have been a strange decade indeed when The People actually allowed this report to be published without mass street protests or a general strike.

In the event not all the closures proposed in Beeching's report actually happened, but a significant mileage of railway and number of stations were closed in a very short time span. Various figures that I have seen suggest an approximate closure 1963 – 1970 of around 4000+ miles, with about 3000+ having been closed between 1950 – 1962 (with a noted spike of 780 miles closed in 1962). Whatever the exact figures may be, the Beeching closures, based on some dubious statistics and biased thinking changed the nature of our railways forever.

Much has been written about Dr. Beeching and the immediate consequences of his report, so I will refrain from detailing them here. If, however, one could use the analogy of a headache, and assuming the problems of Britain's railways in the early 1960s were analogous to a *bad* headache, then the good Dr. Beeching's cure was to cut off the head. Having said all that, and to be fair to Beeching, the real villains of the piece were the 'Road Lobby', championed by the then transport secretary Ernest Marples (who had well documented and significant road interests himself), with Beeching acting merely as an allegedly impartial and objective front-man for a pre-determined policy.

The road-lobby (i.e. the car-makers, oil companies, construction companies and biased politicians) remain all powerful today. Witness the massive, and controversial, expansion of the road network versus the pitiful expansion of the rail network, not to mention the disastrous and disgraceful privatisation of the railways. We are left with the logical conclusion of car-based transport policies and the concomitant rail closure folly: the 'cult of the car'. As recently as 1989, the then Prime Minister Margaret Thatcher, publicly declared her support for the "great car economy", whilst simultaneously showing her extreme disdain towards the railways. It is therefore no surprise that private cars are now ubiquitous across our small island. How many people do you know who do *not* drive or own a car? Cars have long ceased to be just a means of transport. They have, through relentless and clever marketing, transcended into objects of desire to satisfy all manner of human whims, most of which have nothing whatever to do with getting from A to B. This may seem an exaggerated and apocalyptic view, but I would argue that our transport infrastructure, our environment, and the economy would be in a far healthier state had a more measured and unbiased approach been taken by politicians and their Civil Servants back in the mid 1950s and early 1960s. The leviathan that is the road-lobby was successful in dismantling a massive part of our rail network, and we now live with the consequences of a transport free-for-all, so often discussed but never truly addressed by our timid, mealy-mouthed politicians, who run scared from that cruel beast known as 'the motorist', or should that be *'votorist'*. Our great railway pioneers must be turning in their graves.

The above synopsis presents me with a haunting dilemma every time I set foot on the trackbed of some long forgotten railway. Would I rather explore dismantled railway lines as a recreational activity, gaining much personal pleasure, or would I rather see the majority of these lines still functioning as an integrated railway system? My heart seeks the enjoyment of exploration, but my head tells me that the functioning railway is obviously the right answer. I am sure the reader will have a view.

# Walking Dismantled Railways

Little did I know at the time but a casual discussion over a few pints during December 1999 would set in progress a dismantled railway odyssey of a scale then unimagined. I suspect, however, that whilst the majority of such alcohol-assisted occasions end in nothing more than a vague memory the next day, I am also sure that many mountains have been climbed and even continents explored after such verbal doodles in a pub. My suggestion, therefore, to explore the dismantled railway line between Barnard Castle and Darlington, County Durham (Walk I) just after New Year 2000, was accepted by Chris Harrison and Dave Nolan, and was the first step to writing this account.

Why would anyone want to walk dismantled railway lines? This is a difficult question to answer as, the reader's interest will most likely stem from an ethos as unique as their own genetic make-up, so I can only offer a personal explanation.

Having always liked the outdoors, both walking and cycling gave me the practical skills to read maps and sometimes the desire to explore those black dashed lines: "cse of old railway" or "dismantled railway" so faithfully reproduced by the Ordnance Survey. My initial forays were often solitary and ad-hoc affairs. One that stands out in my mind was the exploration in 1986, by mountain bike, of the Cuckoo Line, between Polgate and Heathfield in East Sussex, prior to it's transformation into part of the 'Sustrans' network. Somehow, I subconsciously knew even in the mid-eighties that the old lines had a fascination, and a pull on my imagination that went far beyond just going for a walk or a bike ride.

When it comes to exploring dismantled railway my main motivational forces, are primarily born out of a kind of nostalgia for something that I have missed, something that I wish I could have used for its intended purpose. For me, the old lines just *go somewhere*. That *somewhere* remains unknown until you reach it, with their linear nature having a unique fascination. Unlike climbing a mountain, a dismantled railway line does not reveal itself clearly until you are actually right there, on the trackbed itself. This linearity once gave the line a unique and understood purpose, now long forgotten by most. The spirit of adventure, created by what features lay ahead is integral to my enjoyment. Getting to that *somewhere* always delivers treasures along the way: the ivy-covered tunnel portal gently emerging into view as you enter a cool cutting, the vista offered from a magnificent viaduct, the overgrown station platform or maybe the remains of an old signal box. The list is enormous and varied. The dismantled railway walker will also see, smell, hear and be scratched or stung by the many natural inhabitants who have replaced the trains in this vast linear museum. Wherever your interest lies, I hope this book will encourage and help you in your explorations.

A word of caution is required; although dismantled railway lines are 'flat' by design, the dedicated railway walker will encounter all manner of obstacles, usually man-made but sometimes natural, during their explorations. In the walk descriptions I have tried to detail the main obstacles but minor ones (and there are many) such as small fences are not described.

# Layout and Use of This Book

The walks are presented as chapters in primarily chronological order with some walks being joined together where it seemed appropriate. The walk descriptions are written with the intention of being used in conjunction with the appropriate Ordnance Survey 1:50 000 Landranger (OSLR) maps, with the maps required for each walk being detailed in the Walk Summary at the start of each chapter. Points of interest or importance are detailed by 8-figure alpha-numeric grid references (the two letters are the OS 100 Km grid squares followed by the six-figure grid reference) in brackets in the body of the text, with the first two/three digits being the corresponding OSLR number. Of course nowadays the reader may wish to enter the grid references into the 'Get-a-Map' feature available on The Ordnance Survey website, and follow a walk electronically.

There is also a 'PGAG' reference in the Walk Summary at the start of each walk. This refers to page numbers in: 'The British Railways Pre-Grouping Atlas and Gazetteer', published by Ian Allan (see further reading list for details). This excellent little book gives an excellent overview of our railway network before the 'grouping' of 1923 when 'the big four' railway companies i.e. GWR, LNER, LMS & SR were formed. With this book in one hand, and an OS map in the other, the reader should soon see the extent of dismantled lines across our green and pleasant land.

At the start of each walk chapter I have also included a brief section of highlights, usually consisting of railways features, that the walker will encounter along the way. There is also a brief section on public transport. Apart from wanting to use public transport out of principle, the linear nature of dismantled railway walking often makes the use of a car awkward, so the obscure, heavily subsidised rural bus is a real boon for the dismantled railway walker.

# Equipment For The Dismantled Railway Walker

Walking dismantled railways presents a few extra challenges that the rambler will rarely encounter, usually in the form of overgrowth and other obstacles. The table below details my 'essential list' for a day walk where camping out is not required.

*Table 1 - Equipment for the Dismantled Railway Walker*

| |
|---|
| Walking boots (robust, waterproof – leather recommended) |
| Gaiters to fit boots (robust, waterproof) |
| Long, hard wearing trousers (combat-style trousers ideal) |
| Long sleeved hard wearing shirt (green or drab colours recommended) |
| Jacket – an old combat jacket is ideal (green or drab colours recommended) |
| Cap and woolly hat |
| Tough leather gloves (gardening or builders gloves ideal) |
| Waterproof jacket and overtrousers (green or drab colours recommended) |
| Good quality rucksack about 40 litres capacity (green or drab colours recommended) |
| Sunglasses and/or safety spectacles (handy when negotiating dense undergrowth) |
| Torch and spare batteries (for tunnels – headtorch ideal) |
| First aid kit including foot care kit |
| 1 x 8ft climbing sling (handy for getting over awkward fences etc.) |
| Camera, spare film, batteries etc. |
| Lightweight binoculars or monocular |
| OS map and waterproof map case |
| Notebook and pencil |
| Pocket knife (Swiss Army type ideal) |
| Roll of 'duck tape' (handy for all manner of repairs) |
| Food and drink for the day, including treats and snacks |

# Access to Dismantled Railways

The condition and access rights of any given stretch of dismantled railway since closure varies enormously. From a legal point of view, access to dismantled railways can be divided into two areas: England (and Wales) and Scotland.

## 1. England (and Wales)

Some substantial progress has been made, chiefly by Sustrans (www.sustrans.co.uk) and some local authorities, in opening dismantled railways to the public. However, the vast majority of the dismantled railways in England still have little or no right of public access.

You will have to either seek permission from landowners before you go, seek permission as you go, or be prepared to just have a wander. If you choose the latter course, and as long as you do not damage anything or impede a lawful activity, you should be OK, as simple trespass is not a criminal offence, and most landowners are not usually motivated to take any action other than to tell you to leave their land. If you did happen to find yourself on a dismantled railway line that has no public access, it is best to go quietly and try not to be seen, and if you are seen wear a smile and be courteous. I would, however, like to stress that whatever the reader decides to do regarding access, it is solely their responsibilty, and that inclusion of a walk in this book does not imply that it is a public right of way.

## 2. Scotland

Scotland is way ahead of England in terms of public access to the land, with the Land Reform (Scotland) Act 2003 now enshrining in law a traditionally progressive and tolerant approach. In England the presumption is: no public access unless you are on a right of way, a permissive path or on 'access land' (as defined in the Countryside and Rights of Way Act 2000 – see www.countryside.gov.uk/access), Scotland has the presumption of public access unless there is a good reason otherwise. The 'Scottish Outdoor Access Code' (an excellent publication – see further reading and references) requires tolerance and responsibility from landowners and the public alike. This makes the vast majority of the dismantled railway network legally accessible north of the border.

The condition of the trackbed whether publicly accessible or otherwise varies from tarmac (e.g. cycleway) to impenetrable overgrowth. My favourite is somewhere in between, where the line is not in regular public use, but with a bit of effort can be walked and explored. Whatever your preference it is better to understand both the practical and legal aspects of access before setting out.

# Boots or Slippers?

Finally, whether you are an active railway walker or an armchair enthusiast, I hope that the walk descriptions of the dismantled railways in this book provoke a thought or two. With the walks spanning Britain from the far north of Scotland to the south of England, I hope that some interest or enjoyment can be gleaned by most readers.

I can honestly say that I have had an immeasurable amount of pleasure over the last six years or so, and every one of those 1000 miles walked has provided mc with many lasting memories. Some may wonder what my most favourite line has been. The answer is without question: The Waverley Route and its branches. Whatever your favourite line may be, I hope you enjoy and appreciate what the Railwaymen, both engineers and labourers alike, gave to us.

# SECTION 2

# 1000 MILES OF DISMANTLED RAILWAY

# Walk Orientation Map

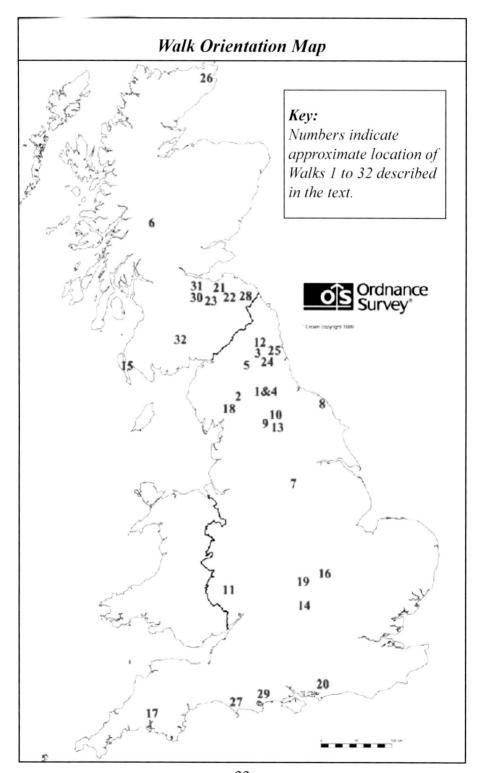

**Key:**
*Numbers indicate approximate location of Walks 1 to 32 described in the text.*

Ordnance Survey®

* Crown copyright 1999

# WALK I
# The South Durham & Lancashire Union Railway
# (Barnard Castle to Darlington)

| Walk Summary | |
|---|---|
| Date walked | 3rd January 2000 |
| Line mileage | 15 ½ |
| OSLR Maps | 92,93 |
| Opened to Passengers | 08 07 1856 |
| Closed to Passengers | 30 11 1964 |
| PGAG Reference | 27 & 28 |
| Pre-Grouping Company | North Eastern Railway |

**Walk Highlights**

Broomielaw Station and Signalbox, Winston Station, West Tees Bridge, and Gainford Bridge.

**Public Transport**

Barnard Castle can be reached from Darlington town centre by Arriva buses 75 and 76. Darlington is on the East Coast Main Line (ECML).

**Walk Description**

It was a bright and frosty morning when I met Chris and Dave outside the 'Jet' petrol station in Barnard Castle for our inaugural walk. The cold morning helped dissipate that vague feeling one has after the New Year festivities.

Our starting point was the perimeter fence of the GSK pharmaceutical plant (92 NZ 058176), that was easily reached by a public footpath. The monolithic plant sits right across the line where the public footpath goes under the dismantled Barnard Castle to Bishop Auckland Line (see Walk IV) via a small stone overbridge (92 NZ 058176). The Barnard Castle to Darlington Line, heading east across fields, was easily accessed beside the embankment of the bridge. The railway junction, Barnard Castle Station, and surrounding lines have been erased by the GSK plant and associated car parks. Only Barnard Castle Station House (92 NZ 054174) remains as a private house, predictably being called 'Station House', and has sadly been incorporated into surrounding housing developments. No trace of the level crossing remained, however the GSK staff canteen is called (or was in 1997) 'The Crossing', as a vestigial reference to the old line. I wondered if any customers ever pondered the historic origins implied in the canteen's title whilst munching their subsidised snacks.

From the bridge the trackbed was clear and grassy making easy walking to the A688 (92 NZ 063175), where no signs of the original level crossing remained. The line proceeded in a north-easterly direction until reaching the signalbox and Broomielaw Station (92 NZ 083182). The signalbox eased into view, and was largely intact, if somewhat skeletal with missing windows resembling oblong eye sockets. Broomielaw Station was less easy to spot until arrival at the platform end, for even in January the undergrowth was considerable. Broomielaw Station was a Halt originally built to allow the Royal Train to drop off members of the Royal Family to the nearby (now demolished) Streatlam Castle, and latterly to allow soldiers stationed at the nearby Stainton Camp to travel to and from Darlington.

Our arrival at Broomielaw still remains one of my most evocative and haunting memories gained from our railway explorations. On the overgrown stone platform was a redbrick base with intact wooden canopy, weathered and bleached white, like some ancient skeleton. Outlines of LNER posters could just be made out on original notice boards, giving the faintest hint of the structure's original purpose. A doorframe had 'LNER' embossed in the paintwork; a shadow remaining from original lettering that had no doubt been removed by a souvenir hunter.

From Broomielaw Station the line continued east across a farm track with public access (line in-filled) past the old army barracks of Stainton Camp. The grassy trackbed was flat or slightly embanked, and easily walked until the minor road at Little Newsham village (92 NZ 126179), where the road crossing was in-filled but easily negotiable. After another 1½ miles of easy walking on a clear trackbed we reached the site of Winston Station (92 NZ 139177). We had to box round the station site in adjacent fields as it was now home, ironically, to a road haulage company. The station building, a substantial structure with rendered white walls complete with 'WINSTON' in large white letters, was in use as an office. Even the station clock was present. Sadly, since our visit the station building has been demolished, with a private house built in its place. The substantial stone engine shed remains, however, still giving good service to the truckers.

After crossing the B6274 the trackbed continued east, passing under a redundant stone bridge straddling the line (92 NZ 145179). We reached the line's first significant cutting near Langley Beck (92 NZ 153178) which was dotted with seed bins for feeding pheasants, and judging by the spent shotgun cartridges littering the trackbed, was obviously in use for bird-killing activities. The cutting gave way to a well walked embankment and soon descended to the A67 (92 NZ 156175), as no trace remained of the overbridge. A short length of public footpath took us to West Tees Bridge, an impressive 4-span stone viaduct over the River Tees (92 NZ 157173), offering good views up and down the river, with access to the viaduct being easy via a gap in the security fence. Beyond West Tees Bridge the trackbed melted into arable fields. Just west of Gainford village the line crossed the Tees via Gainford Bridge (92 NZ 164169), another grand 4-span stone viaduct which was unfenced and easily negotiated. The trackbed at the eastern end of the viaduct disappeared into a ploughed field, forcing us to skirt the edge of the field to the edge of Gainford. The afternoon had turned cloudy and chilly, so we had some lunch in the bus shelter in Gainford. The now private dwelling of Gainford Station House and part of the platform remained, being situated in the centre of the village on the north side of the A67 (92 NZ 168171).

After lunch we regained the line via a stone bridge (92 NZ 177173). Unfortunately we had to deviate round a field to a bridleway heading north at this point as a man, boy, and dog were engaging in a bit of pheasant killing along the alignment of the trackbed. After a detour to the north we managed to regain the line via a public footpath that bisected a quiet cutting (92 NZ 189168). Our detour meant that we missed the junction of the Forcett freight branch (92 NZ 187169), but a subsequent visit has confirmed that it is visible, and easily walked. Another redundant stone overbridge straddled the line near White Cross (92 NZ 198166), over a boggy but passable cutting. With the light beginning to fade, we followed the line east across open country until reaching an animal feed plant (93 NZ 204164) where the trackbed was obliterated. After skirting the plant, and crossing a minor road, the line disappeared under arable land, necessitating some dead reckoning across a field until reaching the B6275, just north of Piercebridge Station (93 NZ 213162). The grand, although largely unrecognisable station house, was in use as a boarding kennels. A careful box-round of the station behind a screen of pines took us past an impenetrable cutting (93 NZ 215163). To the east of the minor road north of Carlbury, the line once again had succumbed to agricultural pressures before crossing another minor road (93 NZ 226164), to re-appear as a good grassy trackbed. Proceeding carefully in the gloaming we disturbed numerous roosting pheasants that screeched out their loud alarm calls, before flying off in a feathered panic in all directions. The line passed under the A1(M) on the outskirts of Darlington (93 NZ 256164), before skirting the Branksome housing estate. The line from the Branksome estate has now been surfaced with tarmac forming a cycle route to the Bishop Auckland branch line near the Rise Carr area of Darlington (93 NZ 285165).

The gloaming gave way to darkness as we arrived at Chris's Mum's for tea. Later that evening over a few pints in a Darlington hostelry, we excitedly recounted the days exploits, and agreed that our walk had been a resounding success. Plans were hurriedly made for further exploration of dismantled railway lines, and we agreed upon the eastern section of The South Durham & Lancashire Union Railway between Kirby Stephen and Bowes.

*The signal box at Broomielaw Station (92 NZ 083182) remains largely intact, but a worrying hole in the roof will inevitably hasten the demise of the structure.*

*Echos of the past on a door frame at Broomielaw Station.*

*Winston Station (92 NZ 139177) complete with station clock, has sadly been demolished since this photgraph was taken.*

*The fine structure of West Tees Bridge (92 NZ 157173).*

# WALK II
## The South Durham & Lancashire Union Railway
## (Kirkby Stephen to Bowes – 'The Stainmore Route')

| Walk Summary | |
|---|---|
| Date walked | March 2000 |
| Line mileage | 16 ¾ |
| OSLR Maps | 91, 92 |
| Opened to Passengers | 04 07 1861 |
| Closed to Passengers | 22 01 1962 |
| PGAG Reference | 31 |
| Pre-grouping Company | North Eastern Railway |

**Walk Highlights**

Stone viaducts: Podgill, Merrygill, and Hatygill, Belah Signalbox, Belah Valley, Barras Station, the crossing of Stainmore Summit and the beautiful moorland scenery.

**Public Transport**

Kirkby Stephen Station is on the Settle to Carlisle line, between Leeds and Carlisle. Bowes is served by Arriva buses service 79 to Barnard Castle or Richmond, North Yorkshire, with subsequent bus connections to Darlington (on ECML).

**Walk Description**

It was a gloriously sunny March morning as we drove over the Pennines to our starting point at Kirkby Stephen. We had decided that this walk would entail an overnight stop, at an unknown location. To keep our pack weight down we decided to forgo a tent, so we would have to find a rudimentary shelter for the night. I had a vague idea that we could find one of the refuges used by Pennine Way walkers and sleep there. Remarkably, neither Chris nor Dave queried my somewhat Gung-Ho approach to a night out in the open on The Pennines in March!

After leaving the car in the pleasant market town of Kirkby Stephen, we quickly accessed the line by a bridleway from the B6279 that crossed the line on a stone overbridge (91 NY 776075), about ½ mile east of Kirkby Stephen East Station (91 NZ 769075). Kirkby Stephen East is undergoing restoration work, and is now home to a heritage railway organisation known as 'The Stainmore Railway Company', and is well worth a visit. Details can be found at: www.kirkbystepheneast.co.uk.

The trackbed from the bridge was muddy but clear of vegetation as it had been trampled by cattle. About ½ mile of easy walking took us to the 11-arched Podgill viaduct (91 NY 782079), constructed in stone and 155 yards long. From Podgill Viaduct the line entered a clear cutting, skirting Hartley Castle. At the end of this cutting was the 9-arched Merrygill viaduct (91 NY 784083), also constructed in stone and 122 yards long. This viaduct is now owned by the Northern Viaduct Trust (www.nvt.org.uk), as is the trackbed between Stenkrith and Hartley, and is due for conversion to a cycleway, thereby eventually becoming legally accessible. Beyond Merrygill Viaduct the line traversed across open country, contouring at about 220m, with good views across the Eden valley. For the next 2 ½ miles or so, the line was clear with a grassy surface crossing a few culvert bridges, and a joy to walk on such a sunny morning. With the line veering southeast the next feature of note was Hatygill Viaduct (91 NY 815103), similar in construction to Podgill and Merrigill and 108 yards long. Almost immediately after Hatygill Viaduct the line entered the spectacular rock-hewn cutting at Howgill. As we emerged from the cutting with Howgill farm on our right, we were spotted by the farmer who was just coming down the track that bisects the line in his pick-up. He informed us rather tersely that the track was not a road, and seemed perplexed about 'rights of way' in general, probably due to the possibility of the line re-opening as a cycle/walkway. We were forced to take his farm track to Heggerscales, and follow the minor road before re-gaining the line just west of the Belah Valley (91 NY 833100). Passing a couple of sheds we entered a shallow grassy cutting leading to the Belah valley. As we emerged from the cutting the remains of Belah signalbox came into view (91 NY 838103),

31

looking like a tired sentinel, with slates and windows missing, but still guarding the spectacular approach to Belah valley. We paused for a while to take in the magnificent scenery. Just beyond the signalbox were the remains of the western abutment of the now demolished Belah viaduct (91 NY 839105). Sitting on the massive abutment gave us fantastic views across the surrounding moorland, with the beauty amplified as it was a cloudless early spring day.

Belah viaduct was a spectacular 16-span iron trestle viaduct at 347 yards long. There is a good picture in Paul Atterbury's book: 'Discovering Britain's Lost Railways', of Belah viaduct with a 'banked' mixed freight train crossing on the climb towards Stainmore Summit. As was often the case, it was the iron structures that were demolished first (before stone structures) on a disused line for their scrap value. The conspiracy theorist in me, however, suspects that these key structures were removed as part of a political strategy to ensure that the line was physically severed, and therefore economically impossible to re-instate, with the alleged scrap value being merely a spin-off. Besides, the cost of removing a large structure, such as a 1000ft long iron viaduct, in a remote location such as the Belah valley must have been significant, and would surely have eaten into any returns on the scrap.

We made the steep descent into the Belah river valley on a public footpath, crossing Belah River on a footbridge (91 NY 838106). The descent into the lush valley gave an excellent understanding of what a remarkable structure Belah Viaduct was, and how difficult it must have been to construct across such terrain. There was another convenient footpath from the footbridge that joined a bridleway/farm track past New Hall Farm that bisected the line just to the east of the cutting on the eastern side of the Belah Valley (91 NY 842108). With the line now heading due north, and still climbing, we made good progress on the grassy trackbed for about a mile to Barras Station (91 NY 844121).

Barras Station with its large house and platform remnants was well preserved and now in use as a private house. Looking at the station in this bleak and lonely location at almost 350m above sea level, I wondered about its past glories, and how many passengers boarded or alighted here. We skirted the station to the east at a discreet distance, respecting the privacy of the owners, before crossing a minor road at the site of the demolished Mousegill Viaduct that was constructed in stone, 6-spans and 82 yards long (91 NY 846123). Basking in the bright spring sunlight, we had a long lunch on the remains of the viaduct abutment. From Barras the line continued to climb to Bleathgill, scene of the famous 1955 British Transport Film: 'Snowdrift at Bleathgill', a highly entertaining and evocative film about attempts to rescue a snowbound train.

The section of line from Bleathgill with its stiff gradient and clear trackbed was pure joy to walk, with magnificent views, which would have been even better if it were not for the ugly omnipresence of the A66 trunk road. Sadly we realised that the famous Stainmore summit was now partially assimilated into the widened A66, complete with lay-by and burger van. The rail summit was at a lofty 1,370ft, with the original twin iron summit marker signs now preserved at the National Railway Museum, York and North Road Station Railway Museum, Darlington.

I tried to imagine the summit as it was, but the presence of the dual carriageway and noisy traffic clouded out my dreams. The sun was now beginning to dip into the haze across the Eden valley, so our thoughts turned to finding somewhere to sleep. On the hillside just to the south of the summit we spotted an old concrete 'pillbox', probably of WWII origin. A brief reconnoitre revealed that it was in good condition, and after removal of a dead sheep, which came out in three pieces, we had our shelter for the night. We lined the pillbox with plastic sheet and set off to scavenge for combustible materials. The pillbox had small gun ports but no chimney, but we found a bit of old pipe that we rigged to a gun port for the chimney. Unfortunately the pipe was plastic and once our fire was going it melted and dripped into the fire giving off noxious fumes, sending us tumbling out of the small entrance door. Chris cooked an excellent pasta dish, which we washed down with a few beers whilst we mulled over an excellent days walking. We bedded down listening to Lionel Richie's late night show on Radio 2, which progressed from dreadful to farce when he started to play his own music.

We awoke to the eerie sound of a woodcock and a cold and misty Stainmore morning, and the nearby A66 could be heard but not seen. I re-kindled our fire for a hurried breakfast before we set off to regain the line next to the A66. The line from Stainmore summit was obviously well used for farm access, and we felt vulnerable, as there were very few trees alongside the line, and the mist soon melted away to give another glorious sunny morning. The trackbed was in excellent condition, with no major obstacles, and was a wonderful way to traverse the moor. A particularly scenic section was where the line crossed the River Greta (91 NY 926114), as the embanked line then hugged the river more or less all the way to Bowes. We had to take a detour round The Otter Sanctuary (91 NY 947120) via the A66, as the line went behind a 5000v security fence. We regained the line from the A66 via a bridleway at God's bridge (91/92 NY 957126). For the next 2 ½ miles the line became indistinct, melting into the fields, then re-emerging for short sections, until finally being buried under the A66 to the west of Bowes. The line through Bowes was obliterated by the A66, but Bowes Station remained (92 NY 996138) defiantly overlooking the dual carriageway. The station building was in a sad tumbledown state of dereliction, with the roof entirely missing. A large farm shed that was built right across the trackbed dominated the station site to the east. I have since heard a rumour that this shed was built around a signalbox that the farmer was not allowed to demolish, but I have not been able to verify this one way or the other.

We ended our traverse of Stainmore summit in the Ancient Unicorn, Bowes, at lunchtime where the very jolly landlord welcomed us with several good pints of Black Sheep Bitter.

*Hatygill Viaduct (91 NY 815103) bathed in sunlight is a pleasing sight.*

*The western abutment of Belah Viaduct (91 NY 839105) can be clearly seen from the valley below. Picture in your minds eye a massive iron trestle viaduct straddling this deep, wide valley.....*

*A roofless Belah Signal Box (91 NY 838103) still guards the western approach to Belah Valley.*

*Two views of the magnificent trackbed east of Stainmore Summit.*

# WALK III
## The Border Counties Railway (Hexham to Riccarton Junction) & Part of The Waverley Route (Riccarton Junction to Hawick)

| Walk Summary | |
|---|---|
| Date walked | May 2000 |
| Line mileage | 55 |
| OSLR Maps | 79, 80, 87 |
| Opened to Passengers | 01 07 1862*, 01 06 1858♦ |
| Closed to Passengers | 15 10 1956*, 05 01 1969♦ |
| PGAG Reference | 27, 31 |
| Pre-Grouping Company | North British Railway |

*The Border Counties Railway, ♦The Waverley Route

## Walk Highlights

Reedsmouth Junction, Kielder Viaduct, Deadwater Station, Saughtree Station, Riccarton Junction, Whitrope Tunnel, Shankend Viaduct, Stobs Station and the magnificent scenery.

## Public Transport

Hexham is on the Newcastle to Carlisle line. Hawick is connected by the First Borders X95/95 bus to Carlisle, Edinburgh, and other Borders towns. Interestingly, it is still possible to buy a train ticket to some of The Scottish Border towns, as a bus add-on facility exists from Edinburgh or Carlisle when using the above bus services.

## Walk Description

Buoyed by the success of our first two walks we decided to tackle something more ambitious over the May Bank Holiday weekend. I had researched the Border Counties Railway that started at Hexham and joined the famous Waverley Route (See Walk XXI) at Riccarton Junction. We decided to include a stretch of The Waverley Route, finishing at Hawick, as unlike Riccarton Junction Hawick had a bus service. The stretch of line between Riccarton Junction and Hawick was also one of the best sections of The Waverley Route for walking and interesting railway relics. To keep the weight of our packs down, we had booked ahead in a combination of Youth Hostels and B&B at convenient stopping places.

## Hexham to Bellingham (17 miles)

The market town of Hexham sits a couple of miles to the east of the confluence of the North and South Tyne rivers. We headed north from Hexham Station, crossing the River Tyne on the A695 road bridge, as according to the map the Border Counties Railway Viaduct over the Tyne was demolished. The Border Counties Railway followed the River North Tyne Valley, whilst the existing Newcastle to Carlisle Railway follows the River South Tyne west of Hexham. We followed a public footpath (87 NY 931654) from the A69 along the north bank of the Tyne to the site of The Border Counties Railway Viaduct (87 NY 956653). The abutments and three supports were all that remained of the viaduct, with the iron platform having been removed long ago. The footpath hugged the riverbank for about 1½ miles until the trackbed became easily discernible. At this point we left the line and headed up the road into Acomb for our overnight stop at Acomb Youth Hostel, which proved to be a good traditional rural hostel.

We explored the pubs of Saturday night Acomb, and after getting a frosty welcome by some locals in The Sun, we settled for The Miner's Arms, where we were entertained by a sozzled bloke sporting loud yellow corduroys desperately trying to chat up the barmaid. We surmised that this was not this hapless Chap's first attempt, nor would it be his last.

The following morning we rejoined the line where we left off, with a good trackbed quickly running through a wet cutting, that was used for vehicle access (87 NY 918671). The lined hugged the eastern bank of the North Tyne, and was walkable until we had to detour round Wall

39

Station (87 NY 916684), that was now a private residence complete with railway carriage in the garden, via the A6079. When we assessed possibilities re-gaining the line, however, it looked very difficult due to the surrounding cropped fields barring access, so we decided to walk down to Wall station and see if the owner would let us have a look round, as from the presence of the railway carriage we thought they may have had an interest in the line. No one was home, so we just pushed on past the nicely preserved station regaining the line to the north, which now offered excellent views down to the lush river valley. The line was in excellent condition until the villages of Humshaugh and Chollerford, where the overbridge that carried the B6318 (87 NY 921704) was bricked up. After a scramble up onto the road we joined a public footpath and passed Humshaugh Station, now a private house in picturesque setting in a glade of trees by the North Tyne (87 NY 922705). We rejoined the line just before reaching the stone overbridge carrying the A6079 (87 NY 929708), where the trackbed was overgrown but still walkable. A short distance beyond the A6079, the trackbed opened out and passed some lime kilns (87 NY 932709), which were obviously once served by the operational railway. The line crossed over the A6079 just south of Chollerton via a stone bridge, but access to the line north of the bridge was difficult due to vegetation and fences. There was a station serving Chollerton (87 NY 931718) but we saw no remains as we passed by. Following a minor road that hugged the line northwest out of Chollerton for about ¼ mile we entered an overgrown cutting, where the going was difficult, especially as it was a hot and humid day. Upon reaching the minor road leading into Barrasford, we detoured into the village in search of some lunch and cold beer, which we duly found at The Barrasford Arms. It was truly one of those 'Ice Cold in Alex moments'; as anyone who has seen said film will understand the magnificent relief brought about by a cold beer in a condensation beaded glass on a hot day.

Foolishly, we followed the minor road northwest out of Barrasford causing us to miss seeing Barrasford Station. This was a symptom of our early walks, in that we had not yet become truly systematic during our explorations. Subsequent research, however, has confirmed that Barrasford Station is well preserved, complete with platform, and is in use as a private house. Getting back on the line, however, was easy via a public footpath/quarry track accessing the line (87 NY 909740), which followed the line for about ¼ mile, before veering away northwards. The trackbed was in excellent condition and easily walked until we reached a cutting (87 NY 885757) close to Chipchase Castle. The cutting was very overgrown and boggy, necessitating a walk on the steep slope of the cutting. We persevered and pushed on for about another mile to a shallow cutting (87 NY 873767), where we were forced to backtrack and leave the line on a public footpath running from Comorgan Farm (87 NY 876765) as a private house that turned out to be Wark Station (87 NY 871768) blocked the trackbed. Wark Station, easily viewed from the minor road, looked like an ordinary stone house but turfed platforms belied its railway heritage. It was possible to rejoin the trackbed just northwest of Wark Station by crossing a grassy field.

Our next treat came in the shape of a remarkably well-preserved signal box (87 NY 866776), which appeared to be in use as some sort of bunk or playhouse. Another detour on a minor road was forced upon us where the trackbed was in use as a private drive (87 NY 866778). The minor road crossed the line further north as it headed into a peninsular of the North Tyne, which provided an easy access point onto the trackbed that was a walkable and mostly wooded track all the way to Reedsmouth Station (80 NY 865820) (*note: the spelling of the station differs from the village of 'Redesmouth'*) and junction. This section for a couple of miles south of Reedsmouth was a beautiful walk in the dappled evening sunshine. Our arrival at Reedsmouth Junction was heralded by a converted signal box perched on an island platform that separated the junction, with the station buildings behind, one of which looked like a water tower converted into a house. The line heading northeast out of Reedsmouth Junction was for Morpeth (see walk XII), 25 miles distant, with the trackbed now a private garden. Our route to the northwest was a well-used and muddy farm track, with an overgrown brick waiting shed sitting on the platform. Nobody seemed to mind as we wandered about taking a few photographs of the various relics. To the north of the station site sat a tired looking engine shed that had been unsympathetically modified into a cattle shed. The entire north side of the station was a sad sight that was now just an untidy farm yard area.

The sun was starting to fade, and we were meant to be at Bellingham Youth Hostel by 19:00, so we pushed on quickly for a short distance along a sapling-covered embankment that ended abruptly at the road bridge crossing the River Rede (80 NY 863823). The railway bridge was demolished, but the stone/brick abutments and supports were present, now acting as supports for the road bridge. On the north side of the river, the line hugged the minor road towards the village of Bellingham, with the trackbed blending into the fields that made easy walking for the final couple of miles into the village. The line into Bellingham became indistinct, but the station house (80 NY 842833) remained and was in use as a council depot.

The Youth Hostel Warden had gone out before we arrived, but a guest who obviously knew we were coming showed us to our dormitory in the largely wooden hostel. Bellingham had a few pubs and places to eat, and proved to be a good overnight stop after the long haul from Acomb. We returned to the hostel to find the female warden with a large gin and tonic in hand in deep discussion about the world wrestling federation, and wrestlers' bodies in particular, with one of the male guests. In the ensuing conversation the somewhat inebriated warden provided an entertaining, if a little frightening, end to a long day.


**Bellingham to Falstone (9 miles)**
Another sunny morning greeted us as we pursued the line northwest out of Bellingham via a cutting (80 NY 836836) running behind some houses. The line left the village and traversed grazing fields on an excellent trackbed. After passing under an elegant footbridge (80 NY 817845), supported on slender stone pillars the line passed the site Charlton Station (80 NY 805846) of which there was no trace. After passing under another fine footbridge at the western end of a cutting (80 NY 804846), the line passed close by, and in full view of a couple of houses at Newton. Fortunately a public footpath runs close to the line at this point if a detour is required. After passing Tarset Station (80 NY 789853) the line traversed a couple of small overbridges before entering a fine grassy cutting with a splendid lineside hut at the western end (80 NY 789853). The line then crossed Tarset Burn on a fine three-arched skewed stone viaduct (80 NY 786856). A splendid trackbed continued with a couple of notable embankments and bridges before becoming a well used farm track about 2km south of Falstone. Falstone Station House, a substantial stone building (80 NY 726873), was well preserved, complete with platform and signal box. The station was converted so

42

that the signal box was now joined to the main house. Falstone is a pretty village that forms the gateway to Kielder Water; a man-made reservoir flooding the upper reaches of the North Tyne Valley. Our accommodation was at Braefoot B&B and was an excellent stay with a warm welcome. The Blackcock Inn served good food and ale, and proved a most agreeable place to discuss our next day on the line.

### Falstone to Riccarton Junction (16 miles)

Heading northwest out of Falstone the trackbed was a public bridleway all the way up to Kielder Water Dam (80 NY 708882), which contains the impressive Kielder Water Reservoir. When the reservoir was created in 1980 about 7 miles of The Border Counties Railway were submerged, along with the remote stations of Plashetts and Lewiefield Halt. Wanting to be as true as possible to the route of the line (and save us some foot slogging), we opted to take the Kielder Cruise Boat, which set off from Tower Knowe (80 NY 698869) on the south side of the dam and dropped us at a small cove called Plashetts, close to the submerged station site (80 NY 674901). We followed a designated cycle route/bridleway through the forest to rejoin the line at the point where it emerged from the reservoir's murky depths (80 NY 640916). It was good to be back on the line, and we were soon rewarded with the fine 155 yard long, skew-arched Kielder Viaduct (80 NY 632924), crossing Kielder Burn at the head of the reservoir. Apart from the skew arch construction, the stone viaduct had castellated parapets and was decorated with Maltese Crosses between the seven arches, and is now preserved as a monument. After bypassing an overgrown cutting just north of the viaduct we detoured into the forestry village of Kielder for lunch.

From Kielder Forest Station (80 NY 626934), now a private house, the line continued climbing with the trackbed being a well used vehicle track making it an easy walk along the increasingly scenic valley. The pine forested valley opened out as we approached the Scottish border. Just prior to the border was the remarkable and isolated station of Deadwater (80 NY 604968). The station was now a private house and appeared to have changed little from period photographs that I had seen in various books. I wondered why Deadwater Station was ever built as the population was, and remains, tiny in this remote area.

Crossing the border into Scotland the trackbed provided superb walking as it continued climbing steadily up the picturesque valley. As the line veered round to the west, entering the valley of Liddel Water we emerged from the forest to see a notable isolated stone overbridge (80 NY 583985), with the scenery opening out giving excellent views back towards Kielder. The line contoured along the valley before entering a shallow cutting, containing the stone pillars of a derelict footbridge (80 NY 573979) before ending at the B6357. The bridge across the B6357 was demolished, but it was an easy scramble down to and up from the road. We had a surprise as we clambered up the bank to get back on the line: laid railway track on the trackbed. The track stretched for a few hundred metres to Saughtree Station (80 NY 564981), now screened behind some pines. Near the wonderfully preserved station, the line had a run round loop and there was a diesel shunter, some wagons, and a brake van present. The station owner, who was obviously an enthusiast, was nowhere to be seen, so we paused to take some pictures of the remarkable site.

Leaving Saughtree, the easily walked trackbed continued to contour up the Liddel Valley across open country until reaching the cutting below Shiel Knowe (79 NY 547965). The cutting quickly became a dramatic embankment offering stunning views south down Riccarton Burn (79 NY 545966), and across the surrounding densely forested hillsides. The country now seemed lonely and isolated as the line had veered away from the road, climbing towards Riccarton Junction. The embankment gave way to another cutting where the line veered north, acting as a gateway to the site of Riccarton Junction; the terminus of The Border Counties Railway. I had visited Riccarton before, but not from the south, and I envied Chris and Dave the experience of what they were about to see for the first time. The cutting quickly opened out into a flat expanse of open land surrounded by pine trees. Forestry roads now took the place of the line and appeared to mark out the actual junction between The Border Counties Railway and The Waverley Route faithfully (79 NY 540976). On a bright sunny evening we had the place to ourselves, and we wandered the site to take in the magic of Riccarton Junction. A badly overgrown platform remained, with a small hut opposite, containing some replica memorabilia owned by 'The Friends of Riccarton Junction'. Riccarton Junction had once been a thriving railway community of over one hundred people, largely isolated from the outside world, connected only by the steel threads to which it owed its existence and survival. There is an excellent book detailing the history of Riccarton Junction, written by a former resident: "Riccarton Junction; Just a Few Lines" by Christopher 'Kit Milligan', available from The Waverley Route Heritage Association (www.wrha.org.uk). For me Riccarton Junction was an eerie, evocative place, and I could not help but feel a tinge of melancholy as we explored this place that seemed to be just quietly laying dormant, waiting for the return of the railway. Riccarton is difficult to photograph due to the surrounding forest, so I urge the reader to visit this site above any other dismantled railway site mentioned in this book, and take in the atmosphere that is unique to Riccarton.

Our overnight stop was to be at 'Will's Bothy' located close to Riccarton Junction. Friends of a chap called William Ramsbotham, who died in a climbing accident in 1993, built the bothy as a fitting monument to him. Aside from being ideally located for the railway explorer, this was the best bothy that I had ever stayed in. Chris and Dave attended to supper as I cooled the beers in the burn and chopped some logs for the wood burning stove. Wandering back to the junction after supper in the twilight, gave us the truly eerie experience of the wonderfully isolated site of Riccarton Junction.

**The Formation of NEDRAT**

After our wanderings we retuned to the cosy bothy and began a candle lit discussion about the days walk and our future continued exploration of dismantled railways in general. I felt that we needed to be more systematic in our approach, and suggested some sort of club, partly tongue-in-cheek, recognising the 'anorak' potential of a small group of blokes walking dismantled railways. The notion of a name and logo was discussed, and we decided that any name had to encapsulate the lines, our somewhat anarchic approach to walking them, and the region where we lived at the time. Dave began putting his artistic talents to the project, and after some more self-mocking banter he coined 'NEDRAT', i.e. *'North East Dismantled Railway Assault Trio'*. It sounded so absurd that we all instantly agreed on our group name. It also seemed fitting that NEDRAT was born at Riccarton Junction.

## Riccarton Junction to Hawick (13 miles)

NEDRAT's first official morning on the line was a cold and misty affair. We were now traversing part of the famous 'Waverley Route' that once connected Edinburgh to Carlisle serving the Scottish Border towns. When The Waverley Route finally closed in January 1969 it was highly controversial, with the closure effectively turning The Scottish Borders into a rail desert.

From Riccarton Junction the line climbed steeply with the trackbed continuing as a forestry track. The surrounding country was steep pine covered hills that looked rather mysterious when shrouded in the morning mist. We made good progress to the overbridge known as 'Golden Bridge' that crosses the B6399 (79 NY 525999). Just north of the bridge lay Whitrope Cottage (*'Signalbox Cottage'*), that was now a private residence. There was a siding and signalbox here but no trace could be seen of either structure, as we glided quietly past. Just north of Whitrope Cottage was the highest summit of the Waverley Route: Whitrope Summit at 1006ft above sea level. The gradients either side of Whitrope summit were once a severe test of man and machine and were at around 1:90 – 1:75 and quite noticeable to the walker. North of Whitrope Summit we entered a deep, damp cutting, that marked the run into the south portal of the 1,208 yard long Whitrope Tunnel (79 NT 526007) that was guarded by some imposing brick buttressing, covered in all manner of plants like some ancient tomb. Whitrope Tunnel curved to the left so was it was some time before the light at the north portal was visible. We heard running water and saw the remains of damaged drainage pipes. Some of the roof had caved in close to the south portal, but the rest appeared sound as we walked the near ¾ mile to the north portal (79 NT 522017), with the trackbed surface consisting of the original ballast. Unfortunately since our walk there has been a significant collapse (March 2002) of the tunnel roof, completely blocking Whitrope Tunnel. The walker would now need to detour up and over Sandy Edge. We were indeed privileged to have passed through this iconic part of The Waverley Route before its sad demise. The cutting at the north portal was quite boggy underfoot, but was passable with careful footwork. The feeling of complete isolation returned at the north portal, as we were well away from any roads, in thickly forested countryside, with the morning mist adding considerable atmosphere. The trackbed was more of a path than a track and for our money this was dismantled railway walking at its very best. As the line neared the B6399 once again (79 NT 531037) it became forestry/farm track, and was excellent walking down to Shankend Station (79 NT 524057).

The signal box and overgrown platforms at Shankend Station (now a private house) provided another evocative location, and I pondered why a station would be here at all. Just to the north, however, was the even more impressive 199 yard, 15-arched Shankend Viaduct (79 NT 522060). Traversing this magnificent viaduct gave one feelings of wonder and admiration at the engineering feats required for the construction of a railway in such a remote area. Beyond Shankend the line veered away from the road again, and an excellent trackbed contoured at a more gentle gradient down the valley of Slitrig Water, alternating between cuttings and raised embankments. We met a shepherd and his flock who were using the trackbed as a drove road. The shepherd eyed us curiously, and nodded good morning, before whizzing off down the line on his quad bike.

After struggling through an overgrown cutting we arrived at Stobs Station (79 NT 505097). The platforms were looking neglected and the skeletal remains of a footbridge still straddled the trackbed offering unsafe passage over a now safe trackbed. The station house was in use as a private residence, and the line was fenced off at the north end of the platforms, so we skirted round in a neighbouring field. The line continued north along the valley following the B6399 more closely, and was walkable with few obstacles, going through cuttings and across embankments for the next 2 ½ miles until it reached the B6399 at the site of Lynwood Viaduct (79 NY 502134). The viaduct crossed both the road and Slitrig water at this point, but was demolished with little trace remaining. To avoid a considerable detour, we forded the fast flowing stream using the remains of the viaduct as stepping-stones. Clambering up the embankment on the north side of the road we found the line entering a deep cutting hewn out of rock, with the damp, mossy, black walls glistening with water droplets. The cutting emerged on the southern outskirts of Hawick, with the trackbed walkable to the A689 where it ended abruptly at a steep grassy embankment (79 NY 504144) opposite a roundabout, and the Safeway supermarket.

Hawick, once a bustling woollen mill town, used to have a large viaduct with a high-level station bisecting the town, but all these structures were long gone to make way for the A-road and the uniform blandness of a Safeway supermarket car park. After the delights of our long walk, Hawick seemed a bit of an anti-climax, as there were no significant remains of The Waverley Route left.

*The wonderfully isolated Deadwater Station (80 NY 604968) looking south (above) and looking north (below).*

*Kielder Viaduct (80 NY 632924) looks splendid with its castellations and ornate embedded cruciforms.*

*Riccarton Junction (79 NY 540976) site looking south. The Border Counties line is on the left, and the trackbed of The Waverley Route heading down to Steele Road on the right.*

*Whitrope Tunnel south portal (above) (79 NT 526007) and north portal (below) (79 NT 522017). The Tunnel suffered a collapse in March 2002, and is now blocked and sealed off by security gates.*

*The curious sight of track and train at Saughtree Station (80 NY 564981).*

*A well restored Shankend Signal Box just south of Shankend Station (79 NT 524057) towers over a clear trackbed on The Waverley Route.*

*Looking south along the magnificent 15-arched Shankend Viaduct (79 NT 522060).*

*The decaying footbridge at Stobs Station (79 NT 505097) looks forlorn on a grey morning.*

# WALK IV
## Bowes to Evenwood and
## The Middleton-in-Teesdale Branch

| Walk Summary | |
|---|---|
| **Date walked** | February 2001 |
| **Line mileage** | 21 ¾ |
| **OSLR Maps** | 92 |
| **Opened to Passengers** | 1863 |
| **Closed to Passengers** | 22 01 1962*, 30 11 1964♣, 18 06 1962♠ |
| **PGAG Reference** | 27 |
| **Pre-Grouping Company** | North Eastern Railway |

*Bowes to Tees Valley Junction, ♣Tees Valley Junction to Barnard Castle, ♠Barnard Castle to Bishop Auckland, ♠Middleton-in-Teesdale to Tees Valley Junction.

## Walk Highlights

Bowes Station, the sites of Deepdale Viaduct and Tees Viaduct, Percy Beck Viaduct, Forthburn Viaduct, Langleydale Viaduct, and the remains of Lands Viaduct.

## Public Transport

Arriva Bus service 79 connects Bowes and Barnard Castle, Go Ahead Northern Bus service 8 connects Barnard Castle and Bishop Auckland. Bishop Auckland is the terminus of the branch line from Darlington.

## Walk Description

### Bowes to Barnard Castle (6 miles)
It was still very dark at seven o'clock as we climbed the steps to Bowes

Station (92 NY 996138) to continue north from walk II. The reason to start so early on a cold February morning was due to the exposed nature of the first section of line; so in an attempt to avoid being seen, we found ourselves stumbling around in the dark at a very spooky Bowes Station. It was also very cold with a strong wind picking up, but we were fortunate that it was blowing in from behind us. Skirting the large farm shed built right across the trackbed at Bowes Station, we picked up the line in a shallow cutting. At the end of the cutting was a large chicken shed (92 NZ 003140), again built right on the trackbed. This was easy enough to skirt round except for the large amount of chicken muck deposited right on the trackbed. Even on a cold morning the stench was awful as we blundered right into the festering pile. At this point the line was indistinct but a public footpath more or less followed the alignment for a few hundred metres before veering away from the trackbed. A good, clear trackbed was either flat or slightly embanked with no trees until the line went into a cutting and under the A67 (92 NZ 023148).

As we passed under the stone road bridge it was now light with an ominous looking leaden sky with snow just starting to fall. We hurried under the A67 on a soggy trackbed across some open ground before entering the seclusion of a wet cutting (92 NZ 023152) that ran for about a mile and curved northwest. This well preserved cutting was also unusual in that it had a metal aqueduct (92 NZ 024154) carrying a stream high across the trackbed. Towards the end of the cutting there was a fine three arched stone overbridge carrying a farm track (92 NZ 019159). The snow was now coming down hard as we emerged from the cutting into a wooded section of line, and a few hundred metres further on was the southern abutment of Deepdale Viaduct (92 NZ 017162). The long demolished viaduct was of similar design to Belah Viaduct (see walk II); an iron trestle structure 247 yards long, that spanned the deep, wooded, gorge of Deepdale. We descended the steep and slippery slope to the beck below as the snow fall gathered momentum. Deepdale Beck was running high and we had to cross barefoot; an early test of our combined mettle. After a scramble up the equally steep north bank, we were soon at the snow covered north abutment (92 NZ 016164), with the bare winter trees allowing good views across, up and down Deepdale. It was a great shame that such a magnificent viaduct no longer enhanced this beautiful location. The trackbed was now a well used track, and not far north of Deepdale we passed a brick built signalbox (92 NZ 016165) that was largely intact except for the boarded up windows.

The snow had eased as we arrived in the village of Lartington. Just across the B6277 road that runs through the village was the grand and very well preserved gabled Lartington Station House (91 NZ 017178). We detoured round the station house as it was a private dwelling, with the landscaped trackbed forming part of the garden, before rejoining the line via a bridleway off of the B6277 (92 NZ 014180). It was possible to walk back along the line a short distance to the perimeter fence of Lartington Station to get a view of this fine building from the north. The trackbed veered eastwards on a high embankment and was obviously well walked with a good cinder surface. The Middleton-in-Teesdale branch line could be seen coming in on our left (see below), finally joining our trackbed at Tees Valley Junction (92 NZ 034176), although the exact location of the junction was hard to pinpoint on the ground.

Just over ½ mile east of Tees Valley Junction was the enormous solid stone western buttress of the once mighty Tees Viaduct. Tees Viaduct had also been demolished, but unlike Deepdale Viaduct, this viaduct was a 7-span iron platform on stone pillar structure, and was 244 yards in length. The views looking down the Tees from the abutment were dramatic towards Barnard Castle, and a good head for heights was required to perch on the edge of the buttress. There was no possibility of fording the Tees, so we had to take a lengthy detour along the Teesdale way into Barnard Castle. We had a welcome respite form the atrocious weather by having a late breakfast in Stables café.

A public footpath led out of town up to the eastern abutment of Tees Viaduct (92 NZ 042174). Although this location was not as dramatic as the western side, we gained a good view of the western buttress and the river way below. The snow had turned to heavy sleet as we set off from the eastern abutment with the line now traversing very open country, before passing under a stark and redundant over bridge (92 NZ 045175) that straddled a flat and very wet trackbed. In less than half a mile the line crossed Percy Beck Viaduct; an elegant 8-spanned, 87 yard long, stone (with white brick arches) viaduct over Percy Beck (92 NZ 049175). The trackbed onto the viaduct was fenced off as it now formed an access for a stable complex. We scouted for a way across, in an attempt to avoid the steep descent to Percy Beck when a toothless old man who was mucking out the horses spotted us. The old chap beamed a friendly, gummy, smile and gestured via hand signals without uttering a word that we could use the viaduct to cross. The trackbed to the east of the viaduct was tarmac and disappeared into an industrial estate, passing Barnard Castle Station House (see Walk I). After skirting around the GSK pharmaceutical plant we were at the overbridge (92 NZ 058176, see walk I) that was starting point of our inaugural walk. We clambered up the embankment by the bridge to join the Bishop Auckland Branch Line.


**Barnard Castle to Evenwood (9 ¾ miles)**
The line was walkable for just over a mile to a minor road (92 NZ 057188), where there was no sign of the level crossing that once guided the line across the road. On the other side of the road the line was in an impenetrable cutting that we had to skirt round in the adjacent field, before the trackbed became walkable to another minor road (92 NZ 055195) where no trace of the original bridge could be seen.  After passing under a couple of isolated overbridges (92 NZ 057201 & 059204), the sleet had now turned to constant cold rain as we approached the stone viaduct across Forthburn Beck (92 NZ 061205).  Forthburn Viaduct was a more squat structure than Percy Beck Viaduct and the arches were faced in stone rather than white brick.  The viaduct was half-heartedly fenced off and easily crossed, with the line continuing to be walkable but very wet in places to the B6279 (92 NZ 071218) where the overbridge had been demolished.

After crossing the B6279 the line continued north in a cutting that was guarded by a Durham County Council (DCC) warning sign to 'Keep Out'.  From this it seemed likely that the trackbed was owned, if not maintained, by the council, which was plausible since DCC has one of the best records in the UK for opening up old lines as walking and cycling routes. We wondered if the Barnard Castle to Bishop Auckland Branch was maybe earmarked for a future conversion. Along a clear trackbed from the B6279 two stone overbridges were visible, with the most distant bridge forming a hazy outline under the nearest bridge, which appeared like a mirage in the thick misty rain.  The rain was now atrocious with water lying on top of icy sheeted puddles making the going tough on a very slippery trackbed. Just north of the second overbridge was Langleydale Viaduct (92 NZ 069225), constructed to the similar design as Percy Beck Viaduct, but with 11 spans and longer at 137 yards. Langleydale provided a much more open and spectacular location than Percy Beck, to give the walker an excellent view of another fine viaduct, even though the weather was doing its utmost to dampen the views.

For the next 3 miles the line crossed bleak, open country, and was walkable to Cockfield Fell Station (92 NZ 113248). The station house, complete with ugly satellite dishes, was in use as a private dwelling. A detour to the north of the station site took us to a minor road (92 NZ 113249) and Cockfield Fell. The fell is covered in a myriad of public footpaths and the clear trackbed had become absorbed amongst these as a de-facto right of way. It was late in the day as we crossed the fell and came to the valley of the River Gaunless. Our earlier struggles were about to be rewarded with an unbelievable sight. Overlooking the valley was a stone viaduct abutment, which gave a panoramic view of the enormous and devastated cylindrical brick pillars that lay below on the valley floor (92 NZ 127252) like fallen giants. Towering 93ft above the valley, the 214 yard long Lands Viaduct once consisted of a 4-span iron girder platform supported by circular white brick pillars with granite capstones. On the eastern bank of the Gaunless the pillars survived, towering above the valley, showing what the toppled giants below would have been if they had not been so callously slain by explosives. The collapsed pillars looked forlorn like the result of a ferocious struggle between two unearthly Titans, and with this we nicknamed this surreal location: 'The Clash of the Titans'.

It was now getting dark, so we descended quickly to see the fallen giants, and each picked up a white brick with 'PEASE' embossed in the frog, and weighing about 4 Kg each, that was just what we needed in our packs after long day on the line! We assumed that the embossing of 'PEASE' was derived from the Pease family of Stockton to Darlington Railway Company fame. Rather than climb the valley on the other side of the Gaunless River, we crossed via a footbridge (92 NZ 130251) and took the trackbed of the old Haggerleases Branch that would have originally passed under Lands Viaduct and up the Gaunless Valley to Haggerkleases/Butterknowle. This short stretch of line brought us to a minor road where we rejoined the line (92 NZ 134253) a short distance north up the hill. We had to go steady now, as darkness had fallen and the rain continued to pour as we groped along the treacherous icy and wet trackbed to the village of Ramshaw, which was the site of Evenwood Station (92 NZ 148260). Entering the brightly lit bar of The Trotter's Arms, Ramshaw, I remember a feeling of exhilaration, with my face stinging from the weathering it had received from a long day on the line. The landlord and customers were very friendly, but struggled to understand what three, soaking wet blokes would be doing walking about after dark on such a foul night. It was not an easy inquiry to answer.

**The Middleton-in-Teesdale Branch (6 miles)**
As this route is a public right of way, and easily walked, the following is only a brief outline of the route. We walked this picturesque branch as a short separate walk, but due to its proximity I have included the walk description in this chapter.

The Middleton-in-Teesdale branch runs from Middleton-in-Teesdale to a point east of Cotherstone village and is a public right of way, courtesy of Durham County Council. The public right of way runs from just east of Middleton Station (92 NY 951245), to a public bridleway (92 NY 031179), close to Tees Valley Junction. It is possible to follow the overgrown trackbed from this point to Tees Valley Junction and beyond to the site of Tees Viaduct as described in the Bowes to Evenwood walk detailed above.

Middleton-in-Teesdale Station (92 NY 947247) is now a caravan park. There are two notable viaducts on the route: Lune Viaduct (5-arched) (92 NY 958241) and Balder Viaduct (9-arched) (92 NY 995201). Cotherstone Station (92 NZ 013191) is now a private house.

*The derelict Bowes Station (92 NY 996138) makes a sad sight. This photograph was taken on a subsequent visit.*

*Coal drops at Bowes Station. The station site sits right next to the busy A66 trunk road and is now in use as part of a farm yard.*

*A fine three-arched overbridge (92 NZ 019159) straddles a cutting south of Deepdale.*

*A redundant overbridge (92 NZ 045175) takes a track over a slushy trackbed close to Barnard Castle.*

A relic from the days of The Stockton and Darlinton railway can still be found on a small stone cottage in Barnard Castle opposite the GSK factory.

Percy Beck Viaduct (92 NZ 049175) (above) provides a difficult subject for the photographer due to the surrounding trees.

Langleydale Viaduct (92 NZ 069225) (right) is a larger version of Percy beck Viaduct in a more open and dramatic setting.

*The massive remaining brick pillar of Lands Viaduct (92 NZ 127252) towers above The Gaunless valley. This photograph was taken on a subsequent visit.*

*The Middleton-in-Teesdale Branch sports two remarkable Viaducts:
Balder Viaduct (92 NY 995201) (above) and Lune Viaduct
(92 NY 958241) (below).*

# WALK V
## The South Tynedale Railway
## (Alston to Haltwhistle)

| Walk Summary | |
|---|---|
| **Date walked** | November 2001 |
| **Line mileage** | 13 |
| **OSLR Maps** | 87 |
| **Opened to Passengers** | 17 11 1852 |
| **Closed to Passengers** | 01 05 1976 |
| **PGAG Reference** | 27 |
| **Pre-Grouping Company** | North Eastern Railway |

## Walk Highlights

Alston Station, Slaggyford Station, Lambley Viaduct, Featherstone Park Station, and Alston Arches Viaduct.

## Public Transport

Haltwhistle is on the Newcastle to Carlisle Line. Various bus companies run to/from Alston. There are buses to: Haltwhistle (464, 681), Carlisle (680), and Durham (X85). The South Tynedale Railway www.strps.org. uk runs seasonal trains from Alston on a narrow gauge preserved line as far as Kirkhaugh.

## An Agricultural Problem

Shortly after our Bowes to Evenwood walk the foot and mouth disease outbreak occurred. Although the risk of a walker transferring an infective dose of the foot and mouth virus is infinitesimally small, the authorities opted for a blanket closure of the countryside, rather than taking a risk-based approach by closing 'high-risk' areas. This draconian and in many

65

peoples' opinion misguided closure policy, shut the countryside for the duration. The cases of foot and mouth correlated very closely with the movement of livestock, i.e. the principle vector for foot and mouth virus transmission, with outbreaks continuing long after the closure of rights of way. If the Government were honest, it would admit that this closure policy was just a PR sop to the prevailing prejudices of many farmers and landowners, who resist public access to the countryside as a matter of course. It was also interesting to note at the time, that large sections of moorland were miraculously 'clear' by 12 August 2001, to allow the grouse shooters (i.e. influential landowners) onto moorland for their 'glorious' annual blood-fest, whilst many footpath bans were still in force. Whatever the politics of the situation, this blanket ban put a stop to our dismantled railway walking activities for the best part of a year.

## Walk Description

With large chunks of the countryside shut we decided to play safe and look for an easy way back onto the line. We decided on the Alston to Haltwhistle Branch, which has public access for its entire length, and had just been re-opened to the public at the time of our walk. As the route is a public right of way, and easily walked, the brief walk description concentrates primarily on points of interest.

### Alston to Haltwhistle (13 miles)
We arrived at Alston market square on a grey morning in heavy rain. Alston Station sitting at 905ft is well maintained and is still in use by the South Tynedale Railway, a preserved narrow gauge line (the original line was single track standard gauge). The station housed a tearoom and gift shop, but was closed up for the winter. The narrow gauge line ran for about 2 ¼ miles to the terminus at Kirkhaugh Halt (87 NY 696496). It was easy walking alongside the preserved line before the trackbed proper started. The rain stopped once we were on the trackbed, with the emerging sun bringing a lift to a dull November day.

The line followed the valley of the River South Tyne, which was a beautiful display of autumn colour, enhanced in the sunlight. We came to the delightfully named Slaggyford Station (87 NY 676523)

4 ¾ miles north of Alston. The substantial station house was now a private residence, and there was a tired looking wooden waiting shed still present on the platform opposite, but no trace of the level crossing remained. Just north of Slaggyford Station, was the fine 4-arched stone Slaggyford Viaduct (87 NY 673528) taking the line over Knar Burn.

The next point of interest and highlight of the line was the magnificent 16-arched, 246m long, Lambley Viaduct (87 NY 675583), crossing the River South Tyne. On the south side of the viaduct were the remains of Lambley Station (87 NY 674582) now a private house that was sadly, unsympathetically maintained. Lambley Station was also the site of the junction to the short Lambley Fell branch that was closed in 1960. The public access route detoured from the line slightly, avoiding Lambley Station before rejoining trackbed to cross on the wonderfully restored viaduct. We had a good view of the surrounding treetops from the 110ft high viaduct, and were lucky to see a red squirrel close up in its natural treetop habitat.

It was good walking to Coanwood Station that was only ¾ mile from Lambley Station (87 NY 677588), which had the remains of a very overgrown platform. Another mile down the line was to Featherstone Station (87 NY 682608), again a private house, but this time nicely restored with a platform complete with station totem. With the line curving north-eastwards we entered a straight, mile long cutting as the afternoon light faded. We pushed quickly on to the 6-arch Alston Arches Viaduct (87 NY 709637) that crossed the South Tyne just southeast of Haltwhistle Station. Since our walk, I have discovered that this viaduct will be restored with help from a £2,000 donation from the Railway Ramblers. We walked across the viaduct right to the site of the junction with the existing Newcastle and Carlisle Railway and then along a path on the edge of the line to Haltwhistle Station.

# WALK VI
# The Callander & Oban Railway and The Dunblane, Doune & Callander Railway (Crianlarich to Dunblane)

| Walk Summary | |
|---|---|
| Date walked | March 2002 |
| Line mileage | 40 ¼ |
| OSLR Maps | 50,51,57 |
| Opened to Passengers | 1870 & 1873 |
| Closed to Passengers | 28 09 1965 |
| PGAG Reference | 33 |
| Pre-Grouping Company | Caledonian Railway |

## Walk Highlights

The highland scenery, viaducts in Glen Dochart, the Glen Ogle Viaducts, and Drumvaich Signal box.

## Public Transport

Crianlarich is on the West Highland Line and can be reached by services from Glasgow Queen Street. Dunblane can be reached by either Edinburgh or Glasgow services.

## Walk Description

Due to the length and remoteness of the route, this was to be our first full camping outing, which meant a considerable weight increase in our packs. Our over indulgence of the buffet offerings on the Friday night rail trip to Glasgow was seen off by a pre-booked breakfast waiting for us at the highly recommended Crianlarich Station tearooms. Forget your chain café nonsense here; this was how a station café is meant to be, with good honest fresh cooked food at a reasonable price.

## Crianlarich to Killin Junction (10 miles)

A glorious March morning helped us on our way as we left Crianlarich Upper Station to join the trackbed at the site of the former Crianlarich Lower Station (50 NN 386254), of which we found no trace. Just east of the station site we found some old sleepers and rail chairs that were marked: 'LMS', which were unfortunately much too heavy to carry. We did, however, find a pile of rail keys, and although they were still substantial lumps of iron we decided to add to the weight of our packs by taking one each. The trackbed heading east out of Crianlarich was obviously well walked, sandwiched between the busy A85 and the scenic Loch Dochart, complete with ruined castle on an islet, which cast a perfect reflection in the still water. The trackbed was walkable until we reached Benmore Burn (51 NN 413259) where the bridge was demolished. Towering above was the gigantic mass of Ben More (1174m), creating a wonderful backdrop to the line. Benmore Burn was running low making it easy to cross on some well placed rocks. Just beyond Benmore Burn about ¾ mile of trackbed had been obliterated by the A85 (51 NN 416261).

We rejoined the line on a shady wooded section on the south side of the A85. The line hugged the A85 until emerging at the site of a demolished bridge (51 NN 443273) to cross to the north side of the road once again. The trackbed now hugged the north side of the A85 passing under a stone overbridge (51 NN 454276) and then quickly over a delightful 3-arched stone bridge (51 NN 456277) crossing the Allt Coire Chaorach. The trackbed became more open running through fields as it once again crossed the A85 at the site of another demolished bridge (51 NN 473280). We crossed the road and clambered up the embankment to a boggy wooded section of line that soon ended at a caravan site that was the site of Luib Station (51 NN 478280); of we which there was no obvious trace to be seen. As we were carrying rucksacks we thought it would be fine to just follow along the trackbed through the caravan site and pick up some water on the way. We passed a caravan that obviously housed the (English) owner who very curtly asked us where we had come from. Of course, what he really meant was: 'what are you doing coming in the back way onto *my* campsite?' In the ensuing exchange I enquired how much camping fees were, to which, he rather too quickly, informed us that the site was full, which was obviously not the case. Although we had no intention of camping here I did think it was an odd way to treat potential customers! This up-tight 'Little Englander' was obviously very rattled and we left him fulminating over his Daily Mail, and carried on along the trackbed.

Beyond the caravan site the line became very scenic, contouring along the south side of Glen Dochart to give excellent views. The bridge across Luib Burn (51 NN 501275) was missing, but the shallow burn was easily forded. With the trackbed now in use for farm access, it went through a short cutting with a ganger's hut at one end (51 NN 504273) and under a stone overbridge (51 NN 526283) before reaching an elegant viaduct across Ardchyle Burn (51 NN 528273). This 3-arched viaduct, although not grand in scale, seemed to grow out of the surrounding landscape, and guided the trackbed into a pine forest that concealed the ruins (house and platform) of Killin Junction Station (51 NN 531287) and Killin Junction (51 NN 533290), that was clearly visible on the ground as the trackbed was now a well-surfaced forestry road. The 4-mile branch line terminated at the small town of Killin at the head of Loch Tay.

It was late in the day so we decided to camp just inside the forest boundary under the trees next to Ardchyle Burn, that gave us an excellent view and enabled us to survey the viaduct as we ate dinner. It was just as well we camped under the trees, as it was a ground frost that night and we were a probably a degree or two warmer as a result.

### Killin Junction to Strathyre (10 ½ miles)
Pausing at Killin Junction Station we opted not to walk the branch line to Killin, as it would have meant an 8-mile roundtrip, which our time constraints made impossible. Therefore we proceeded on past Killin Junction on the the main Callander & Oban Railway. Not far beyond Killin Junction we came across an old railway telegraph pole that still had some white porcelain insulators intact. By climbing an adjacent tree I managed to retrieve two insulators marked 'LMS'(London Midland & Scottish Railway), making a couple of nice souvenirs.

The line curved sharply to the south dropping into Glen Ogle, coming close to the A85 once again. At this point the trackbed became 'The Glen Ogle Trail'; a walking and cycleway, passing Glenoglehead Station platform (51 NN 558284) and houses, that were in private use. Apart from the views, the highlights of the cycleway were the two Glen Ogle Viaducts (51 NN 570265 & 572263). The 46 yard 12-arched and the 23 yard 3-arched structures enabled the line to cross two gullies and contour along the glen. Our progress was swift on the Sustrans path, and needing some lunch we made the steep descent into the village of Lochearnhead. Lochearnhead had a station on the former Lochearnhead, St. Fillans & Comrie Railway, which joined the Callander & Oban Railway at Balquidder Junction (51 NN 574211). The landlord of The Lochearnhead Hotel warmly welcomed us, providing us with beer, and fried food; the much-loved staple of the railway walker. The landlord was a former merchant seaman, and he kept us entertained with over lunch with tales from his life on the high seas, a life which he obviously missed.

After lunch we retraced our steps back up the steep climb to the Glen Ogle Trail to continue south, passing a fine, well preserved, ornate iron footbridge (51 NN 575218) that carried a footpath over the line. As the line approached the A84, the compensation for the loss of tranquillity was a fine view westwards down the glen towards Balquidder. The bridge across the A84 (51 NN 576212) was demolished, thus requiring a short clamber down the embankment to the road. A frontage and underpass were the only visible remains of the former Balquidder Station (51 NN 574211) and junction, as a campsite now occupied the site. Therefore we had to follow the A84 to rejoin the line on the north side of a bend in the road at 51 NN 565205. After a few hundred metres we crossed a minor road close to the obliterated site of Kingshouse Halt (51 NN 562203). Although mainly walkable, the trackbed lost some of its charm as it hugged the A84 into the village of Strathyre, which sat snugly in the forested valley bottom. Strathyre Station (57 NN 559168) was sadly lost forever under a car park and picnic site, so we walked on and camped at the campsite on the south side of the village.

**Strathyre to Callander (8 ½ miles)**
It was Easter Sunday and we awoke to an overcast morning. Rejoining the line was a straightforward affair as a footbridge had been placed on the site of the original rail bridge in Strathyre (57 NN 559168). The trackbed was now a footpath running close to the scenic western shore

of Loch Lubnaig. Some short sections of the trackbed were flooded but still walkable to the southern end of the loch. A short section of line (57 NN 587088) was isolated on the eastern side of the river by two missing viaducts, near The Falls of Leny. We opted to stay on the western bank after peering over the remains of the viaduct abutment, thus avoiding a significant detour. It was hard to understand why the viaducts were demolished, unless they were removed to make way for the A84, or were constructed in iron and taken down for scrap. The remaining few miles was an easy and scenic walk along the trackbed used as a path into Callander.

It had been hard graft carrying camping kit over the last couple of days, so we treated ourselves to a B&B in Callander. The town proved lively, with a selection of pubs and a good Chinese restaurant.


**Callander to Dunblane (11 ¼ miles)**
The weather had improved overnight and we set off to look for Callander Station (57 NN 625082), but, sadly all we could find was a car park. Callander was the start of The Dunblane, Doune & Callander Railway, and the trackbed heading southeast was a tarmac footpath running on the northern side of the town along the edge of a golf course to a minor road (57 NN 649069). A short grassy section of line became a vehicle track, and we made good time to the signal box at Drumvaich Crossing (57 NN 675043). The signal box appeared to be the home of an avid Scottish Nationalist as 'BRAVEHEART' was daubed in huge letters on a hoarding accompanied by the Saltire. We were in plain view of the signal box but managed to glide past unseen into the sanctuary of a grassy cutting (57 NN 676042).

A good trackbed ended at the A84 at Buchany (57 NN 706030) as the bridge was missing. This required a difficult detour round a field and across a couple of barbed wire fences, to regain an indistinct line (57 NN 707029) running through grassy fields. With another bridge missing we had to cross the A84 again on the outskirts of Doune, where there was some curious graffiti on a corrugated tin shed: 'CARS KILL OUR WORLD, SAVE OUR WORLD'. I wondered why this was written on a shed in Doune. Cars may have arguably killed the railway in Doune, but claims for killing the world seemed, well, a world away.

We saw no trace of Doune Station (57 NN 722019) and in persistent rain we skirted Doune on a clear trackbed past a nature reserve. The trackbed first a path, then a farm track was walkable as far as Ardoch Burn, where the bridge was demolished (57 NN 754017). The track deviated to a minor road that we followed to regain the line at an overbridge (57 NN 755017). The last mile or so of the line to the A9 was well used by cattle and very boggy, with some persistent rain not helping conditions underfoot. The A9 dual carriageway was the effective end of the line (57 NN 770018), as housing had been built over the remainder of the alignment into Dunblane. From this point the walk was just an anti-climatic trudge through the streets of Dunblane to the railway station.

*An old chair lies quietly rusting away on a moss covered, rotting, sleeper on the trackbed close to Crianlarich Station.*

*An elegant viaduct (51 NN 528273) takes the line over Ardchyle Burn, close to Killin Junction.*

*The rugged lines of Glen Ogle Viaduct (51 NN 570265) blend in well with the surrounding hills. Today the viaduct carries a cycleway.*

# WALK VII
## The Hull & Barnsley Railway
## (Cudworth to Hull)

| Walk Summary | |
|---|---|
| Date walked | May 2002 |
| Line mileage | 53 |
| OSLR Maps | 105, 106, 107, 111 |
| Opened to Passengers | 27 07 1885 |
| Closed to Passengers | *01 01 1932, ♦01 08 1955 |
| PGAG Reference | 21, 22 |
| Pre-Grouping Company | North Eastern Railway |

*Cudworth to South Howden, ♦South Howden to Hull (Walton Street Junction)

## Walk Highlights

Brierley Tunnel, South Kirkby Tunnel (Barnsdale Tunnel), Weedly Tunnel, Sugar Loaf Tunnel, Drewton Tunnel and Little Weighton Cutting.

## Public Transport

Both Hull and Barnsley are served with connecting trains to Leeds and York. Cudworth is connected to Barnsley Central Station by bus service 306.

## Walk Description

The main line of the Hull & Barnsley Railway originally ran from Cudworth near Barnsley, South Yorkshire, to Hull (Alexandra Dock Station) on the River Humber. A short section of line in Hull remains in use as a freight only branch to this day. The route of the line meant a traverse significant geographical features, including the Yorkshire Wolds and the River Ouse, as it headed east from the South Yorkshire coalfields to the east coast. Therefore the prospect of substantial structures and earthworks was a tantalising prospect.

Dave and I had taken the unusual step of carrying out a reconnaissance of the main features of the line as the map showed several bridges missing, and the route had at least four tunnels, whose condition was unknown. The major bridge across the Ouse near Drax was missing, and with the nearest crossing being Boothferry Bridge, an 8-mile detour would have been required. To save some foot slogging we decided to purchase a dinghy to get across the river, close to the original site. In theory this plan was merely questionable but in practice it was insane.

### Cudworth to Carlton (22 miles)

We took an early morning service from Leeds to Barnsley, and then a local bus to Cudworth. Using a public footpath/bridleway we joined the trackbed just north of Cudworth (111 SE 378095) at the site of a small bridge. The northbound trackbed was a low embankment with a well-walked cinder surface. The line soon veered eastwards with a lot of old mine workings and associated waste visible to the west. The trackbed was easily walkable except for minor obstacles such as the odd burnt out car and rubbish until a waterlogged cutting (111 SE 386117), which had to be negotiated with care. Beyond the cutting a good walkable trackbed took us to a minor road where we discovered another flooded cutting (111 SE 404117) that guided the trackbed to the western portal of Brierley Tunnel (111 SE 412119). The trackbed in the flooded cutting was easily bypassed from the road by using a convenient public footpath, running along the cutting's southern edge. Donning newly purchased hard hats and leather gloves, Chris and I descended a steep and slippery slope to Brierley Tunnel, with the flooding from the cutting abated by the gradient at the portal. The portal was bricked up with breezeblocks but the metal security gate was open. From our reconnaissance we knew that the tunnel (originally 685 yards in length) was blocked, as the eastern portal had been buried under a new road, but this was our first time inside the tunnel. An airshaft had been sealed off, and was now just a cascade of water, and after about 100 metres we came to a sloping wall of sandbags and rubble that completely blocked

76

the tunnel, that forced us to retrace our steps. A public footpath running above the Brierley Tunnel emerged at a roundabout on the A628 (111 SE 415118). It was this road that had been built over the eastern portal of Brierley Tunnel and the trackbed for about 2 miles as a bypass for the village of Hemsworth. We used the foot/cycleway running alongside the bypass to follow the original alignment as closely as possible.

The trackbed proper reappeared just before the B6422 (111 SE 435122) as a short overgrown embankment that was quickly crossed by the B6422 at the site of the former Hemsworth & South Kirkby Station (111 SE 436122), which was demolished except for the Station House, now in private use. At the existing Doncaster to Wakefield Line we were forced to detour over a footbridge (111 SE 442127) on the eastern edge of Hemsworth, as the original Hull & Barnsley overbridge (111 SE 444125) had been demolished. Much to our amusement someone had written "Sex Pistols" on the wall of the footbridge, thereby dating the bridge as at least pre-1976. On the other side of the railway, the trackbed became indistinct, traversing grassy fields with sections of the line having been filled in, until reaching the Sheffield/Rotherham to York Line (111 SE 454129), where the rail bridge was gone but a footbridge remained.

A delightful, well-walked and tree-covered section of line, shady in the afternoon sun brought us to Upton & North Elmsall Station (111 SE 474130), where only the overgrown platforms remained. On the outskirts of Upton we crossed the site of the Wrangbrook Junction (111 SE 495135) (not visible on the ground) where other Hull & Barnsley lines once radiated southwest towards Wath and southeast towards Denaby, before we entered the deep cutting approach to South Kirkby Tunnel (aka Barnsdale Tunnel). The western portal of South Kirkby Tunnel (111 SE 498137) was not easy to see until we were very close due to the dense foliage, but the trackbed was very dry and easily walked. The brick built portal with a stone keystone was in excellent condition, and only slightly plagued by graffiti. The tunnel was dead straight and 1,226 yards long, being dry and walkable throughout, except for a slightly damp section at the eastern portal. The eastern portal sits below, and adjacent to, the A1 (111 SE 504147), with the trackbed being completely filled in by the A1's embankment. We climbed the embankment to the A1 close to a service station only to find that the footbridge was closed, thereby necessitating a hazardous foot crossing of the thundering A1. After getting some cold pop from the petrol station shop we dropped into an overgrown but cool cutting on the eastern side of the A1. The trackbed continued in a northeast direction across arable fields and was walkable to a minor road (111 SE 524160), where it disappeared into a wheat field. The absent trackbed and Chris's hay fever gave us a good excuse to head round field margins to The Fox at Little Smeaton village, for a couple of cold beers that were most welcome on a hot afternoon.

Due to some bad planning we rejoined the line at the 1 km long cutting just out of Little Smeaton, therefore missing the remains of Kirk Smeaton Station site (111 SE 531164) completely. There is a building still marked on the map and I understand that it is the station house now in private use. The cutting from the station was badly overgrown, forcing us along the southern edge for about a third of its length before we could enter to enjoy the shade. The overbridge (111 SE 546172) across the existing freight branch running between Knottingley and Shaftholme Junction (closed to passengers in 1947) was demolished. We detoured to cross the railway on a public footpath just south, where we followed an excellent trackbed to the A19 (111 SE 566185). No remains of the level crossing could be seen and we had to carefully skirt the house on the eastern side of the road via a nearby gate to a field. A ditch (111 SE 567186) with the bridge missing abruptly impeded us. Instead of the bridge was a feeble looking plank that took some care in getting across to prevent a muddy bath. The trackbed became indistinct in the open fields so we detoured via a minor road (111 SE 573191) to a crossroads. It was obvious from the map that the bridge across the Knottingly & Goole Canal (105 SE 588208) was missing so we stayed on the minor road with a good view of the embanked line, to cross the canal west of Great Heck. It was easy to pick up the line from Great Heck and the trackbed was walkable to some quarry workings (105 SE 593215) where it disappeared. Fortunately no one was around in the quarry so we were able to escape to a minor road through the main gate close to the M62 bridge. Just beyond the M62, the line crossed the East Coast Main Line, (105 SE 597217), but the bridge was long gone forcing us to follow the minor road to the A645 and examine the bus options to Carlton, for our overnight stop. This meant missing only a short section of line, as beyond this point the Hull & Barnsley remained in use as freight branch for about 4 miles serving the enormous coal-

78

fired Drax power station, complete with its 12 massive cooling towers that dominated the skyline.

It had been a very long day and the buses to Carlton were non-existent, so we tried our luck at hitching. To our surprise a car driven by a young bloke; a sound, 'rocker-type' from Goole, stopped almost immediately after our thumbs went out and took us into Carlton. Our B&B was The Foresters Arms, which was a basic room behind the pub, and as this was not a tourist area, we assumed that the rooms were probably used by workers at the Drax power station.

## Carlton to South Cave (18 miles)

The weather had changed from a scorcher to persistent drizzle overnight, and we left Carlton via a northbound public footpath that had been ploughed up and planted with wheat, making the going very wet and sticky underfoot. We joined the existing freight railway close to Drax (106 SE 656256) and walked along a path close to its edge to the buffer stop on a siding close to a roundabout on the A645. Just across the road was Drax Station, (106 SE 667264) now a private house, that did not look much at all like a former station. After a detour round the station house on a public footpath through some woods, we regained the line at a pond (106 SE 671267) where the leviathan of Drax power station was curiously reflected on the murky surface. The trackbed from the pond was indistinct and in plain view of a nearby farmhouse, running across a grassy field. We had to rely on the miserable weather as a deterrent to any curious landowners. Whilst crossing this field I did, however, do my good turn for the day by righting a distressed sheep whose fleece had firmly anchored it to the wet ground. Crossing a minor road (106 SE 676274) the line became embanked and was walkable, but very wet due to the overhanging vegetation. We descended from the embankment onto a minor road next to the River Ouse (106 SE 684270). The remains of the bridge abutments had been incorporated into a private garden, so we set off southwards on the minor road for about 100 metres before hopping over a fence to find a concrete mooring platform that Dave and I had previously reconnoitred.

This was to be the launch pad for our river crossing. Stifling guffaws of laughter we quickly pumped up our two dinghies complete with 'Action

Man' logo, purchased from a toyshop for £12 each. Our plan was for one man to paddle a dinghy across with a cord attached, then using the cord to pull it back, load up with gear and pull it back across the river, before repeating the process for the two remaining NEDRAT members. This stretch or the river was tidal, and the tide was going out quickly, leaving a very muddy slope to launch the dinghies into the water. The dinghies took a while to inflate with the foot pumps, and it was at this point that we realised that they were rather small for three men all over 6ft tall. As it was my harebrained idea in the first place to be "true to the line", I had to be first in to establish the link across the river. Sitting in the dinghy with my life jacket inflated, Chris lowered me down the muddy bank into the water by the cord attached to the back. I was only about a metre from the bank when the current took hold and I quickly disappeared from sight behind a huge moored barge. Because I had the oars arranged in the rollicks they trapped my legs as the cord pulled tight folding the tiny dinghy up pulling me towards the anchored barge. I just managed to throw the oars overboard and went to get my knife to cut the cord when it snapped, as Chris still had a hold, leaving me hurtling downstream. Fortunately, I had had the foresight to take a canoe style paddle as a reserve, and with this I began to paddle for all I was worth. Once out of the main current I reached the far shore quite easily, about 500 metres down river, much to the concern of Chris and Dave, who eventually came running down the southern bank only to find me on the northern side. After a brief discussion we decided to abandon any more amphibious crossing attempts i.e. Chris and Dave had seen my efforts and were not persuaded to follow! This left us with only one option: to walk down the riverbank and rendezvous at Boothferry Bridge, about 4 miles for me, and even further for Chris, Dave who also now had to carry my backpack.

At lunchtime we met at the impressive Boothferry road bridge. After an exciting and wet morning it was a relief to get some hot food at The Ferryboat pub that sits right next to the bridge. Over lunch the sky blackened and the rain became torrential, dosing a wedding party who were holding their reception in the pub. With the weather staying bad we consulted the map for our next move. The surrounding landscape was very flat and the line looked disjointed, with large sections not marked and some of the trackbed being under the M62. In other words this was the least interesting section of the line. After a few drinks, lethargy had set in and we decided to catch the bus to our overnight stop at South Cave. Having been soaked and swept down a river, and feeling very tired, I only slightly regretted this decision. Our room at The Fox & Coney Inn in South Cave soon resembled a youth hostel drying room as our gear was hanging from all available hooks, shelves, chairs etc. A good night's food, drink and sleep set us up nicely for the next day and the highlights of the Hull & Barnsley Railway.

### South Cave to Hull (13 miles)

The weather had improved overnight to bring a fresh bright morning. We rejoined the line at some quarry workings just off the A1034 (106 SE 918327). The flat land of the Ouse valley quickly gave way to the hills of The Wolds, and we soon entered a leafy cutting used as a farm track (106 SE 926332), with a delightful overbridge (106 SE 932333) carrying a bridleway over the line two-thirds the way along the cutting. At the end of the cutting lay the western portal (106 SE 934331) of Weedly Tunnel (132 yards long). Weedly Tunnel with its brick arch and stone keystone was open and obviously in use as a farm track. Beyond Weedly Tunnel the trackbed ran in a dramatic deep cutting through the chalky hill, and was about 1km long, with the western portal of Sugar Loaf Tunnel (106 SE 946334), also 132 yards long, marking the end of the cutting. Just in front of the portal was a three-arched, brick, overbridge that straddled the cutting. With the walls on top of the bridge missing, it was now essentially a platform. The bridge and portal so close together was a dramatic site.

Unfortunately, Sugar Loaf Tunnel was partially filled with rubble, wire and assorted rubbish, but was passable with a bit of scrambling. Emerging from the eastern portal of the tunnel, we came upon a scene of utter devastation. Just a short distance beyond the eastern portal the once deep cutting was full of rubble. We could hear men and machines at work, so we scrambled up the south side of the steep cutting out into a field to get better views of the destruction taking place right before our eyes. The site appeared to be part quarry and part landfill, and somewhere in that heart-breaking mess was the western portal to Drewton Tunnel; a monster at 2,114 yards long. As there was so much activity on the site, we could not descend the bare hillside and enter without being seen. After a while the big yellow machines stopped work and most of the

81

occupants wandered off to a hut for lunch.

Our reconnaissance had paid off as we knew roughly where the portal lay, and this was our chance to get in. Quickly, we tumbled over the barbed wire fence and scrambled down the steep slope into the workings, using what cover we could. Eventually we came out on a track thick with wet chalky clay. A couple of trees and a clump of stinging nettles marked the location of Drewton Tunnel's western portal (106 SE 952335) that was almost completely filled in with chalky rubble, with just the keystone and the very top of the arch visible in the morass. Just as we were looking down on the tunnel a voice yelled out at us. There was a workman about 200 yards from us who had spotted us. He told us to get out, so we turned and walked off for a few metres until he turned back towards his machine, at which point all three of us literally threw ourselves down the drop to the tunnel and careered through the nettles landing in a heap at the bottom. Not waiting around to be seen again, we slid down the extremely muddy slope into the tunnel, hearts pounding. Helmets and torches were quickly produced and we set off into the cold, wet, darkness. For the first 20 yards the tunnel floor was covered in ankle deep wet silt that had run off the soil used to fill the portal, and was very slippery, but it soon gave way to firmer ground. The tunnel was dead straight and we could see the far end, but a strange glow seemed to appear before this. This glow of course, was the light coming from an airshaft, and Drewton Tunnel has five of these structures allowing a ghostly light in at intervals along the tunnel. Small sections of the tunnel walls had caved-in, but generally they were in good condition, although quite a lot of water was dripping down the airshafts. It took us about an hour to reach the eastern end of the tunnel. The eastern portal had a security fence accompanied by a tangle of razor wire, and in front of this was a pool of some foul smelling agricultural slurry of some description that acted as a moat. After a struggle we negotiated both obstacles, emerging in a leafy cutting (106 SE 971337). This was our longest tunnel to date and all the trouble getting in and out added to our excitement. We wondered how long it would be before the western portal of Drewton Tunnel would be lost forever?

Outside the tunnel there was building and agricultural debris scattered around, with the cutting partially infilled. The trackbed became indistinct in a series of fields to the village of Little Weighton. The impressive brick built Little Weighton Station (106 SE 982334) was in use as a private house. Just across the road in Little Weighton was the spectacular Little Weighton Cutting. At almost ¾ mile long, up to 82ft high and only 120ft wide at the top it was truly a unique cutting, guiding the line through the chalk of the Wolds. Sadly we heard a bulldozer working in the cutting. It appeared that the magnificent Little Weighton Cutting was now a landfill site. The narrow cutting gave us no cover and the bulldozer driver quickly spotted us. He informed us that this was a working site and we'd better not be seen by his boss somewhere up ahead in the cutting. At least he seemed aware of the awful destruction that he was involved with. Thanking him for the tip, we proceeded cautiously along the remains of the magnificent cutting. We made good progress along the broad well used trackbed to a minor road (106 TA 009316) that marked the boundary of the works undetected, after having to take cover a couple of times for passing vehicles. The trackbed on the other side of the road disappeared into an already filled in landfill site that was busy with traffic. This marked the end of the line for us, and we detoured round to Willerby for a bus into Hull for the train home.

*A bright sunny day highlights the western portal of South Kirkby Tunnel (111 SE 498137). The light from the eastern portal can just be seen.*

*The western portal of Weedley Tunnel (106 SE 934331) reveals the curve in this short but fine tunnel.*

*The eastern portal of Drewton Tunnel (106 SE 971337) is both heavily fortified and overgrown.*

*The once magnificent Little Weighton Cutting (106 SE 984333) was being used for landfill when we passed; another wonderful relic of our rail heritage in the process of being erased forever.*

*The substantial house of Little Weighton Station (106 SE 982334) makes a fine private dwelling.*

# WALK VIII
## The Whitby, Redcar & Middlesbrough Union Railway
## (Whitby to Staithes)

| Walk Summary | |
|---|---|
| Date walked | November 2002 |
| Line mileage | 11* |
| OSLR Maps | 94 |
| Opened to Passengers | 1883 |
| Closed to Passengers | 05 05 1958 |
| PGAG Reference | 28 |
| Pre-Grouping company | North Eastern Railway |

*Approximate distance quoted from Larpool Viaduct to Staithes (Line mileage from Whitby West Cliff to Staithes is 10 miles).

## Walk Highlights

Larpool Viaduct, Sansend Tunnel, Kettleness Tunnel, Kettleness Station, and the magnificent coastal views.

## Public Transport

Whitby is at the end of the picturesque Esk Valley line from Middlesbrough. Steam trains also run from the North York Moors preserved railway from Pickering to Whitby. Staithes is connected by Arriva bus X56/56 to Middlesbrough and Whitby.

## Walk Description

The northern section of The Whitby, Redcar & Middlesbrough Union Railway remains in use as a freight only line serving the potash mine at Boulby on the Cleveland coast. To the south of Whitby, the former Scarborough & Whitby Line is now an excellent cycle/walkway to

87

Scarborough.

Having taken the first service out on the Esk Valley line from Middlesbrough to Whitby, we joined the line at the northern end of the 13-arched brick built Larpool Viaduct (94 NZ 896096). This magnificent structure towers 125 feet above the River Esk and is 305 yards long, giving splendid views up the Esk valley and across the town of Whitby. As well as taking the line over the River Esk, Larpool Viaduct also straddles the existing Esk Valley Line. The Esk Valley Line was once connected to The Whitby, Redcar & Middlesbrough Union Railway via a steep curve that ran from Prospect Hill Junction (94 NZ 893103) under Lapool Viaduct along the north bank of the Esk to Bog Hall Junction (94 NZ 899103), north of Whitby Town Station.

The Scarborough & Whitby Railway Path ceased just north of the Larpool Viaduct, and we were soon off the right of way. The line quickly disappeared into housing developments but could still be followed until we emerged onto the A174 (94 NZ 894107). Walking through the West Cliff area of Whitby we observed that Whitby West Cliff Station House (94 NZ 890111), had been converted for private residential use, and did not resemble a former railway station. Beyond the station we had to skirt the trackbed via the coastal path as it had been usurped as part of a golf course (94 NZ 884117) just beyond West Cliff, and the golfers were out braving the November drizzle. There were two viaducts (Upgang Viaduct and Newholm Beck Viaduct) on this stretch of line but both had been demolished. Beyond the golf course the line ran adjacent to the A174 as a barely recognisable grassy mound as far as East Row. Walking along the beach we arrived at the village of East Row, and found the stunted remains of the supporting pillars from East Row Viaduct (94 NZ 864126) on the beach. A short distance along the beach and perched high above Sandsend was Sandsend Station (94 NZ 860129), now in use as a private house with a commanding view out into the North Sea. Beyond Sandsend Station the trackbed, now part of The Cleveland Way, started its convoluted route round the cliffs. The gradient was severe and provided good walking on a cinder trackbed with excellent panoramic views out to sea.

The public footpath left the trackbed at the south portal of Sandsend Tunnel (94 NZ 854142), veering off up the hill. The moss-covered stone portal was bricked up to about a third of its height.  In the centre of this wall there was hole about 1 metre off the ground.  The tunnel was flooded to a depth of about 18 inches, with the wall effectively acting as a dam for water running down the gradient inside the tunnel, and we could not see how far the water extended into the tunnel from our vantage point in the wall.  Deciding to chance wet feet I donned gaiters and Dave put a couple of fertiliser sacks over his boots, while Chris opted for removal of socks and insoles.  I squeezed through the hole and perched precariously on some rubble before sprinting into the blackness.  To my surprise I reached dry land after about 20 metres, managing to keep my feet dry.  Dave's fertiliser sacks were not quite so successful at keeping the water out, but he did look entertaining as he splashed through the flood like a man possessed!

We put on helmets and got out torches and moved carefully into a very wet tunnel.  The walls were very slimy and sooty, and there was a virtual stream running down the gradient, with many holes in the floor and bits of debris everywhere.  The tunnel, being only single track, gave a more claustrophobic feel than we were used to, and at 1,652 yards was a good test of our collective mettle.  We came upon a side tunnel to the right that went all the way out to the sea-cliff, probably used during construction.  We did not explore this tunnel as it looked in a very dangerous condition.  The northern portal (94 NZ 842149) of Sandsend Tunnel was like something out of 'The Land That Time Forgot' with damp clumps of vegetation hanging from the roof of the portal.  We had emerged into a steep, narrow, and wet cutting, and because the cutting sat between Sandsend and Kettleness Tunnels, it was an isolated and infrequently visited sanctuary.  The cutting was only about 200m long before reaching the southern portal (94 NZ 839152) of Kettleness Tunnel, where we were rewarded with a marvellous sea view.  Kettleness Tunnel was 308 yards long and was bricked up at each end but with open doorways that provided easy access.  Although a lot shorter than Sandsend Tunnel it appeared very dark as it was on a slight curve.

We emerged from the north portal of Kettleness Tunnel (94 NZ 838154) into a much more open and exposed area of countryside, and a strong sea breeze blowing in the damp air made it feel very cold.  The line was a lovely grassy track that curved sharply to the west, following the profile of the coastline to the small settlement of Kettleness.  Approaching

Kettleness we veered off onto a public footpath as the trackbed was in use as a farm track running very close to a farm house with resident dogs barking frantically at our presence. Over the minor road in Kettleness was Kettleness Station (94 NZ 832156), a sympathetically preserved and substantial three-chimneyed house with platforms intact. We walked past the station on a track before joining the line just beyond the end of the platforms. I envied the owners of an old station in such a dramatic setting. The line was now a muddy but walkable track that followed the convoluted coastline with the occasional cutting and stone overbridge. The trackbed continued to be muddy but walkable to the minor road heading into Runswick Bay (94 NZ 804156). It was now raining hard so we detoured into the village Runswick Bay and found shelter and a coal fire in The Runswick Bay Hotel.

We dawdled for a long time over food and beers waiting for the rain to ease before retracing our steps to rejoin the line where we had left off. The trackbed was very walkable until it disappeared into some fields on the outskirts of Hinderwell (94 NZ 799161). It was quite a difficult walk round fields in the wet grass until eventually we emerged onto the A174 on the edge of Hinderwell. The late hour and fading daylight was not helped by the dark low clouds that occasionally doused us in a shower of cold rain. We managed to pick up the line that was now a road in Hinderwell close to the site of Hinderwell Station (94 NZ 795163) that appeared to be long gone. Just north of Hinderwell we descended an embankment to the A174 (94 NZ 788174) to find the line obliterated in agricultural land on the other side of the road. There was no option other than to follow the A174 into Staithes. Staithes Station (94 NZ 783184), a large red-brick house remained as a private dwelling. Just west of Staithes Station there once stood the spectacular 700ft long, iron girder, Staithes Viaduct (94 NZ 779186) that was now sadly demolished. Fragments of trackbed exist beyond Staithes to the existing freight branch at Boulby mine.

*The wonderfully clear trackbed north of Sandsend, climbing steeply, hugs the cliffs on the approach to Sandsend Tunnel.*

*The heavily overgrown north portal of Sandsend Tunnel (94 NZ 842149) provides a haven to put on dry socks.*

*Dave emerges from the northern portal of Kettleness Tunnel (94 NZ 838154).*

*Kettleness Station (94 NZ 832156) sits in a wide open and windswept location.*

# WALK IX
## Colne to Skipton

| Walk Summary | |
|---|---|
| Date walked | February 2003 |
| Line mileage | 11 ¼ |
| OSLR Maps | 103 |
| Opened to Passengers | 1848 |
| Closed to Passengers | 02 02 1970 |
| PGAG Reference | 21 |
| Pre-Grouping Company | Midland Railway |

**Walk Highlights**

Although there are no notable structures on this line, the countryside is very pleasant and the trackbed is in excellent condition for most of the route.

**Public Transport**

Colne is the terminus of line from Blackburn and Burnley. Skipton is served by frequent trains from Leeds.

**Background**

If you look at the map, this short line looks like a missing link that should most definitely not have been taken out, considering the centres of population it linked. Indeed, this short section of line was not included in the 1963 Beeching Report as a candidate for closure. I have been unable to find out why this line was closed, but there is a real possibility for the line to be re-opened, as the trackbed had been largely protected from development and is in remarkably good condition. Since our walk I have discovered a group dedicated to re-opening this line. The Skipton

East Lancs Railway Action Partnership (SELRAP) can be found at www.selrap.org.uk, where there is an excellent series of photographs showing the entire length of the trackbed.


**Walk Description**

The once through-station of Colne was fenced off at the northern end, with the former link to Skipton disappearing into playing fields (103 SD 881399). After a magnificent breakfast at the Istanbul Café in Colne we joined the line under the B6274 iron overbridge (103 SD 879402). The line, obviously well-walked, curved north-eastwards to cross the Leeds & Liverpool Canal at Foulridge Wharf (103 SD 888426). A detour via a track round the old station yard (103 SD 886425), now an untidy works yard, into Foulridge was required as the bridge over the canal was absent.

From Foulridge the trackbed was easily walkable, paralleling the busy A56, through pleasant countryside to Earby. We opted not to explore the short branch to Barnoldswick from Barnoldswick Junction (103 SD 899452). The trackbed became more overgrown as it ran behind Earby, and apart from the predictable domestic detritus one expects on a dismantled railway running close to houses, it was easily negotiable. Although Earby Station site (103 SD 904463) had been built on, the small station house remained as a private house. Just north of Earby we stopped for lunch at The Punch Bowl, as it looked a better option than the other pubs in the village itself.

The line continued as a good walkable trackbed to Elsack Station (103 SD 926495) where the bridge was demolished, and the station was now a light industrial site. A scramble down to the minor road was required before rejoining the line (103 SD 927497) round the former station site via a convenient public footpath. The line continued into the River Aire valley with a good trackbed, offering fine views of the surrounding hills. The bridge crossing the River Aire (103 SD 968509) was missing, necessitating a detour via a minor road south before walking along the riverbank to cross on a public footpath bridge (103 SD 974505). It was a simple task to walk back along the north bank of the River Aire and rejoin the line on an overgrown embankment (103 SD 969509). After about 400 metres the embankment ended at the A629 Skipton bypass marking the end of the walkable line (103 SD 974511). The former Skipton North Junction with the existing railway could just be made out, and a public footpath passed under the existing railway close to the junction site, that gave easy access into the town of Skipton.

*The B6274 bridge (103 SD 879402) marks the start of the trackbed in Colne.*

*The clear trackbed of the Colne to Skipton Line makes fine walking.*

# WALK X
## Harrogate to Crossgates via Wetherby

| Walk Summary | |
| --- | --- |
| **Date walked** | May 2003 |
| **Line mileage** | 17 ¾ |
| **OSLR Maps** | 104, 105 |
| **Opened to Passengers** | 1848 |
| **Closed to Passengers** | 06 01 1964 |
| **PGAG Reference** | 21, 42 |
| **Pre-Grouping Company** | North Eastern Railway |

## Walk Highlights

Prospect Hill Tunnel, partially demolished viaduct at Spofforth, and the bridge at Scarcroft Hill.

## Public Transport

Harrogate and Pannal are served by trains on the scenic Leeds to York Loop Line. Crossgates is 5 minutes from Leeds and is served by trains on the direct Leeds to York Line.

## Background

Harrogate was once supplied by a complex railway infrastructure with lines radiating out to Ripon, York, and Leeds and up Nidderdale. Today Harrogate is just a stop on the scenic Leeds to York Loop Line.

## Walk Description

### Harrogate (Crimple Junction) to Wetherby (7 ¾ miles)

We alighted at Pannal station and headed for Crimple Junction (104 SE 323527) via a bridleway that crossed the existing Leeds-Harrogate-York Railway (104 SE 320524). It was possible to skirt the top of the cutting to reach the dismantled line just south of Crimple Junction, as there was a private house located close to the actual junction site. We descended to the trackbed through woods on a muddy, heavily rutted farm track. Within a few yards we were inside the damp northern portal of Prospect Hill (also known as Crimple) Tunnel (104 SE 324526). Although damp, the tunnel was in good condition and tyre marks indicated that it was in use as a thoroughfare for farm/estate vehicles. Prospect Hill Tunnel was dead straight and 825 yards to the southern portal (104 SE 330522) which was also clear. Once out of the tunnel we were soon confronted with the embankment of the A658, where the trackbed was infilled. Crossing the A658 we found that the cutting to the south was also infilled in with very sticky mud. After about 500 metres of this quagmire, the cutting reappeared and was in use as a vehicle track. The track emerged from the cutting and diverted from the trackbed to the right after crossing some flat open country (104 SE 343516). The line then entered another, shorter cutting, (104 SE 346516) before becoming vague in some open fields.

We reached a minor road west of Spofforth village where the overbridge was filled in (104 SE 353515). Crossing the minor road we dropped into a damp overgrown cutting. Due to the proximity of a golf course we found several golf balls sitting like mushrooms on and around the trackbed. We arrived in Spofforth on the partially demolished stone viaduct (104 SE 361510), that overlooked houses that had been built across the line. It was an easy descent from the truncated viaduct to a bridleway into the village of Spofforth, where we found no trace of Spofforth Station (104 SE 364507).

The trackbed from Spofforth (104 SE 365506) had been converted into a walking/cycleway, that provided an easy but not very interesting walk for about 3 miles into Wetherby. The walking/cycleway included the southern spur from Wetherby West Junction (104 SE 398491) bypassing Wetherby, but we headed straight into Wetherby for a pie and a pint as

97

the heavens had opened.


**Wetherby to Crossgates (10 miles)**

The line continued east from Wetherby to Tadcaster but our destination was south. After leaving the town centre we arrived at Wetherby Golf Course, situated just southwest of Wetherby. The embanked line bisects the golf course between the River Wharfe and a minor road. The place was swarming with (judging by the cars in the car park) affluent golfers, who we surmised, would definitely not appreciate a visit from some railway walkers. Fortunately, a public footpath crossed the golf course giving us access to the line's embankment. The heavens opened again sending the cashmere-clad golfers running for cover and gave us a golden opportunity to clamber up onto the line at the site of a former overbridge (104 SE 393476). The embankment was thickly wooded and initially had a good track on it, but this soon petered out into thick undergrowth. Stealth was the order of the day as we crept along the embankment. We came to the site of a second demolished overbridge and we could hear some golfers chatting whilst sheltering from the rain. All we could do was wait for them to move off before we nipped off the line across the gap and back into the sanctuary of the trees. The embankment abruptly ended at a tee, with golfers present. Again extreme stealth was called for as we waited for them to move on. Near the end of the embankment was a public footpath (104 SE 391468) that provided our escape route. We had managed to cross the busy course but had taken us more that an hour to go one mile.

The rail bridge across the River Wharfe (104 SE 389464) was missing so we crossed on the minor road bridge just north of Collingham village. We tried to pick up the line in Collingham, but were thwarted by a housing estate. Backtracking, we made our way out of Collingham on the A659 before following a hedge down the edge of a field to rejoin the line (104 SE 373453). The embanked line quickly crossed Keswick Beck in a scenic valley, curving round to head due south. We arrived in East Rigton under a dark and threatening sky, where the rail bridge was missing so we left the line at a car park (104 SE 365440). Housing largely obliterated the line south of East Rigton, so we followed the A58 to a bus stop to catch the bus back to Dave's place in Leeds for the night.

The following morning promised a better day as we retraced our steps to East Rigton. We joined the line from the A58 (104 SE 369430), which was a well-surfaced track, and the scenery continued to improve as we got further south. The trackbed was somewhat overgrown and damp in places but it was a joy to walk for about 1½ miles to Scarcroft Hill, to a magnificent 3-arched red-brick overbridge (104 SE 374413), carrying a minor road across the line. Passing under the bridge we negotiated the wet, overgrown cutting before the line emerged into open country. Entering a cutting (104 SE 376409) just north of Thorner, we had to backtrack due to the presence of farm buildings. There was an easy diversion into Thorner via a public footpath (104 SE 375410), just in time for some lunch. Unfortunately The Mexborough Arms was not doing lunch, so we headed to The Fox where a rather grumpy landlord served us a very mediocre toasted sandwich.

Heading south out of Thorner we joined a public footpath (104 SE 378403) that crossed the line via a stone bridge (104 SE 379399). It was easy to access the flat, grassy, trackbed from the bridge, and it was good walking for about 2 miles to the A64. Passing under the A64 the line skirted a row of houses on the north side of Scholes. Although not a right of way at this point the line was obviously well walked. Just by the road crossing in Scholes (104 SE 376372) the old station had been turned into a rather plastic looking pub named 'The Buffers'. The line south of Scholes was a well-used path as far as a minor road (104 SE 373358). Beyond the road the trackbed was obliterated until we reached a cutting (104 SE 370351). The cutting however was extremely overgrown and full of domestic rubbish and was a real struggle to negotiate before we could escape at the next minor road crossing (104 SE 369347). The last short cutting to the junction with the Leeds – York line was also badly overgrown so we skirted along the top before making our way through a housing estate to Crossgates Station for the train back to Leeds.

# WALK XI
## The Hereford, Ross & Gloucester Railway
## (Hereford to Grange Court)

| Walk Summary | |
|---|---|
| Date walked | August 2003 |
| Line mileage | 22 ½ |
| OSLR Maps | 149, 162 |
| Opened to Passengers | 01 06 1855 |
| Closed to Passengers | 02 11 1964 |
| PGAG Reference | 9 |
| Pre-Grouping Company | Great Western Railway |

## Walk Highlights

Ballingham Tunnel, Fawley Tunnel, Lea Line Tunnel, and the scenery of the Wye Valley and Forest of Dean Area.

## Public Transport

Hereford is on the Crewe, Shrewsbury and Newport Line. Hereford can also be reached from Worcester via the Great Malvern Line. Stagecoach bus number 73 runs from Gloucester Railway Station to Westbury-on-Severn. It is about a 2-mile walk from Westbury-on-Severn to Grange Court.

## Walk Description

### Hereford to Ross-on-Wye (12 miles)

A Friday night drunken Irishman with mad eyes greeted us on the road-over-rail bridge as we made our way into Hereford for a few pints. Amongst his ramblings was the lucid phrase: "Here we are fellas, stuck on a bridge between two stories". Did he mean the dominance of road over rail as physically reflected by our present location, or was it just some random product of struggling synapses? Whatever the meaning, it gave us a focal point for discussion over some chips with curry sauce. Hereford was a lively place on a summer Friday night, and we struggled to find a quiet pub to discuss the walk.

It was a hot morning as we made our way to Hereford Bus Station. Unfortunately during my planning I had omitted finding a bus to the start of our walk close to Holme Lacy. We had opted to miss out the first section of line from Rotherwas Junction (149 SO 523388), as from looking at the map the alignment appeared obliterated by a sewage works. This was our first mistake as it meant we would miss exploring Dinedor Tunnel (110 yards long) (149 SO 540376), which I had not noticed at the time of planning. Subsequent research has revealed that Dinedor Tunnel is accessible via the north portal, but the south portal is blocked.

The bus driver dropped us a mile south of the village of Mordiford at Even Pits, where we crossed the River Wye before joining a public footpath (149 SO 559360) that followed the west bank of the river. This was our second mistake, as the path was not well used and extremely overgrown, costing us a lot of energy and time. Eventually we found the trackbed (149 SO 550360), and we walked into a cool cutting close to Holme Lacy. The morning was hot, and it promised to be a blistering day; not good for the dismantled railway walker having to bash through some very thick undergrowth.

We arrived at the remains of Holme Lacy Station (149 SO 553357), nestled in a leafy cutting. The location was barely recognisable in the dense vegetation, with only the platform in evidence. Climbing out of the cutting at the B4399 road bridge (149 SO 554356) we picked up a public footpath running along the top of the cutting to avoid the dense jungle-like growth below. A bonus was a plum tree next to the footpath laden with ripe plums. The cutting became clearer close to where the footpath joined a minor road, so we rejoined the trackbed for about 500 metres before emerging on a minor road junction (149 SO 558351) at the site of a demolished bridge. At this point we opted to take the minor road shadowing the line as the trackbed was severely overgrown, and this fact, combined with the hot weather meant we were moving very slowly. This section of line was very flat, running on the flood plain of the River Wye and was hard to make out from the road as we shadowed the trackbed. We scrambled onto the trackbed again (149 SO 564332) just before a bridge that took us over the road and onto the approach to the north portal of Ballingham Tunnel (1,208 yards long) (149 SO 565326). Appearing like a lost temple, the portal slowly came into view through the dense vines and undergrowth, and the still coolness of the cutting was a relief. Ballingham Tunnel was open, and being dead straight we could see the light at the southern portal. Inside the tunnel it was dry and the walls appeared in very good condition. The approach to the southern portal (149 SO 566315) was damp, with the shear cutting walls covered in lush mosses that steamed in the heat. It looked, and felt, more like a jungle somewhere in South East Asia. Upon spotting a large shed further down the line we opted for a difficult climb out of the cutting to an adjacent field. Skirting a plantation of trees we emerged at a minor road (149 SO 568311). Ballingham Station House (149 SO 573300), now a private dwelling was visible from the minor road bridge. The map indicated that the nearby bridge across the River Wye (149 SO 569306) was missing, so a detour into Hoarwithy village was required.

During the morning we had made slow progress, but Hoarwithy proved to be a delightful oasis on a hot lunchtime. The New Harp Inn with a cheery welcome from the staff, very cold lager and gigantic bowls of chips proved a suitable tonic. It was with some reluctance that we set off from the shady beer garden into the blistering heat. Because of the bridge being out, it meant about a 5-mile road walk to regain the line. I have since found out that the reason that the viaducts across the Wye are gone is that their platforms were of timber construction. With a bit of dead reckoning we left the road (149 SO 569302) and cut across a very exposed and recently harvested field, until we reached the woods along the steep riverbank. The woods provided shade, but were thick with the pink flowered, and foul smelling Himalayan Balsam (*Impatiens glandulifera*), which was above head height. More dead reckoning took us to the cutting and the north portal of Fawley Tunnel (540 yards long) (149 SO 570305). The portal was bricked up but had a partially bricked up doorway that allowed easy access. Looking back from the cutting it was just possible to see the remaining stone pillars of the viaduct across the River Wye. The southern portal (149 SO 572300) was bricked up in a similar fashion to the northern portal, with the cutting being rather damp. Taking no chances, we scaled the steep bank out of the cutting to avoid a building situated a short distance along the line, to join a public footpath that took us to a minor road (149 SO 574299). Just over the road was Fawley Station, which was in use as a private house. The presence of the house plus the late hour made access to the next section of line difficult. Adding to the problem was the fact that the next viaduct (149 SO 577286), was also missing, meaning another significant detour. After some deliberation, we opted to follow the minor road to Sellack Boat, to cross the Wye on an unusual suspension footbridge (149 SO 565280). A long road-walk took us to the site of Backney Bridge (162 SO 583270), where the area on the bank had been converted into a picnic area that offered a good view of the remaining stone pillars of the viaduct. There was no trace of Backney Halt (162 SO 584273). In hindsight a dinghy would have very useful on this walk, as there were many crossing points over the slow flowing River Wye. As crossing the river was impossible at this point we had to walk the rest of the way into Ross-On-Wye via minor roads and public footpaths. During the walk into Ross, we could see sections of line that looked very overgrown.

Although Ross was very busy we managed to get a basic and cheap room at The Riverside Inn. The landlord even reduced the price by £3 a head, as we did not want breakfast.


**Ross-on-Wye to Grange Court (10 ½ miles)**
The site of Ross-on-Wye Station (160 SO 606244) had been re-developed as an industrial estate. Ross-on-Wye was once the junction station for the former Ross & Monmouth Line that followed the Wye Valley south to Monmouth.

Emerging on the A40 we saw an indistinct line traversing some very open country, and with a lot of activity in the fields we were unable to access the line until reaching an overbridge (162 SO 627239). Due to buildings on the line we could only follow about 500 metres of line before being forced into a detour at Weston-under-Penyard, where we found no sign of the Halt (162 SO 632234) that once served the village.

A short detour to an overbridge (162 SO 634234) brought us back

103

to the line, where it was easy walking until the trackbed completely disappeared into an infilled cutting and ploughed field (162 SO 642228). Another detour via minor roads to a public footpath (162 SO 649213) led to the edge of a deep cutting (162 SO 650213). The footpath skirted along a field of ripening maize to the edge of the cutting, where there was a farmer feeding his cows. As we were on the public footpath he was happy to chat to us about our walk. When we informed him that we were walking to Gloucester, he proclaimed in his fantastic strong West Country accent: "You must be *outta* your *moinds*!" which provided a few laughs. During our conversation he even suggested that we go down into the old railway cutting for a bit of shade. At this stroke of luck we scrambled down into the deep cutting. Chris and I walked to the western end of the cutting to see that the line westwards had been totally obliterated by agricultural development.

Thanks to the cattle the trackbed had been well grazed and was walkable until we saw a recent housing development built across the line (162 SO 656212) at the site of Mitcheldean Road Station, which necessitated another detour via a public footpath to a minor road (162 SO 655212). Following the road to the other side of the housing development, we were able to access the line via an embankment (162 SO 658213). The trackbed was easily walked until we reached the A40 (162 SO 665214) where the bridge was infilled and the cutting was completely overgrown and rubbish-strewn. Dropping into the cutting on the other side of the A40 required caution, as there was a stable and sheds present, but the area was deserted. Moving rapidly, we came to the western portal of Lea Line Tunnel (782 yards long) (162 SO 668212). The portal was completely bricked up with only a small hole close to the bottom that was blocked up with loose stones. After removing the stones, it was just possible to slip through the hole into the tunnel after removing our packs, and passing them through the hole one at a time. I replaced the stones and we proceeded carefully through the tunnel towards the clear greenish light of the eastern portal (162 SO 674210). When we emerged from the eastern portal into the cutting we could see a garden ahead right across the trackbed, so we were forced to climb out of the cutting to a public footpath running above the portal back to the A40.

East of Lea Line Tunnel the trackbed was inaccessible as it was occupied by private gardens, but after a short detour down the A40 to

104

a minor road we gained access to the line via an overbridge (162 SO 682205). Some easy walking on a good trackbed took us to the outskirts of Longhope where we took a track and minor road back to the A40. The line disappeared under some houses in Longhope so we took a public footpath that lead to a private track (162 SO 691184). Longhope Station (162 SO 689189) also appeared to have been demolished. The private track ran adjacent to the overgrown line, thus providing an easy alternative route. At the point where the track crossed the line and rejoined the minor road (162 SO 693173) we climbed over a gate to rejoin the trackbed. After moving round a short overgrown section of trackbed we descended into a shallow cutting.

It was here that Dave tripped on a bramble and fell headlong into the cutting. By the expression on his face I knew he was hurt. As he fell he had twisted his ankle, and, as we would latterly discover, he had damaged some ligaments. After a brief inspection I could see swelling already starting, so I advised keeping his boot on. Dave could only hobble, so Chris and I had to carry his pack between us. Due to Dave's injury we took the shortest possible route to the A48. We left the line after a delightfully wooded, and easily walkable section of trackbed at an overbridge (162 SO 702162), close to the site of the long gone Blaisdon Halt (162 SO 703162), thus missing the final short section of line to Grange Court.

*The lush vegetation in the cutting can be clearly seen when looking out of the north portal of Ballingham Tunnel (149 SO 565326).*

*The south portal of Fawley Tunnel (149 SO 572300).*

*The missing platform of Backney Bridge (162 SO 583270) makes a formidable obstacle to the railway walker.*

*A fine section of embanked trackbed close to the site of Mitcheldean Road Station.*

# WALK XII
## The Wansbeck Railway
## (Reedsmouth Junction to Morpeth)

| Walk Summary | |
|---|---|
| **Date walked** | October 2003 |
| **Line mileage** | 25 |
| **OSLR Maps** | 80, 81 |
| **Opened to Passengers** | 01 05 1865 |
| **Closed to Passengers** | 15 09 1952 |
| **PGAG Reference** | 27 |
| **Pre-Grouping Company** | North British Railway |

## Walk Highlights

Although this line has no spectacular structures of note, the trackbed is mostly in excellent condition, passing through some marvellous and remote Northumbrian countryside. Anyone walking this line should also call in at The Ox, Middleton; an excellent country pub.

## Public Transport

Morpeth is on the East Coast Mainline and is served by local services from Newcastle. Redesmouth does not have a bus service but nearby Bellingham is served by infrequent Royal Mail Postbus (route 277) from Hexham. Hexham is on the Newcastle to Carlisle Line and has a taxi company outside the railway station.

## Walk Description

### Reedsmouth Junction to Middleton (16 miles)
The Wansbeck Railway was a link line from Reedsmouth Junction on The Border Counties Railway (Walk III) to the East Coast Mainline at

Morpeth. After I got the bus times wrong we had to take a taxi from Hexham Station to Reedsmouth Junction (note: the village is spelt *Redesmouth*).

We accessed the line from the minor road through a gate onto the trackbed (80 NY 866822) that was now a well used track with permissive access. A glorious, bright and crisp autumn morning gave us a pleasant start to our walk. The first feature of note was a picturesque overbridge (80 NY 872834) at the end of a short wooded cutting. About ½ mile up the line from the overbridge was a junction (80 NY 876836) with a short branch up the valley of Broomhope Burn that must have been used for some (disused) quarry/mining workings nearby. The trackbed was fenced off with 'Private' signs and had a stone gangers hut with a rusty tin roof still standing guard. From Broomhope Burn the line contoured along the hillside above the valley of the River Rede, that allowed excellent views of the surrounding countryside. Further easy walking on a good trackbed took us to a thickly wooded cutting below Cragg Farm complete with stone overbridge carrying a public footpath (80 NY 887853). Beyond the cutting, the line became an embankment across open country with the trackbed turning due east and soon entering a short overgrown cutting, which was just about walkable. Upon reaching the A68 we had to pick up a public footpath to Woodburn Station (80 NY 902861), now in use as a single-storey private house.

The trackbed from Woodburn Station flattened out and crossed some very open grazing land, with the only obstacles being a few fences. With the clear afternoon rapidly dipping into evening we found an excellent spot for a wild camp just inside a plantation of pine trees with running water in Risey Burn (80 NY 935851), and enough space for a couple of tents.

It was a splendid morning, with the sun shining brightly and the frosty ground glistening white, as we left our campsite and joined the trackbed that had been tarmaced, and now formed part of a farm track (80 NY 935850) as far as Summit Cottage (80 NY 938846). The trackbed continued southeast as a gravel track through a gate. The low sun was blinding as we proceeded east along an excellent section of trackbed that offered superb views as the line descended from the summit. We came across the remains of a gangers hut, consisting of a moss covered brick chimney and clay pot, standing like a broken finger; a rather melancholy monument to the line.

A short distance beyond Ray Demesne the farm track left the line (81 NY 972858) and the trackbed was fenced off. There was a lot of activity at the nearby farm so we hurried over the fence into a short overgrown section before reaching a public footpath, which was also a farm track, near Blackhalls (81 NY 976858). At this point the trackbed had been planted with pines and was difficult going for about ½ mile. At the end of the plantation the line emerged into open fields onto the A696, where we left the trackbed via a gate (81 NY 988858). As it was mid-morning we could not let a breakfast opportunity go by, so we stopped at the café at Knowesgate Filling Station, which was a proper and independently owned 'greasy-spoon'. We were served by a large, tattooed woman, clad in a grubby 'Iron Maiden' T-shirt; no bland corporate staff uniforms at this eatery!

The trackbed on the eastern side of the A696 was obliterated for a short distance, so we picked up the line via a public footpath that led to Knowesgate Station (81 NY 990858), which was similar in construction to Woodburn Station. The line was easily walkable and very scenic, varying between open sections and avenues of birch trees, to a minor road (81 NZ 015868) where the trackbed became a permissive path to the junction of the Rothbury Branch (81 NZ 034866) (walk XXV) just to the west of Scot's Gap. Under a leaden sky we walked a short section of the Rothbury branch before doubling back just as the rain started. The permissive path ended at Scot's Gap (81 NZ 038864), where the trackbed was occupied by buildings present on the eastern side of the B6343 road bridge. Scot's Gap Station House (81 NZ 039864) had been unsympathetically modernised, with the station site now in use by an agricultural supplies company. We boxed round the station site to join the line via a track (81 NZ 041865). The trackbed was wet and overgrown and indistinct through a wood to a minor road (81 NZ 047863), where the overbridge was demolished. A gate allowed easy access to the trackbed that was now a farm track to Middleton. Very little remained of Middleton Station (81 NZ 065852), with only part of the very overgrown platforms visible, and we left the line at the overbridge and walked into Middleton. Prior to the walk I had telephoned Peter, the landlord of The Ox in Middleton, and asked him if we could camp for the night in his beer garden. Peter was very obliging, and immediately agreed to my request. The Ox was an excellent, unspoilt country pub with Peter being a first class landlord. After pitching tents in the garden, we had an entertaining evening chatting with the locals by a cosy coal fire, whilst listening to the rain pouring down outside.

## Middleton to Morpeth (9 miles)

The rain had abated overnight, giving way to a bright autumn morning. We were on our way before anyone was about, regaining the line where we had left off at the road bridge. The trackbed was still in use as a farm track and easily walkable to a public footpath (81 NZ 079846), where the line was fenced and signed as 'Private'. A short distance beyond the fence we came across a fallen signal gantry and an upright telegraph pole. The telegraph pole had still had four insulator pots present. I scaled the pole, but could not dislodge any of the pots. Not wanting to push our luck we moved quickly to the bridge over the River Wansbeck (81 NZ 082843), a fine twin-arched stone structure. Beyond the River Wansbeck Bridge, the trackbed became more overgrown but remained walkable until a minor road that was once a level crossing. On the eastern side of the former crossing was Angerton Station (81 NZ 087840), that was now a private house. We skirted to the south of the station site, and rejoined the line in a shallow cutting (81 NZ 087839) where the trackbed was walkable, passing under two overbridges carrying minor roads over the line, before reaching Meldon Station (81 NZ 122834), again occupied as a private house.

With the line being blocked at the overbridge, we exited to the minor road and detoured south round the edge of a ploughed field, rejoining the line just east of Meldon Station. The trackbed continued in excellent condition across predominantly flat and open country. As the line passed through a wooded section, I found an insulator pot just lying by the trackbed. It was in perfect condition and was embossed: 'LNER', making it an excellent souvenir. Apart from the odd small overgrown section, the line was walkable before disappearing into fields around grid reference 81 NZ 169842. From this point it was possible to use an overbridge (81 NZ 174843) as a landmark for some dead reckoning walking, as the trackbed was long gone under arable fields. Just to the east of the overbridge sat a line side hut, that was roofless but still had a brick chimney-stack and partial sleeper walls. From the hut to the A1 trunk road the line was all but obliterated under arable fields. We joined a public footpath crossing the A1 (81 NZ 183844) before rejoining the line at a minor road overbridge (81 NZ 185844), where the remainder of the trackbed was a pleasant bridleway to the A197 (81 NZ 198848), and the end of our walk.

Morpeth once had a complex set of junctions as it was at the centre of lines radiating north, south, east and west. Today, Morpeth is just a quiet station on the ECML, ignored by most of the Inter-City services. Just north of Morpeth station, however, the former branch line to Bedlington remains as a freight only line, swinging away to the east.

*The well preserved building of Woodburn Station (80 NY 902861), now in use as a delightful private house.*

113

*A quiet, leaf-carpeted, section of embankment west of Middleton.*

*Early morning sunshine illuminates a sturdy bridge (81 NZ 068851)*

*A battered lineside hut (81 NZ 174843) is no longer able to provide shelter for the railway walker.*

# WALK XIII
## The Lancs & Yorkshire & Great Northern Joint Railway
## (Halifax to Keighley)

| Walk Summary | |
|---|---|
| Date walked | January 2004 |
| Line mileage | 14 |
| OSLR Maps | 104 |
| Opened to Passengers | 1878 - 1884 |
| Closed to Passengers | 23 05 1955 |
| PGAG Reference | 21 |
| Pre-Grouping Company | The Lancs & Yorkshire & Great Northern Joint Railway |

## Walk Highlights

North Bridge Tunnel, Lee Bank Tunnel, Queensbury Tunnel, Queensbury Station site, Thornton Viaduct, Well Heads Tunnel, Hammer's Hill Tunnel, Doe Park Tunnels, Hewenden Viaduct, Cullingworth Viaduct, and Lees Moor Tunnel.

## Public Transport

Halifax and Keighley stations can be reached by services from Leeds or Bradford. Keighley is also home to the Keighley and Worth Valley preserved steam railway running to Oxenhope (www.kwvr.co.uk).

## Walk Description

The Lancs & Yorkshire & Great Northern Joint Railway from Halifax to Keighley ran through some very hilly terrain between Halifax and Keighley, with the aid of no less than ten tunnels and three spectacular viaducts. The route deserved its nickname of 'The Alpine Route'.

116

## Halifax to Ovenden (1 ¾ miles)

During our original walk in 2004 we missed out the short section between Halifax and Ovenden. The following details are from a walk in July 2007.

Remains of the platform used by trains on 'The Alpine Route' can still be seen at Halifax Station, where the trackbed is now a car park (104 SE 097249). On the north-east side of the car park the remains of some coal drops were still present and in a hazardous condition. The line north from Halifax Station was conveyed on a viaduct which has now been demolished. After a wander through the streets it was possible to pick up a re-emerging trackbed in the far northern corner of a car park beyond Sainsbury's and a leisure centre (104 SE 094257). North Bridge Station has been completely obliterated by the car parks and surrounding development. Below a huge mill chimney that dominated the skyline, the trackbed ran in a deep, buttressed cutting for about 200 yards to the south-eastern portal of the 402 yard long North Bridge Tunnel (104 SE 092258). The stone portal was bricked up with a locked steel security gate barring entrance. Although there was a hole in the security gate, we knew that the tunnel was blocked further along, so we decided not to enter.

The trackbed north from North Bridge Tunnel was very difficult to locate, due to the presence of a domestic refuse plant and probable in-filling. Following minor roads to a bridge that crossed the trackbed (104 SE 085265) we were able to access a very overgrown trackbed and walk a short distance south to the north-western portal of Lee Bank Tunnel. The stone portal of the 267 yard tunnel was completely bricked up. Leaving the overgrown portal, we clambered up onto the A629, and headed back south along the road. From the road it was impossible to see either the south-eastern portal of Lee Bank Tunnel or the north-western portal of North bridge tunnel. We assumed that the cutting had been infilled, or possibly the trackbed was so overgrown that the portals were obscured.

## Ovenden to Keighley (12 ¼ miles)

Ovenden Station (104 SE 084271) was in use as a scrap yard, although what appeared to be an original timber station building remained. The trackbed beyond Ovenden Station was largely occupied by industrial units. We had to walk north for about ¾ mile on the minor road towards Holmfield before getting our first real taste of the line at an overbridge (104 SE 084284) in the form of an overgrown and rubbish-filled cutting, that was the site of the now demolished Holmfield Station. The surrounding area was in use by industrial units.

The going was difficult, and with the trackbed suffering more development ahead, we left the cutting at the next overbridge (104 SE 084286) and joined a public footpath (104 SE 085287) which was also used as an access road to a factory. Below the path on the western side the trackbed ran in a deep cutting. About 100m from the south portal of Queensbury Tunnel (104 SE 087292) the cutting was dammed off, and consequently the trackbed was flooded right into the tunnel to about half of the portal's height, with slimy-looking blue-green water. The portal was not physically blocked and would have been accessible by dinghy. This first disappointment forced us to continue on the footpath right up over the hill to Queensbury Village. A convenient track with public access (104 SE 100307) descended the steep northern slope of the hill to a minor road where the line crossed on a stone overbridge (104 SE 105312). Access to the trackbed was easy from this bridge and we walked back along the line to the north portal of Queensbury Tunnel (104 SE 104308). The rubble-strewn portal, secluded in a wet and leafy, cutting was bricked up but had an entrance gated with galvanised steel security gates. One of the slats was missing in the fence allowing just enough room for a (thin) person to squeeze through. I was the only one willing to go inside and explore the 2,501 yard Queensbury Tunnel, and after donning my helmet I proceeded inside and found a very wet black hole with considerable rubbish and rubble present, and some large holes in the floor. Keeping as close to one side or the other as possible to minimise the risk of being hit by falling masonry I pushed on slowly right to the flooded south portal. I estimated that the flooding from the cutting penetrated the tunnel by about 100 metres. After a slow, cautious walk out it was a relief to join the lads again at the northern portal.

A few hundred metres from the northern portal was the complex triangular formation of Queensbury Station and Junction. The junction was divided into north, south, and east junctions, with the east junction taking the former line to Bradford through the blocked Clayton Tunnel

(104 SE 110311). The west portal of Clayton Tunnel was open and accessible via a steep descent down the earth and rubble of the infilled approach cutting. Queensbury Station (104 SE 105310), and the surrounding junction sites were completely obliterated, with the whole area now a muddy wasteland. There were, however, some small fragments remaining of the demolished Queensbury Viaduct (104 SE 106311). Despite the obliteration, Queensbury Station remained an interesting if somewhat sad dismantled railway location, nestled among the steep surrounding hills.

From Queensbury Station the trackbed, boggy in places, was walkable to the superb 20-arched, 300 yard long sandstone and brick Thornton Viaduct (104 SE 095325). A fence of railway sleepers topped with barbed wire barred access to the viaduct. Using a climbing sling and a bit of brawn, we managed to scale the fence much to the amusement of some nearby golfers on the adjacent Thornton Golf Course. The trackbed over the viaduct was clear and had 6ft walls on each side, and peering over the walls gave some wonderful views. On the northern side of the viaduct was the site of Thornton Station, that was completely demolished and now home to Thorton Primary School. We skirted on the eastern side of the school to the B6145. The trackbed east of the school was obliterated for about 500m where it was possible to rejoin the line via a path under an overbridge (104 SE 090327). The trackbed quickly became an overgrown cutting, and we emerged again on the B6145, having to cross over the road due to an infilled bridge (104 SE 085327). A few hundred metres from the B6145 with the line now in a cutting, lay the south portal of the 662 yard long Well Heads Tunnel (104 SE 083328). The portal was bricked up with steel doors, but one door was open, allowing us to explore inside. At probably ¾ of the tunnel's length we were confronted with a pile of sand and earth retained by plywood shuttering that completely blocked the tunnel. Therefore, we had no choice other than to retrace our steps and climb up and over Well Heads Hill, initially on a public footpath before taking a direct route to the site of the north portal of Well Heads Tunnel (104 SE 079332). The cutting and buried north portal were full of earth, rubble and assorted rubbish. Following the edge of the cutting we skirted this eyesore and rejoined the trackbed near a bridge over Denholme Beck (104 SE 076334). The trackbed quickly became a cutting for a short distance to the south portal of the 153-yard long Hammer's Hill Tunnel

(104 SE 075335). The entrance area was extremely wet and boggy, and those without gaiters suffered badly with wet feet. This time we were in luck as the steel door in the bricked up portal revealed light at the northern end. Although Hammer's Hill was only a short tunnel it was tricky to negotiate as the going underfoot was wet with some deep mud. The northern portal of Hammer's Hill Tunnel (104 SE 074336) had a similar open steel door and was also extremely boggy in a shear and very overgrown cutting.

About 100m further along the line was fenced and badly overgrown. This was the site of Denholme Station (104 SE 074337) that was now occupied by a timber yard. After a tricky detour to the east of the timber yard we regained the line just in front of the south portal (104 SE 074340) of the first (145 yards long) of the three Doe Park Tunnels. The portal was open, and scattered inside were a lot of old paint tins and assorted rubbish. The light visible from the north portal proved to be a small hole in the brick wall, but the steel access door was welded shut and could not be budged. Our third major detour saw us backtrack and climb out of the cutting up to a bridleway running along the top of the hill. The trackbed was easily regained via the cutting that housed the northern portal of the first Doe Park Tunnel (104 SE 074341). Just north of the first tunnel was the second (33 yards long) Doe Park Tunnel (104 SE 074342), which was open at both ends and easily walked. At the end of the cutting about 50 metres from the second tunnel was the south portal (104 SE 074343) of the third (northernmost) 112 yard long tunnel. The portal was bricked up with a welded steel access door that was firmly shut. The north portal (104 SE 074344) was also completely bricked up making access impossible.

The trackbed was in very good condition north of the Doe Park Tunnels, and included a fine embanked section, until we were forced to leave the trackbed as it completely disappeared into the grounds of a large house and site of the demolished Wilsden Station (104 SE 075352). Descending from the bridge to a public bridleway we made our way to the magnificent 343-yard long, 17-arched, stone structure of Hewenden Viaduct (104 SE 075357). A scramble up the embankment lead us to the 125 ft high viaduct where the trackbed was fenced off. The fence was easy to negotiate, and the top of the viaduct was clear of vegetation and allowed excellent views up and down the valley. The splendid viaducts of 'The Alpine Route' more than compensated for the disappointing detours caused by the blocked tunnels.

With the line curving northwest we reached the outskirts of Cullingworth on a good trackbed. The galvanised steel security fence of the 9-arched, 150 yard long Cullingworth Viaduct (104 SE 067362) was easier to get round rather than over. Cullingworth Viaduct took us conveniently above and round the village of Cullingworth, and at the northern end of Cullingworth Viaduct the line was impeded by some industrial units, occupying the site of Cullingworth Station, which required a detour to the west onto a cinder track. The cinder track became a public bridleway, and we proceeded quickly before regaining the line at 104 SE 063369. The trackbed was now a wide grassy track having been infilled, and traversed across open fields before dipping into a wet and overgrown cutting, which lead to the eastern portal of the 1,553 yard Lees Moor Tunnel (104 SE 057375). The portal was bricked up with a metal grill enclosing a hole at the top, making access impossible. A public bridleway ran close to the portal that gave easy egress to the village of Barcroft. The northern portal of Lees Moor Tunnel (104 SE 049383) is now inside a caravan park, making access impossible. As we walked north along the A629 we could see the line of the preserved Keighley & Worth Valley Railway running in the valley of the River Worth. North of Lees Moor Tunnel the trackbed was largely built on, and due to the late hour we opted to follow the road into Keighley. This meant that we missed the opportunity to explore the 48 yard long Ingrow East Tunnel (104 SE 057396), but my research suggests that this short tunnel remains open and accessible. Ingrow East Station (104 SE 058397), however, is long gone with the area being occupied by a builders yard.

*The cutting and southern portal of North Bridge Tunnel (104 SE 092258) look out of scale with the towering chimneys of the surrounding old mills.*

*The enormous structure of Thornton Viaduct (104 SE 095325) viewed from the northern end.*

*The southern portal of Well Heads Tunnel (104 SE 083328) remains open, but the northern portal has been completely filled in.*

*Hewenden Viaduct (104 SE 075357) as seen from the trackbed (above) to the south, and (below) the railway walker's view on the viaduct itself.*

# WALK XIV
# The Great Central Railway, Part I
# (Calvert Junction to Rugby)

| Walk Summary | |
|---|---|
| Date walked | March 2004 |
| Line mileage | 34 ½ |
| OSLR Maps | 164, 152, 151, 140 |
| Opened to Passengers | 15 03 1899 |
| Closed to Passengers | 05 09 1966 |
| PGAG Reference | 10 |
| Pre-Grouping Company | Great Central Railway |

## Walk Highlights

The excellent condition of the trackbed, Helmdon Viaduct, Catesby Tunnel, Catesby Viaduct, and numerous other 'blue-brick' structures.

## Public Transport

Rugby is on the West Coast Mainline. Calvert can be reached by local bus 18 from Bicester or Buckingham.

## Background

The inspiration for this walk came from an article in 'Railway Ramblings', the magazine of The Railway Ramblers; a publication always full of useful information. What caught my eye was a mention of the 3,000 yard long Catesby Tunnel. This prompted more research, and the more I read, the more The Great Central Railway (GCR) appealed. Our walks thus far had been largely confined to minor routes and branch lines, so an opportunity to explore a dismantled mainline was an exciting prospect. Originally running from Quainton Road near Aylesbury,

Buckinghamshire to Nottingham, Sheffield and Manchester, the GCR was connected to London Marylebone via Aylesbury. The GCR was the last mainline to be built in England, and remained open for a mere 65 years. Although a mainline, the GCR ran through sparsely populated areas, which contributed to the line's short history. It would, however, have been an extremely useful diversionary and freight route for today's railway traffic had it remained open.

Some of the GCR remains today as mothballed track (Aylesbury to Calvert Junction via Quainton Road), preserved line ('The Great Central Railway', Leicester North to Loughborough Central), and line due to be added to the preserved 'Great Central (Loughborough to Ruddington).

## Walk Description

### Calvert to Culworth (17 ¼ miles)
After an overnight stay in Bicester we caught the bus to Charndon, the nearest village to Calvert Junction. We accessed the GCR trackbed slightly north (164 SP 680258) of Calvert Junction, from a public footpath just north of Charndon (164 SP 674253) that crossed the single-track mothballed Bicester to Bletchley Line (164 SP 676254). The GCR trackbed was in an open, grassy field and was only just discernible on the ground. After arriving at the remains of an overbridge (164 SP 674262) we were forced to detour as a track on the other side of the road lead to a property close to the line. A public footpath allowed easy access to the line at an overbridge (164 SP 669265) that carried an adjoining public footpath over the line. The wide trackbed was in excellent condition, and walkable passing through flat, open country, with several of the GCR trademark 'blue-brick' overbridges to the A4421 (formerly A 421). Just before the road the trackbed was used as a dumping ground for scrapped cars. The bridge over the A4421 was an interesting split bridge structure with the trackbed being divided as it was carried over the road.

On the northern side of the A4421 was the site of Finmere Station (152 SP 629313), which was a large open expanse full of rubble. The island platform was very overgrown but all traces of the buildings were erased. Proceeding north from Finmere we found the long deep cutting shown

126

on the map to be largely infilled with very sticky red clay that doubled the weight of our boots. It was difficult to avoid this quagmire, so we just pushed on until we reached the A421 (formerly the B4031) (152 SP 622329), where the bridge was also infilled. Crossing the road we descended a steep, slippery drop from the infilled bridge to the trackbed. From the A421 the trackbed emerged into open country passing close to a couple of farms before dipping once again into a cutting to reach a minor road (152 SP 618338). On the northern side of the road, the trackbed was barred by some recently built farm buildings, but an easy detour via a public bridleway (152 SP 615339) guided us back onto the trackbed. The line became a conduit for the national grid, with pylons straddling the formation for about 2 miles, with the trackbed forming a convenient access road. The power lines marched away from the line in a northerly direction and the trackbed lost its role as an access road to become less distinct in open fields. We crossed the A422 where the trackbed briefly became a public footpath that soon veered away northwards (152 SP 598367).

Emerging on a high, truncated embankment, we could see the site of the completely demolished Brackley Viaduct (152 SP 595371) in the River Great Ouse Valley. (There is a good picture of this once magnificent structure in Mac Hawkins's excellent book: 'The Great Central Then & Now'). Below us was the noisy A43 dual carriageway, and we had no choice but to descend the embankment and cross the busy road. Our next obstacle was the River Great Ouse, more of a large stream really, but still not fordable. We crossed the river on a footbridge (152 SP 595373) that carried a public footpath into the outskirts of Brackley. It was impossible to regain the line at this point as it was on a high embankment, fenced, heavily overgrown and occupied by an industrial estate, and we had a difficult detour across numerous barbed wire fences before reaching the outskirts of the industrial estate. The remaining structures of Brackley Central Station (now offices) (152 SP 591380) looked incongruous amidst the modern industrial units, but at least it was extant. Having no rail service now, Brackley once boasted two stations: Brackley Central on the GCR, and to the south, Brackley Station on the London & North Western Railway. Sadly, Brackley is now just a blip on the bypass system of Britain's road network, the kind of place that only seems to exist on road signs.

The trackbed beyond Brackley Central's industrial estate had been developed and disappeared into a housing estate, forcing us to trudge down a minor road beyond the boundary of Brackley before following a stream (152 SP 588389) to access the line. The line entered a wide cutting typical of the GCR, with gently sloping sides, with the trackbed remaining clear and easily walked. Halfway along the cutting was the fine structure of Helmdon Bridge (152 SP 587426), with its three blue-brick arches still supporting the B4525 above the cutting. It was getting late in the day when we reached the site of Helmdon Station (152 SP 586431). A high level 'island road bridge', with central passenger access to the island platform, guarded the approach to the station. This type of station architecture was a hallmark of the GCR. North of the bridge only the platform of Helmdon Station remained. Because of the time we did not linger, and some more excellent trackbed took us past Helmdon village to Helmdon Viaduct (152 SP 583437), a superb 9-arched example of the GCR's 'blue-brick' architecture. Passing under Helmdon Viaduct was the trackbed of the former Northampton & Banbury Junction Railway, that also had a station serving Helmdon Village.

North of Helmdon the line was easily walked until we reached the site of a former overbridge (152 SP 564483) and Culworth Station, where the line was blocked, and the station obliterated by farm buildings. Due to fading light we boxed round the obstacle via minor roads to take us to our pre-arranged B&B accommodation at Crockwell Farm (152 SP 557507). It was dark when we arrived at the B&B to be greeted by our hostess, Hermione, who was very pleasant and, I'm sure she wouldn't mind me saying; a bit 'jolly-hockey sticks'. Our accommodation was in a converted barn separate from the rambling farmhouse, and very comfortable. I had also taken the precaution of booking a table at The Royal Oak in the nearby village of Eydon for eight o'clock. As it was gone seven o'clock when we arrived, Hermione's husband, Bay, very kindly offered us the use of one of his vehicles to drive to the pub in, to which we gratefully accepted. The vehicle in question turned out to be an old Range Rover complete with 'Countryside Alliance' sticker in the back window. Since all three of us are vehemently opposed to any form of 'fun-killing', it was beyond irony that we were off to a posh country pub in such a vehicle.

## Culworth to Rugby (17 ¼ miles)

After a slap-up breakfast (Hermione was only slightly perplexed at finding out that two of us were 'veggies') we took a minor road from Crockwell Farm to rejoin the GCR (152 SP 551505) just north of Culworth Junction (152 SP 555500) where the former Banbury Branch joined the GCR. Almost immediately, we came across the remains of an old signal gantry, which looked forlorn on an overcast morning. A short distance beyond a small overbridge (152 SP 546513) was the junction (152 SP 544514) with the former Stratford-Upon-Avon & Midland Junction Railway, veering away northwest and still clearly visible on the ground. This junction was once the southern end of a triangular junction, with the Stratford-Upon-Avon & Midland Junction Railway running through the centre of the triangle to pass over the GCR on a (now demolished) bridge (152 SP 543516).

Just north of the junction the 3-arched overbridge (152 SP 542519), carrying a minor road across the cutting, south of the village of Woodford Halse, could clearly be seen. Upon reaching this bridge we paused just in time as a man (out of sight behind one of the bridge's supports) started a chainsaw that prompted us to scurry up the side of the cutting to the minor road. Re-accessing the line was impossible until we reached the village of Woodford Halse where a short section of the GCR trackbed was a woodland footpath. We found no sign of Woodford Halse Station (152 SP 540523), but the overbridge (152 SP 541525) crossing the road was still intact. Picking up the 'Jurassic Way' out of Woodford Halse we followed this long distance path until it crossed the GCR trackbed on an overbridge (152 SP 543549). The trackbed was muddy but walkable to the infilled bridge at the A361, on the edge of Charwelton. Across the road was the expanse that was once Charlwelton Station (152 SP 535563). No structures remained, and the derelict site was in use for farming purposes. At the north of the station site the line passed under an iron bridge (152 SP 536563) that carried a minor road over the line. Here the GCR became the damp, but walkable Catesby Cutting, which formed the approach to Catesby Tunnel; the Jewel in the GCR crown at 3,000 yards in length. A large stone in the centre of the brick south portal (152 SP 533570) was engraved with the date of construction: '1897', forming a proud reminder of the GCR's vintage. The south portal was gated with rather flimsy metal gates that were unlocked. The tunnel was dead straight and light at the northern end of the tunnel could be seen. Although wet in places, Catesby Tunnel was in good condition, with several airshafts that periodically illuminated short sections of the trackbed with an strange, misty light. Even with the numerous and large airshafts, I would not like to have been working in the middle of Catesby Tunnel as an express barrelled through. The north portal (151 SP 524596) of Catesby Tunnel had similar gates but the trackbed was flooded, and opening them from the inside was a little tricky. The north portal also proudly displayed a keystone engraved: '1897'. Just up the line from the north portal was a 3-arched brick overbridge that straddled the cutting, sporting a 'Private No Access' sign on the central arch. Proceeding cautiously, (the trackbed was in full view of nearby houses) we crossed the magnificent 12-arched, 159 yard long Catesby Viaduct (151 SP 522605) constructed in blue-brick to the relative sanctuary of a well-wooded cutting.

Pausing at the A425 (151 SP 519616) where the bridge had been demolished, for some lunch, Dave decided that he had had enough of walking. Chris and I decided to push on, not wanting to miss probably the best line we had walked to date, after arranging to meet Dave at Rugby Station.

The trackbed north of the A425 was walkable except for a flooded cutting (151 SP 525640) until we reached a wide gulf formed by a demolished bridge (151 SP 525650) that once took the GCR across the former London & North Western Line. It was possible to walk across this broad space and clamber up the north side to a minor road. A small cutting (151 SP 525652) just north was wet and partially infilled making the going difficult. The bridge across the Grand Union Canal (151 SP 525654) was missing, so we took the bridge just to the west that carried a byway across the canal. There was a vibrant community of people living in barges alongside the canal bank who had a few campfires going. Another significant viaduct was missing (151 SP 525660) making the crossing of Rains Brook a bit of a chore. We passed the site of the now completely unrecognisable Braunston & Willoughby Station (151 SP 524672) to cross the A45. Just north of the A45 the line ran closely parallel with the Oxford Canal for about 2 km, with some of the cuttings in this section being very overgrown and unwalkable, but easily avoided by using the Oxford Canal towpath. Along this section we also came across another signal gantry similar to the one near Culworth. This time the gantry had a rickety ladder and I could not resist the temptation to climb up for a photo opportunity.

Thankfully, the substantial iron bridge (140 SP 517713) across the M45 was still present, complete with bizarre, probably drug induced, graffiti. Someone had spent some time writing his or her enigmatic musings in large white letters on the side of the bridge thus: "A BRANCH SHORN OF LEAVES. A RAVEN PERCHING ON IT. THIS AUTUMN EVENING". Whatever the meaning of the message, we were thankful to the author for putting a spring in our step for the remainder of the line into Rugby.

At a minor road (140 SP 516725) the trackbed became 'The Great Central Walk', providing an easy walk for the last few miles into Rugby. We passed the platforms of the former Rugby Central Station (140 SP 514745), before emerging at the northern end of The Great Central Walk (140 SP 516757) at the site of the truncated, heavily graffitied GCR bridge that crossed the existing mainline. This 'birdcage' bridge, sadly, has since been removed.

With some time to kill before the train home we set out to find a pub. The closest place we could find was 'The Wheeltapper', which turned out to be a dreadful mistake. If you are ever in Rugby avoid this place like the plague unless you have some stolen goods that you want to sell.

*The derelict remains of Finmere Station (152 SP 629313) look very bleak on an overcast day.*

*A wonderfully wide and clear cutting provides a splendid approach to Helmdon Bridge (152 SP 587426).*

*On the south side of Helmdon Station (152 SP 587426) looking north.*

*The superb 'blue-brick' structure of Helmdon Viaduct (152 SP 583437).*

*Two views of the remarkably clear trackbed of the GCR. Above left shows an overbridge (152 SP 612346), and above right a signal gantry (152 SP 546512).*

*Just north of Catesby Tunnel the railway walker is rewarded by the fine 'blue-brick' structure of Catesby Viaduct (151 SP 522605).*

134

*The 3,000-yard long Catesby Tunnel, seen in this view from the south portal (152 SP 533570), must surely be one of the finest structures remaining on the dismantled railway network.*

# WALK XV
# The Portpatrick & Wigtownshire Joint Railway
## (Portpatrick to Castle Douglas & The Whithorn Branch)

| Walk Summary | |
|---|---|
| **Date walked** | May/June 2004 |
| **Line mileage** | 74 ½ |
| **OSLR Maps** | 77, 82, 83, 84 |
| **Opened to Passengers** | 28 08 1862*, 12 03 1861♣, 02 08 1875♦ |
| **Closed to Passengers** | 06 02 1950*, 14 06 1965♣, 25 09 1950♦ |
| **PGAG Reference** | 25, 26 |
| **Pre-Grouping Company** | The Portpatrick & Wigtownshire Joint Railway |

*Portpatrick to Stranraer Town, ♣Dunragit to Castle Douglas, ♦Newton Stewart to Whithorn

## Walk Highlights

The generally good condition of the trackbed and marvellous scenery, Glenluce Viaduct, Tarf Bridge, Gatehouse of Fleet Station, Big Water of Fleet Viaduct, Loch Skerrow Halt, Stroan Viaduct, and Loch Ken Viaduct.

## Public Transport

Stranraer can be reached by train from Newcastle and Carlisle. Portpatrick can be reached by Stagecoach bus 358 from Stranraer. Castle Douglas can be reached by buses 500, 501, and 502 from Dumfries. Dumfries is served by ScotRail from Carlisle.

## Background

The Portpatrick & Wigtownshire Joint Railway (P&WJR) was originally conceived to exploit trade with Ireland via rail-connected harbours at Stranraer and Portpatrick, as the crossing from these harbours to Northern Ireland is very short at 21 miles. A branch was also later added to Whithorn, primarily for agricultural traffic. The section between Stranraer and Portpatrick was also destined to remain a branch line from the main line due to the difficult terrain between these stations that was compounded by lack of future upgrades after construction.

Crossing some wonderful countryside, the line was constructed over numerous obstacles that required some significant engineering. Many of the engineering marvels that were created to cross this remote landscape remain today, with the highlight of the P&WJR being undoubtedly Big Water of Fleet Viaduct.

## Walk Description

For some time we had discussed the idea of doing a week-long walk. For this we needed a longish line, and P&WJR seemed to fit the bill. The walk was also christened 'NEDSTOCK 2004'; a festival of dismantled railway line walking. In honour of the walk I had commemorative T-shirts printed with 'NEDSTOCK 2004', with an embroidered badge of the NEDRAT logo sewn on the right arm made for each of us.

Due to the length of the route, and the remote countryside we had decided to take full camping equipment, giving us flexibility, but it meant having to carry heavy packs. We took the train to Stranraer from Newcastle via Carlisle; an interminably long trip caused by the fact that the more direct line i.e. The Portpatrick & Wigtownshire Joint Railway had been closed. We camped just outside Portpatrick on a campsite adjacent to the trackbed (82 NX 007535). It was an ideal spot as it allowed us to follow the trackbed past the stark remains of Dunskey Castle, through a short but interesting rock cutting, and down the steep gradient to the picturesque harbour town of Portpatrick for a couple of pints on a glorious late-spring evening.

**Portpatrick to Stranraer Town (7 ½ miles)**

A warm sunny morning greeted us as we shouldered our heavy packs and joined the trackbed from the embankment running past the campsite. The trackbed was well walked and the path wove its way through dense clumps of gorse, looking splendid with their blooms of bright yellow flowers. We soon ran into difficulty as we entered the boundary of a golf course. The trackbed entered a small cutting right on the golf course (82 NX 015542) that was wet and overgrown, so we carefully skirted north, following a watercourse to a track leading to the golf course club house. Getting onto the track was difficult as it was embanked and had a thick hedge and fence. We had considered following the stream but the former rail bridge was fenced off underneath. Once across the track we regained the line and moved quickly on a good trackbed to the A77 (82 NX 026546). There were farm buildings on the trackbed so we bypassed them on the A77 for a short distance before regaining the line just east of the B7042 junction (82 NX 030545). The trackbed had opened out onto a small embankment heading across open fields until reaching a minor road at the site of Colfin Station (82 NX 039548), now the site of a fish smokehouse.

The line had climbed steeply to Colfin Summit, and crossing the minor road now started the descent towards Stranraer, across open fields. So far the trackbed had been largely walkable but a nasty surprise awaited just ahead where the trackbed suddenly became very overgrown (82 NX 044550) as it led to a short cutting hewn through rock. The going underfoot was damp but we managed to continue walking, as the thick vegetation seemed to abate slightly. Although the trees had thinned, lush vegetation was laying thickly like a green carpet covering a bog, as Chris and I found out to our cost as we suddenly sank right up to our crotches in the quagmire. Dave had got wet feet but had sensibly hesitated and decided to try and climb out of the cutting. Chris and I ploughed on through the cutting, keeping as close as possible to the edge before we could escape at an overbridge (82 NX 046552). This was not a good start to our expedition, and after Chris and I extricated ourselves from the morass, we could hear shouts from Dave somewhere back in 'bog-cutting'. During his escape attempt Dave had become stranded on the steep rocky wall of the cutting, and he required a rescue with the aid of my climbing sling. We regrouped on the overbridge to clean out our boots and put on fresh socks, and I took full responsibility

138

for leading us into such a mess.

The trackbed was overgrown to the east of the overbridge, so we followed the A77 that ran adjacent to the line until reaching some houses (82 NX 053558), where the road swung east away from the trackbed. It was impossible to access the trackbed at this point so we pushed on a short distance down the A77 and followed a field margin to reach the line at the site of a wooden overbridge (82 NX 056562). The trackbed, skirting the hillside, arrived at a partially demolished stone viaduct (82 NX 058565) that once crossed a farm track, and now looked like an elevated garden for an abundance of wild plants. A lovely section of line offering fine views, led down to the site of a completely demolished viaduct (82 NX 059574) that once crossed Piltanton Burn. It was a sweat-inducing drop, and climb from the burn on a hot day. Apart from some short overgrown sections, (notably one cutting at 82 NX 062577) we managed to complete the line to the A77 (82 NX 063588) where the bridge was missing. To our dismay the trackbed on the other side of the road was in use for some kind of horse-riding event, forcing us to trudge down the tarmac into Stranraer for about a mile.

### Duragit (Challoch Junction) to Newton Stewart (18 miles)

The stretch of the P&WJR from Stranraer to the former Challoch Junction (82 NX 169570), east of the former station of Dunragit, remains part of the existing line to Stranraer. Therefore, we took a bus from Stranraer to a minor road (82 NX 173567) that gave easy access to the trackbed just east of Challoch Junction. The grassy trackbed crossed open fields, offered grand views across Luce Sands, before entering a cutting on the edge of a wood, which gave some welcome shade. At the eastern edge of the wood was the 109-yard long Glenluce Viaduct, (82 NX 191573); a spectacular 8-arched stone structure. The way was barred by the usual galvanised spiky security fencing that was easily negotiated by going round the side. The trackbed on the viaduct was clear and the railings remained in-situ. After crossing the viaduct, and admiring the views up and down the Water of Luce, we found that the trackbed became a neglected wasteland on the northern edge of Glenluce Village. We left the line at an overbridge on the north side of Glenluce (82 NX 196575), and continued into Glenluce for supplies. As Glenluce Station had been demolished we left Glenluce on a minor road, passing an interesting stone plaque welcoming one to Glenluce with a logo that incorporated a stylized picture of the viaduct.

Time was pushing on as we regained the line at a road junction (82 NX 209576). This section was overgrown and required several detours off of the trackbed. As the line veered away from the road and followed the watercourse of Lady Burn, the trackbed running on a slight embankment, became clear and provided excellent walking sharing the open ground with an old military road and modern pylons. There was a missing bridge across Lady Burn (82 NX 229591), but a telegraph pole and some scaffolding enabled us to scramble across with dry feet. We left the trackbed soon after this obstacle to camp below a small hill on the north side of the line. The site was somewhat exposed, but our green tents blended in quite nicely, besides we had to stay fairly close to the burn to avoid a long walk to get water.

It was not long before the midges arrived. They were quite bad but I have known a lot worse. Dave had never experienced the traumas of the Scottish Midge before and he proceeded to walk about smoking furiously with arms flailing like windmills in a gale in a vain attempt to deter the airborne menace. As the sun dipped a thick mist appeared to seep upwards out of the ground, giving an eerie feel from out hilltop viewpoint, and we watched the tents slowly disappear into the accumulating haze.

A fresh breezy morning kept the midges at bay as we rejoined the trackbed that was now in use as a farm track. The line entered a shallow cutting before running adjacent to the A75 before crossing the road (82 NX 271600) at the edge of a wood. The line became indistinct at this point, forcing us to follow a minor road until we reached an overbridge (82 NX 289596) that gave easy access to the trackbed. The trackbed was once again in good condition and we made good progress to the splendid twin-arched Tarf Bridge (82 NX 296596). From Tarf Bridge the line remained walkable but had several boggy sections that were easy to avoid.

We reached Kirkcowan at around midday, at the site of a stone bridge and the old station house (82 NX 323610) that no longer looked much like a railway station. Although the temperature had cooled we decided on a pie and a pint stop in Kirkcowan. Kirkcowan had a ghost town feel about it, but we found the Craiglaw Arms on the south side of the village but it was closed. As we stood outside looking thirsty, a passing local girl told us to knock door and the landlord would probably serve us. Her information was accurate, and before long we were gratefully tucking into toasted sandwiches and beer. The landlord had not been running the pub for long and was very welcoming telling us all kinds of amusing stories of his past, the pub trade, and how he ended up in Kirkcowan. It was with some reluctance that we left the cosy environs of The Craiglaw Arms.

The cutting (82 NX 326612) just east of a minor road leading from Kirkcowan was overgrown so we skirted the edge, picking up the trackbed at the eastern end. Shortly, the cutting gave way to a low embankment across open fields decorated with bright patches of May blossom, before skirting a wood and entering another short but boggy cutting with a pretty stone overbridge (82 NX 334624). We left the line at the junction of the A75 and B735 (82 NX 338628), as it was necessary to cross Black Burn on the road bridge. At this point the line became indistinct as it ran right next to the road, with a short section of the trackbed probably under the road. Due to this fact and the beginnings of sore feet for Chris, we stopped in a lay-by and caught a bus into Newton Stewart. We opted to camp at the campsite in Newton Stewart for two nights as it meant we could leave our gear to walk the Whithorn branch with light packs.

Newton Stewart Station (83 NX 406649), like so many other stations, has been replaced with an industrial estate, although a locomotive shed on what was once a large and important junction station remained.

**The Wigtownshire Railway, Whithorn to Newton Stewart (19 ¼ miles)**
Our plan was to walk the Whithorn Branch from Whithorn back to Newton Stewart, as there was an early bus to Whithorn from Newton Stewart. After a queasy ride to Whithorn, caused by a combination of the previous night's high spirits, a winding road, and a maniac bus driver, we opted for a late breakfast in a café in Whithorn before setting off.

The former station site at Whithorn was occupied by a Fire Station (83 NX 446409), where we able to join the line. The trackbed continued as a grassy farm track, that provided excellent walking winding its way across open fields past the unrecognisable Broughton Skeog Station site, (83 NX 456441) and under a pretty overbridge, (83 NX 464456) before ending at the B7052 (83 NX 465463) on an overgrown embankment where the bridge was missing. Due to time constraints we opted against walking the short spur to Garlieston, continuing instead westwards along the B7052 as access to the line was barred by the station houses (there were two station sites for Millisle being close together and operating at different times in the lines history) of Millisle (83 NX 464464), now in use as private dwellings. The line beyond Millisle disappeared into the fields forcing us along the road until we picked up the site of the trackbed (83 NX 453468) on a track leading to the ruins of Sorbie Tower. Sorbie Tower, a ruin of a fortified tower house, lay hidden in woods among rhododendrons and was a lovely spot for elevenses.

Beyond Sorbie Tower the trackbed ran straight, traversing open fields that alternated from overgrown to indistinct, with a bridge missing (83 NX 442471) across a ditch, until reaching the A746 (83 NX 435475) at the site of a stone sculpture plant, that was formerly a creamery previously served by the railway. It was possible to skirt the perimeter fence of the plant and get out onto the road opposite Sorbie Station, now a private house that was barely recognisable as a former station.

Following the B7052 for a few hundred metres enabled us to bypass Sorbie Station and walk across a field to the line. Just before we entered a wet, but walkable cutting (83 NX 423483), we were spotted by a farmer who sped towards us on his quad bike. He turned out to be very friendly, and happily chatted about the line's history, before wishing us good luck whilst at the same time warning us that the next farmer up the line had a slightly grumpier disposition towards walkers. Bearing this in mind we set off cautiously, hoping to rely on stealth to prevent a more unpleasant encounter. In the event nothing happened, and we followed an excellent trackbed to the site of Whauphill Station (83 NX 405498), that was now occupied by a works yard of some kind. A short but difficult detour over several fences took us round the busy yard into a quiet but rubbish-strewn cutting (83 NX 405500) adjacent to the B7085. The line opened out from the cutting and passed under a well preserved overbridge (83

NX 411509), providing excellent walking to Kirkinner, where due to recent building on the trackbed south of Kirkinner Station House (now a private house) we cut across a field to the main road running through Kirkinner. It was a short walk up the hill to the Kirkinner Inn, where once again we had to knock on the door for service. Fortunately it was service with a smile and the landlady even allowed us to eat our own sandwiches whilst supping her beer. I also took this opportunity to dress some blisters on Chris's feet. He had been bothered since the soaking at 'bog cutting'. A couple of angry swollen blood blisters exploded their contents once pierced with a sterile needle. The wondrous 'second skin' product 'Compede®' enabled him to carry on, but I feared that Chris's feet would not hold up, as we had a lot of ground to cover over the next few days.

From Kirkinner the trackbed remained walkable for about 2 miles to the River Bladnoch. We emerged in thick trees on a minor road overlooking the bridge site. The bridge was missing (83 NX 424541), but the stone abutments and a central pillar in the middle of the river remained like an aquatic folly. Fortunately for us the tide was out, and a brief perusal of the location gave me the idea that we could ford the river, right at the site of the bridge. After finding suitable sticks to use as 'third legs', we successfully forded the river, avoiding a long detour into Bladnoch. The embankment on the north shore of the River Bladnoch was a delightful well-walked green avenue. Our arrival into Wigtown was close to the station house (83 NX 436548), now a private house named 'The Old Station House', which was easily bypassed by a convenient track. Just north of Wigtown Station the trackbed was inaccessible, but a footpath had been placed alongside the cutting that soon joined the trackbed (83 NX 436552) that led to a picnic site. Beyond the picnic site the line became vague, traversing flat fields, so we shadowed the line on a minor road and rejoined the trackbed from an overbridge (83 NX 434567). The line under the bridge was a well-used farm track, with the overbridge being the only clue as to the original purpose of the track. The line was difficult to follow, and a tricky crossing of Borrowmoss Burn (83 NX 429574) was required as the bridge was missing. Just north of Borrowmoss Burn the trackbed became a rough track before becoming vague in a wooded area, to the A714 close to the site of Causeway End Station (83 NX 420597), now unrecognisable as a station. Due to Chris's sore feet we decided to call a taxi to get us back to Newton

Stewart, thus unfortunately missing about 3 miles of the branch back into Newton Stewart.


**Newton Stewart to Castle Douglas (29 ¼ miles)**

With the viaduct missing across the River Cree (83 NX 435634), we decided to get the bus to Palnure (83 NX 452634) to avoid the very long walk round. It was possible to see parts of the line as it traversed the flood plain of the River Cree from the bus, as it was a bright morning. We alighted from the bus at the site of Palnure Station (83 NX 452634); now a small house but not really recognisable as part of the railway. The iron bridge over Palnure Burn (83 NX 455633) was still intact. We attempted to cross the bridge from the western side but were thwarted by thick undergrowth and a security fence. These obstacles probably could have been surmounted, but we would have been in full view of houses that had incorporated part of the embanked line into their gardens. Retreating, we took the soft option and crossed Palnure Burn on the A75 bridge. Just east of this bridge was a footbridge (83 NX 455632) crossing Graddoch Burn that led into a boggy field. We picked our way carefully across the field joining the line just east of the Palnure Burn Bridge. The embanked line was well tree covered but quite clear with plenty of original ballast still in-situ. After about half a mile the embankment ended at the site of Graddoch Viaduct (83 NX 462631). Graddoch Viaduct was oddly truncated, with just two now purposeless low arches straddling a lawn like a garden folly. On the eastern side of the minor road from Graddoch Viaduct (83 NX 455632) the trackbed now formed part of the Sustrans National Cycle Network (route 7), for about 2 miles to a cutting (83 NX 469604) at Spittal, before leaving the trackbed to rejoin a minor road. We hopped over the fence and continued on the trackbed as it began to curve eastwards, contouring into the valley of Moneypool Burn, with some good view out over the flatlands of the Cree's estuary.

We had to leave the line for a short distance to avoid Creetown Station (83 NX 475599), now a private house complete with original platform. Regaining the line at a sharp bend in a minor road at the site of a large farm building (83 NX 480601) we made good progress across open fields with clumps of bright gorse scattered about, until we reached the site of the demolished Culcroncie Bridge (83 NX 505613). Fortunately the original bridge crossed the minor road as well as the Culcroncie Burn so it was easy to cross using the remaining road bridge.

We found a good spot for lunch right on the trackbed as the line entered a pine forest that surrounded the optimistically named Gatehouse of Fleet Station (83 NX 544624). Before the planting of the pines, the now secret Gatehouse of Fleet Station must have been a bleak windswept place, as it sat in isolation some 7 miles from Gatehouse of Fleet itself. The platform at Gatehouse of Fleet was badly overgrown, but the grassy trackbed was a delight to walk. The station house, an austere solid stone building was now a private house. From the station, the line soon emerged from the pines to run very close to a minor road, giving magnificent views across the Water of Fleet Valley, and the first tantalising glimpses of the delightfully named Big Water of Fleet Viaduct (83 NX 558643), the highlight of the P&WJR The line was now a well-used track as it descended to Big Water of Fleet Viaduct. From a distance I thought Big Water of Fleet looked like a Roman aqueduct, owing to the massive brick buttresses reinforcing the 20 stone arches.

As we approached, the closely cropped grass embankment eased the trackbed onto Big Water of Fleet Viaduct, with the enormity of this magnificent structure becoming apparent. A quaint sign on a twisted bit of metal guarded the western end of the 300 yard long viaduct stating: "Private Property – This land is the property of The British Railways Board and all persons are warned not to trespass." The sign did not exactly have us quaking in our boots, but it was nice to see BR still responsible for something at least. We had intended to push onto Loch Skerrow for the night, but as this was such a dramatic spot we decided to camp right next to the Water of Fleet, with the viaduct towering over us. This gave us time for a leisurely evening meal, and a stroll up onto the viaduct to take a few pictures and watch a few cyclists travelling on the National Cycle Route passing under the viaduct. The warm afternoon gave way to a mild dusk, and out came the midges, in force this time. Forced into the tents we could hear an audible buzz as the bloodthirsty blighters sought desperately to penetrate our defences.

The evening hum of the midges was replaced by a morning drumbeat of rain on the flysheets. Our good weather had evaporated in no uncertain terms, and it was a truly foul morning as we trudged back up to Big Water of Fleet Viaduct. The eastern end of the viaduct was a marked contrast with the western end. Although there was no 'scary sign', the trackbed was covered in dense, high, Broom plants. As we left the viaduct it was like taking a cold shower as the head high and waterlogged Broom released its moisture over us. What was a clear trackbed yesterday had become an overgrown jungle, and in the wet was a real chore to negotiate. It was a couple of miles of struggle, with several short detours, until the trackbed became clear, where it was in use as a forestry road. The proximity of a forestry road running parallel and just north of the tracked gave a good explanation for the overgrown section east of Big Water of Fleet Viaduct. There was a viaduct missing across the Little Water of Fleet (83 NX 586671), but this was easily bypassed on the forestry road. The embanked trackbed appeared again, but we opted to stay on the forestry road that ran very close, as the line was still badly overgrown. The thick, damp, forest gave way to open ground as we rejoined the trackbed (83 NX 602671) close to the head of Loch Skerrow. The trackbed was a delight as it hugged the eastern shore of Loch Skerrow, but the weather was showing no signs of let up, so we took a breather in a boathouse on the loch shore. We left the boathouse at about lunchtime, with the rain easing a bit. Chris was first up on the line as he wanted to get a long a bit, being slow with his sore feet. As I left the boathouse I saw a previously limping Chris leap into the air, yell, and run back down the line. I approached the cause of his panic with caution, and discovered the large Adder coiled up right on the trackbed. This was an excellent example of adrenalin taking away pain, as a visibly shaken Chris (he hates snakes) hobbled back to the line. A short distance from the boathouse were the remains of Loch Skerrow Halt (83 NX 609683). All that remained were a couple of lichen-covered staggered concrete platforms either side of the trackbed, full of atmosphere and looking terribly forlorn on wet day; a good metaphor for the fortunes of P&WJR.

The trackbed from Loch Skerrow Halt became a farm track, providing easy walking to Stroan Viaduct (77 NX 646700), that straddled the Black Water of Dee at the head of Stroan Loch. Although not in the same league as Big Water of Fleet Viaduct, Stroan Viaduct was a welcome site with its four stone arches being in good condition. From Stroan Loch it was an easy walk to the site of New Galloway Station (84 NX 661705), now the site of a private house with evidence of the platform in the garden. As we approached the station we were treated to the site of a Red Kite soaring high above. The Red Kite is a rare and often persecuted British bird for where Galloway is still a noted stronghold.

We stopped for a drink at Mossdale Post Office and decided on our next move. Chris's feet were about done for, so we opted to get to the A713 on the eastern side of Loch Ken and catch a bus, as I noted from the bus timetable that a bus was due in Parton in about an hour. We skirted the overgrown trackbed on a minor road, regaining it from a track (84 NX 681703) just ahead of Loch Ken Viaduct (84 NX 683703). Loch Ken Viaduct was a marvellous 260-yard long, triple lattice arched iron structure on stone pillars, with rickety timber decking that was obviously used for light vehicle access, straddling a narrow point across Loch Ken. There was no fence at the western end of Loch Ken Viaduct enabling us to gain access and cross quickly. The eastern end was a different story however, as our way was blocked by large padlocked gates covered in a ridiculous amount of barbed wire, situated right next to a caravan site. Time was running out for us to get the bus and it was a considerable hassle to get over the gates.

We made the bus with minutes to spare. Fortunately, what remained of the line from Parton (6 miles) ran adjacent to the A713 all the way into Castle Douglas, so at least we could at least observe the line from the bus. The line disappeared into an industrial estate in Castle Douglas, leaving no recognisable trace of the station. Our original plan was to walk the Kirkcudbright Branch from Castle Douglas, but due to Chris's sore feet we had to leave the exploration of the Kirkcudbright Branch for another day.

*A truncated viaduct (82 NX 058565) turned into a hanging garden by extensive growth of ivy and other plants.*

*A wonderfully clear trackbed across Glenluce Viaduct (82 NX 191573).*

*Stations on the* P&WJR *were small, tidy buildings. The above view shows Creetown Station (83 NX 475599), and below Gatehouse of Fleet Station (83 NX 544624).*

*Three views of the magnificent Big Water of Fleet Viaduct
(83 NX 558643), the unrivalled highlight of the* P&WJR.

*The Whithorn Branch: The remains of Bladnoch Bridge (83 NX 424541) (above), and below a view of the trackbed and a fine over-bridge (83 NX 411509).*

*The weathered structure of Loch Ken Viaduct (84 NX 683703) has been converted for motor vehicle use, but the decking has seen better days.*

# WALK XVI
# The Great Northern & London North Western Joint Railway (Market Harborough, Great Bowden Junction to Bingham Road, Saxondale Junction)

| Walk Summary | |
|---|---|
| Date walked | July/August 2004 |
| Line mileage | 38 ½ |
| OSLR Maps | 129, 141 |
| Opened to Passengers | 1879 |
| Closed to Passengers | 06 06 1966* 07 12 1953♠ |
| PGAG Reference | 16 |
| Pre-Grouping Company | Great Northern & London North Western Joint Railway |

*Great Bowden Junction to Welham Junction, ♠Welham Junction to Saxondale Junction

## Walk Highlights

East Norton Tunnel, John O' Gaunt Viaduct, and Hose Tunnel.

## Public Transport

Market Harborough, Melton Mowbray and Bingham Road are all on the rail network.

## Walk Description

For our second visit to the midlands we decided to have a go at a nicely contained line that would have joined two existing lines, giving us a two-day walk with quite challenging mileages per day. The Great Northern & London North Western Joint Railway (GN & LNWJR) also had an evocative name with some equally interesting station names

153

such as John O'Gaunt and Long Clawson and Hose, to stimulate the imagination.


**Market Harborough to Great Dalby (19 ½ miles)**

After an agreeable overnight stop at The Greyhound Inn in Market Harborough we set off on foot to join the line at Great Bowden Junction (141 SP 743894), accessing the trackbed easily by the minor road bridge that sat almost on top of the once complicated multi-level junction with the existing Market Harborough to Leicester Line. The trackbed was walkable and ran across some very open and flat country before we joined a minor road (141 SP 754911). The line disappeared into the fields on the other side of the road. We followed the road due to the absence of the line, but also because we would have to cross three watercourses where the bridges were missing, one being the River Welland. Welham Junction (141 SP 766919) appeared to have just melted away into the landscape. Using a public footpath from the village of Welham we regained the line at a sad looking redundant 3-arched bridge (141 SP 777927) sitting isolated in a field, with the trackbed largely obliterated on either side. Another bridge originally traversing a bridleway (141 SP 779930) was missing entirely. We had to take another detour via a minor road and byway (141 SP 783934) as there were some people working on the trackbed ahead, to rejoin the line at an overbridge (141 SP 792950). The line north of this point was home to a Gypsy or Travellers' camp, so once again we had to box round on a minor road. Curiously, the Gypsy camp had a badly spelt sign attached to a post box that read: "The Old Raile Way Embankment".


We rejoined the line just north of Hallaton Junction (141 SP 792952) via a public footpath. The trackbed was walkable to the site of Hallaton Station (141 SP 794965), now barely recognisable as a former station, and in use as a private house. The line continuing from Hallaton Station was thickly wooded, so we skirted the edge until we came to a public footpath that cut right across the trackbed (141 SP 794968). Emerging from the trees the trackbed went straight across some open fields and unfortunately for us there was a tractor working to the west of the trackbed. After a short pause we picked our moment and moved quickly, sometimes on all fours, using what little cover there was to the next minor road (141 SP 794972). Our luck improved a little as the

154

trackbed was now in use as a farm track, that passed under a couple of fine overbridges, that enabled us to make better progress until we reached the south portal of East Norton Tunnel (141 SP 792993). The approach to East Norton Tunnel was quite overgrown, with the portal being barred only by an easily negotiated low wooden fence. The portal and tunnel lining were constructed of brick, and were in excellent condition, with the bore running dead straight through the low hill for 444 yards. The north portal (141 SP 792996) of East Norton Tunnel was less overgrown, but after a short cutting the trackbed northwards had been infilled, forcing us to follow a fence line to the A47 (141 SK 792002) and the site of East Norton Station, where all that remained were a couple of derelict houses.

To the north of the A47 the trackbed became very indistinct, so we followed a public footpath across open fields, to reach Eye Brook. The 208 yard long East Norton Viaduct (141 SK 7920008) across the brook had been blown up in 2002 and was still marked on my (2001) map. Having seen some good pictures of this once grand viaduct, I wondered why it had to be destroyed as it was in a remote setting that did not seem to be a hazard to anybody. It was easy to cross Eye Brook on a public footpath bridge, but it was sweaty work to clamber up the thickly wooded embankment on the north side of Eye Brook. The sun was now fully out and there were a couple of buzzards circling overhead filling the valley with they mournful cries. The trackbed became very overgrown, and we took the opportunity of a byway (141 SK 786019) to skirt round a particularly bad section via the village of Loddington. A public footpath took us through the graveyard of Loddington church where we startled a young guy working in the churchyard. I asked him if there was a pub nearby but he just stared at us in a disconcerting 'slack-jawed' manner, giving no audible response. A follow-up question again yielded no audible response and we began to get an uneasy 'Village of the Damned' feeling! Moving swiftly on, we rejoined the trackbed north of Loddington (141 SK 785027), but we were only able to walk a short section to an overgrown, impenetrable cutting (141 SK 782033). Passing a crossroads that was also an overbridge we managed to regain the line at the northern end of the cutting (141 SK 774035) with the trackbed being overgrown but walkable. Another enchanting cutting that was in use as a nature walk ran to a minor road at the site of Tilton Station (141 SK 760056). Tilton Station house was not easy to see, and the trackbed northwards was in use to access Vale House Farm. It would have been a difficult detour to get round the farm building so we opted for a late lunch stop in The Rose & Crown at Tilton in the Hill. This was a welcome oasis of cold beer and chips on what was turning out to be a very hot day.

Going back down the hill to Tilton Station was out of the question for access reasons previously mentioned, so we rejoined the line via a public footpath (141 SK 759064). An excellent trackbed continued to Marefield South Junction (141 SK 744074), which was well preserved with the former Great Northern Line to Leicester clearly visible to the west. The grassy trackbed continued to Marefield North Junction (141 SK 741079) forming the northernmost part of the triangular junction, and was also well preserved and clearly visible on the ground. From Marefield North Junction the gated trackbed headed due north through a cutting then onto an embankment before crossing a stream on the impressive 14-arched brick John O' Gaunt Viaduct (141 SK 742091). We paused at the southern end of the viaduct, as it was obvious that not far from the northern end of the viaduct the trackbed had been occupied by large farm buildings at the former John O' Gaunt Station site (141 SK 741096).

After quickly crossing the viaduct we descended the embankment on the eastern side, and followed a tree line to the minor road in John O' Gaunt village, thus bypassing the farm. It was impossible to get a good look at what remained of John O' Gaunt Station. To the north of John O' Gaunt, access to the line was impossible as it had disappeared into the fields and our way was barred by houses. This forced a long detour into Twyford to access a public footpath that crossed the line between two substantial and delightfully clear cuttings (129 SK 734104). It was now getting late, but we were fortunate that the trackbed was easily walkable for about 3 miles to the overbridge at Great Dalby (129 SK 734142) without any need for further detours. The site of Great Dalby Station on the northern side of the road was in use as a substantial farm complex. We left the line at the overbridge to walk up into Great Dalby village to our pre-booked B&B at The Old Dairy. The only pub in Great Dalby was The Royal Oak, which was nothing special, but they served a good plateful of basic pub grub which was most welcome after a long day on the line.

**Great Dalby to Saxondale Junction (19 miles)**

The morning was mercifully cooler, and after a quick breakfast we set off to join the line via a public footpath (129 SK 735148). The trackbed was largely walkable to an industrial estate (129 SK 736175) on the outskirts of Melton Mowbray, where the line was obliterated. At this point Dave announced that he was not going to continue as he was too tired from the previous day's exertions. This was not unexpected, but Chris and I were determined to continue and finish walking the line.

A public footpath (129 SK 741175) took us further into Melton Mowbray, a town famous for its pies. The former bridges of the GN & LNWJR that crossed the existing Melton Mowbray to Nottingham and Melton Mowbray to Syston Lines were missing. This forced us to wander through the streets to pick the line up at a redundant bridge on an embankment (129 SK 742189). This section of line appeared to have 'de-facto' access for local dog walkers. The original rail bridge across the River Eye in the centre of Melton Mowbray was missing, having been replaced by a substantial footbridge (129 SK 744192), built on the original supports, that formed the start of a right of way that curved round the centre of the town. The trackbed right of way was short, running for about ½ mile crossing the A6006 (bridge missing) and ending at the A606 (129 SK 748195). From here the line had been built over with a supermarket, various buildings and car parks. The site of Melton Mowbray Joint Station (129 SK 752196) was also obliterated. It was awkward trying to trace the line but the situation improved when we joined a footpath (129 SK 755196) running adjacent to the remains of the trackbed into a park. We managed to rejoin the trackbed (129 SK 760202) as it veered due north and out again into open countryside.

The trackbed was in excellent condition, and a delight to walk for about three miles past the clearly discernible Scalford Junction (129 SK 758238) of the former Great Northern freight line to Eaton Quarry, to a minor road (129 SK 755241) just west of Scalford village. The bridge was missing, and Scalford Station (129 SK 755242) if anything still existed, was now probably a private house that was screened behind trees as we shadowed the line on a track that ran parallel to the trackbed to Mawbrook Farm House. The trackbed was now either infilled or not recognisable up to the house. Fortunately there was a footpath heading east from Mawbrook Farm House that quickly turned north enabling us

157

to skirt the line, which was now an overgrown cutting, to a minor road (129 SK 747254).

On the northern side of the road the trackbed became a wide open cutting that had some rubble scattered about but was easily walked to the south portal (129 SK 746257) of Hose Tunnel. The portal was brick and similar in design to East Norton Tunnel but the approach had a more open aspect. Hose Tunnel, at 834 yards, had a very slight curve and was in excellent condition being totally dry inside. The north portal (129 SK 746265) of Hose Tunnel was open, but the cutting was steeper with more foliage. The trackbed veered northeast and was in excellent condition. As we passed by the site of Long Clawson & Hose Station (129 SK 746266) we found no remains. Near Brock Hill Farm a large farm shed had been built right on the trackbed (129 SK 753274), but it was skirted by a public bridleway that seemed to end at the barn. It was easy enough to go round the barn via the bridleway and rejoin the trackbed, now in use as a farm track. A short distance up the line we came to a cutting that housed numerous beehives with bees buzzing around furiously. Although the sun had come out and it was getting hot again, we donned waterproofs as a protective measure just in case the bees got nasty. At the end of the cutting the line flattened out and quickly melted into some arable fields (129 SK 758291). There was a huge stack of black plastic wrapped silage bales that were more or less on the line. As we passed we heard a voice greeting us, which was odd, as we could see nobody about. Looking up there was a scruffy bloke in a pork pie hat and donkey jacket lying on top of the silage bales. He started prattling on about the fact that there was no right of way here but "It would be OK for us to get out onto the road". Ignoring his diatribe we walked on, but I remained curious as to why he was up on top of some smelly silage bags on a hot day dressed in a donkey jacket.

We got onto a minor road at the site of a former over bridge (129 SK 759296) and found that the line just disappeared into some cornfields. Consulting the map we could see a public footpath that ran from Willow Farm to cross the line (129 SK 760306) at the site of Harby & Stathern Station, which was now a large rubble-strewn yard with a few scattered buildings, and some evidence of a platform. The trackbed became an embankment with an access road running adjacent. We had just scrambled up the embankment when a truck came barrelling down the access road, that sent us diving for cover amongst the rosebay willow-herb, that fortunately, was prolific on the trackbed. The truck soon left and we hurried to cross the minor road (129 SK 760314) on a fine bridge. The embankment was fairly overgrown and tree covered but remained walkable. We passed Stathern Junction (129 SK 761323) taking the left (northwest) fork. The landscape flattened out and the trackbed became less overgrown as we crossed the Grantham Canal on a low bridge (129 SK 756332). The excellent trackbed literally ended under a minor road bridge (129 SK 739358) in an overgrown and boggy mess, which was the site of Barnstone Station, now sadly gone. Beyond the bridge the trackbed was unrecognisable, and a new house had been built right on the alignment about 200 metres to the north. There were people in the garden of the house, so we had to take a tortuous route across open fields using dead reckoning to reach the line where it reappeared as a cutting (129 SK 733368). Once in the cutting the trackbed was again navigable and was a delightful walk for the last 3 ½ miles into Bingham, with the last mile or so being an official walkway.

*John O' Gaunt Viaduct (141 SK 742091) is best seen from a distance, but this view gives an indication of the length of the 14-arched brick structure.*

159

*The two tunnels on the* GN & LNWJR *are fine structures. Above is the north portal of East Norton Tunnel (141 SP 792996), and below shows the north portal of Hose Tunnel (141 SP 746265).*

# WALK XVII
## Bere Alston to Meldon Quarry

| Walk Summary | |
|---|---|
| **Date walked** | September 2004 |
| **Line mileage** | 21 |
| **OSLR Maps** | 191, 201 |
| **Opened to Passengers** | 1874*, 1890♠ |
| **Closed to Passengers** | 06 05 1968 |
| **PGAG Reference** | 1, 2 |
| **Pre-Grouping Company** | The London & South Western Railway |

*Bere Alston to Lydford, ♠Lydford to Meldon Quarry

## Walk Highlights

Shillamill Tunnel, Shillamill Viaduct, Tavistock Viaduct, Brentor Station, The parallel lines of the GWR and the LSWR between Tavistock and Lydford, Bridestowe Station, Lake Viaduct, and Meldon Viaduct.

## Public Transport

Bere Alston is on the Gunnislake Branch served by trains from Plymouth. Meldon Quarry is linked to Okehampton by The Dartmoor Railway (runs May to November) see www.dartmoorrailway.co.uk. Okehampton is served on summer Sundays by trains from Exeter via Crediton on the Barnstaple Branch.

## Walk Description

Exeter was our rendezvous point at the shabby but comfortable Great Western Hotel, outside Exeter Station. Apart from its historic nature, the Great Western also benefited from a good selection of Real Ale.

161

## Bere Alston to north of Tavistock (About 10 miles)

After a good night in Exeter we caught the train for Plymouth, changing to pick up the Gunnislake Branch Line service for Bere Alston. Unfortunately the unit that was to take us to Bere Alston had a brake problem, so we ended up crammed in a taxi with a surly youth wearing a T-shirt stating: "Its gonna be huge", with an arrow pointing at his crotch.

Bere Alston was once the junction station where the Okehampton Line connected the Tavy Valley with the Callington Branch in the Tamar Valley; an important part of the once substantial rail network of Devon and Cornwall. The remaining line at Bere Alston now forms a reverse junction for services between Gunnislake and Plymouth, as the line from Gunnislake to Callington also fell to Beeching's Axe.

Joining the line could not have been simpler; we just walked east off of the end of the platform past the buffer stop and disappeared into the trees; a splendid way to start a dismantled railway walk. A short distance from the platform, the line, thick with lush vegetation, entered a short cutting. At the end of the cutting we came to an abrupt halt as a bridge (201 SX 443674) was missing. Whilst attempting to cross a track where the viaduct would have been, we were startled by a resident in a nearby house that yelled at us for not being on the footpath. As this was our first visit to the southwest, we feared that the 'Little Englander' population might be quite high, so we immediately vowed to be more careful. The nearby footpath almost immediately took us into a sheer black rocky cutting, with glistening rocks, and tropical looking vegetation clinging to its sides. The trackbed was overgrown but rarely unwalkable, frequently in cuttings or with a good shield of trees. We passed under several delightful overbridges and a permanent way hut being slowly consumed by arboreal growth. In one of the cuttings I found a white insulator pot stamped: 'BR(W)'- a nice reminder that we were in BR's Western Region. A slight detour was required where the line crossed a minor road (201 SX 454682), as the bridge and trackbed were very badly overgrown.

A good trackbed became a farm track from Hocklake Farm (201 SX 466691) that subsequently utilised the line as it entered the Tavy Valley. The sun was now out, but due to the trees and thick vegetation, we were often in the shade as we approached the south portal (201 SX 462706) of Shillamill Tunnel. The south portal had steel mesh gates (about 8ft high) that were not locked. Although Shillamill Tunnel is only 593 yards long, it seemed longer due to its curve making it impossible to see any light at the northern end. The inside of the tunnel was wet under foot but in reasonable condition, and appeared to be in use for occasional vehicle access. The north portal of Shillamill Tunnel had similar steel gates, only this time they were padlocked, but were nevertheless easily climbed. The trackbed heading north from the tunnel was a very well used track that left the line close to the southern end of the 12-arched stone Shillamill Viaduct (201 SX 464721), with the trackbed becoming well covered in trees again. High shiny steel plate gates topped with plenty of barbed wire blocked the way onto Shillamill Viaduct. It may have been possible to go over the gates, but that would have put anyone attempting this in full view of nearby farm buildings, and we had already seen some activity down below. As the embankment dropped steeply away, going round the gates was not an option, as it was nigh on impossible to get a hand or foothold on the stone abutments. In the end we opted to build a bridge from a tree on the western side (i.e. out of view) using a plank we found lying nearby. I shinned across and up onto the viaduct where it was then possible for me to pull up our backpacks and then Chris and Dave using a climbing sling. Curving across the River Lumburn, Shillamill Viaduct allowed excellent views up and down the scenic valley. The trackbed on Shillamill Viaduct was overgrown with saplings and ground cover, but this did not impede our progress over the 230 yards to the northern end, that was also blocked by an easily climbed wall.

The line from Shillamill Viaduct entered a cutting before becoming a right of way about a mile south of Tavistock. At the A390 (201 SX 471737) the line became a walk/cycleway, that continued through the north side of the town crossing the impressive Tavistock Viaduct (201 SX 480746); an 8-arched, 160- yard long stone structure, before arriving at the remains of Tavistock North Station, now named 'Station House'. The trackbed was inaccessible, due to new developments, northeast of the station site and the walk/cycleway was diverted onto minor roads, as the line headed for the outskirts of the town to the village of Wilminstone (201 SX 494762), before veering north, with only short sections of overgrown trackbed remaining.

This was a convenient point for us to stop for the day and head off for our B&B at Sowtontown Farm (201 SX 514763), in a picturesque setting below Cox Tor perched on the edge of Dartmoor. The owners at Sowtontown greeted us in the best possible fashion: three beers straight out of the fridge. Our hosts continued to be extremely welcoming even taking giving us a lift to and from the nearby 'Trout 'n' Tipple for an excellent evening meal and a few pints of local ale.

**North of Tavistock to Meldon Quarry (About 11 miles)**
Leaving Sowtontown, we set off to pick up the line close to Wilminstone. Our point of access was actually on the parallel running GWR (the *pre-grouping* GWR company that was latterly absorbed into the GWR) trackbed close to Wilminstone (201 SX 498762), before joining the LSWR trackbed again. Although Wilminstone never had a station, Tavistock was once blessed with two stations: Tavistock North being served by the LSWR and Tavistock South being served by the GWR. The GWR Line ran from Plymouth to Launceston, meeting the LSWR at Tavistock. The two lines then converged in the Tavy Valley before veering off north up the River Burn Valley, a tributary of the River Tavy. Rather than share track, each company built its own line with the trackbeds running right next to each other with the GWR going under the LSWR using a diagonal elongated bridge (201 SX 499772) that remains hidden among the trees today. This bizarre arrangement continued for about 5 miles to Lydford, where both companies had separate stations about 1 ½ miles south of Lydford village. From Lydford the LSWR headed north and the GWR headed west following the Lyd valley.

This stretch of dual line made for interesting walking and a debate ensued as to whether or not we could claim ten miles of line walked for the price of five! The broad swathe of both lines running so close together gave the appearance of a major mainline. From the crossing point of the lines (201 SX 499772) we tended to utilise whichever was the most walkable trackbed, which was generally grassy surfaced and in good condition. We came across an unusual double stone overbridge (201 SX 498787), or to put it more accurately two bridges built, one across each line, and joined by an embankment to form a single crossing point, highlighting the madness of this stretch of line in idiosyncratic fashion. Just north of the bridge was the site of Mary Tavy & Blackdown Station (where only a house, probably the GWR Station House, remained), where the trackbed ran in a boggy cutting, that was walkable with care. Another visible feature of the competition between the GWR and the LSWR was the presence of boundary markers. We saw a couple of GWR boundary markers still in place looking like 3ft high cast iron toadstools, with the sold cast iron cylindrical head being marked: 'GREAT WESTERN RAILWAY Co, BOUNDARY, 1899'. Unfortunately we found no equivalent LSWR boundary markers. Maybe the LSWR had used less substantial boundary markers and they had been carried off as souvenirs long ago?

The excellent trackbed enabled us to make good progress to Brentor Station (LSWR) (201 SX 486812), now a wonderfully restored building, complete with platform, canopy and totem, which was in use as a B&B. The trackbed past Brentor Station formed the garden, and was fenced off. We skirted station site to a minor road leading to the small village of North Brentor. A short walk back down the minor road led to an infilled road bridge. Access to the trackbed was via a gate, with steps leading to some stable buildings. The trackbed continued to be walkable until a high fence was reached (201 SX 498826) forcing a short detour to a public footpath that took us past the derelict site of the two Lydford Stations (201 SX 499827) that were built very close to each other. Looking at the location of the stations, it struck me as odd that they were so close to together but over a mile away from Lyford itself. As only the LSWR ran close to Lydford it was surprising that they had not built their station much closer to the village. The Lydford Station site was also where the GWR diverged from the LSWR, to follow the Lyd Valley to Launceston.

The LSWR continued in a north-easterly direction, skirting Lydford Gorge and village. The trackbed ran adjacent to a dead end minor road (201 SX 506839) on the southern edge of Lydford, and was badly overgrown, so we took the easy option and walked on the road. The road turned into a track/public footpath that allowed us to regain the trackbed from a bend in the footpath (201 SX 512844), with the line now an embankment. The wooded embankment, running past some private houses, led to Lydford Viaduct (201 SX 513847), with its 7 arches spanning the River Lyd. The trackbed on the viaduct was clear with only a few saplings tenaciously hanging on in the ballast. From the viaduct it was about half a mile of good trackbed until we reached a minor road and the start of 'The Granite Way' (see the council leaflet at: www.devon.gov.uk/granite_way_2.pdf), a walking/cycling route forming part of route 27 of the National Cycle Network (201 SX 516853). The Granite Way, a compacted gravel track, followed the trackbed all the way to Meldon Quarry, except for a detour via minor roads round Bridestowe Station (191 SX 523873), now a restored private house complete with concrete footbridge and station totem. The Granite Way was a well-converted route running through lovely scenery on the edge of Dartmoor.

After Bridestowe Station the next highlight was Lake Viaduct (191 SX 534899), a curving stone structure carrying the line over a cleft in the hillside. Just east of Meldon Junction (191 SX 558922), where another LSWR line diverged to Halwill Junction, and just before the trackbed ended at Meldon Quarry, (191 SX 565924) we were treated to the magnificent site of the 183 yard long Meldon Viaduct, a 150ft high wrought and cast iron trestle structure that carried the line over the River Okement. It was a breathtaking finale to a magnificent railway walk.

We left The Granite Way at Meldon Station, now the home of The Dartmoor Railway, a private preserved railway company. After some meticulous planning by Chris, we joined a Class 73 and Class 47 locomotive 'top and tailed' hauled train for the short trip to busy and well kept Okehampton Station, where we joined a 'summer Sunday' national rail service to Exeter.

*The secluded south portal of Shillamill Tunnel (201 SX 462706) provides welcome shade on a hot day.*

*This view looking north along Shillamill Viaduct (201 SX 464721) shows extensive vegetation on the trackbed and parapets.*

*Tavistock North Station (201 SX 480746), above, is a fine old railway house. Bridestowe Station (191 SX 523873), below, still sports many features from its past to keep the railway enthusiast happy.*

*The splendid iron trestle structure of Meldon Viaduct (191 SX 565924) is indeed a rare and unusual relic of our railway heritage, as all too often metal viaducts were removed for their scrap value.*

*Another interesting lump of metal; this picture shows an '1899' boundary marker from the pre-grouping GWR. A few of these unusual markers still survive on the stretch of line between Brentor and Lydford, where the GWR and the LSWR ran side by side.*

# WALK XVIII
## The Lune Valley Railway
## (Low Gill to Clapham)

| Walk Summary | |
|---|---|
| **Date walked** | October 2004 |
| **Line mileage** | 23 |
| **OSLR Maps** | 97, 98 |
| **Opened to Passengers** | *1861, ♦1849 |
| **Closed to Passengers** | 01 02 1954 |
| **PGAG Reference** | 24, 27 |
| **Pre-Grouping Company** | *London & North Western Railway, ♦Midland Railway |

*Low Gill to Ingleton, ♦Ingleton to Clapham

## Walk Highlights

Low Gill Viaduct, Waterside Viaduct (Sedbergh), Rawthey Bridge, Leck Beck Viaduct, Ingleton Viaduct, and the generally excellent condition of the trackbed running through picturesque Dales scenery.

## Public Transport

Clapham is on the Leeds to Lancaster line. Low Gill has no direct bus service but service 106/107 runs between Kendal and Penrith (WCML) running close to Low Gill on the A685.

## Background

We were down to just two members for this walk, as NEDRAT had been disbanded in September 2006. As a result of this fact, Chris and I latterly decided to continue with our exploration of the old lines; and what else could we call ourselves but the North East Dismantled Railway Assault

171

*Duo?* Consequently *NEDRAD* was born.

The Lune Valley Railway was originally two branches: The L&NWR from Low Gill to Ingleton and the short MR branch from Clapham to Ingleton, with these companies being bitter rivals. Ingleton originally had two termini, and passengers changing between railway companies had a long and hilly walk between the stations. The two branch lines only became a through route with the construction of the magnificent Ingleton Viaduct.

## Walk Description

### Low Gill to Kirkby Lonsdale (13 ¾ miles)

It was drizzling on a cold and dark morning when my wife, Ruth, dropped Chris and I off under the M6 road bridge at Low Gill (97 SD 615969). Walking back down the B6257 we crossed under the West Coast Mainline and accessed the dismantled line via a minor road overbridge (97 SD 618968), that lead to the scattered dwellings that constituted the settlement of Low Gill, perched on the western side of the Lune Valley. We backtracked from the bridge to get close to the former junction with the existing mainline, where the former Low Gill Station was unrecognisable. From the overbridge, the line curved round to the south giving an excellent view of the 11-arched, stone, Low Gill Viaduct (97 SD 616965). The magnificent viaduct was fenced off at both ends but was easily accessible, and the trackbed was clear right across. The grassy trackbed was walkable as far as the short cutting at Bowers (97 SD 623953), where we took a detour out to the B6257 to avoid a private house.

The overbridge at Bowers provided an easy access point to the trackbed into a short cutting. The trackbed sat high above the River Lune and was a delight to walk, with sections of avenue and a soft carpet of autumn leaves underfoot. The approach to Waterside Viaduct over the River Lune (97 SD 630930) was via a grassy embankment that gave tantalising glimpses of this incredible structure. Waterside Viaduct was an unusual combination of stone and iron, and it was even more unusual as it still remained intact, as iron structures were all too often removed. Waterside Viaduct, at 177 yards long and 100 feet high, consisted of three stone arches, a central iron arch straddling the Lune, followed by a further three stone arches, with the best viewpoint being from the eastern side of the River Lune. A token chain-link fence guarded the approach to Waterside Viaduct with a faded red warning sign detailing a £25 penalty for trespassing. As there was no honesty box we just skirted round the fence whilst trying to stay out of sight of a nearby house below. The approach across the stone section was clear and conventional, but the central iron section was more challenging, as it was just iron girders except for a narrow timber walkway on the right hand (western) side. Fortunately the metal handrail was intact and we moved gingerly across the unnervingly flexible timber, enjoying a panoramic view of a swollen River Lune rushing below.

Just south of Waterside Viaduct the line entered a wet cutting with a very symmetrical three-arch stone overbridge (97 SD 634927) straddling the cutting. The trackbed remained walkable passing under several more stone overbridges to an infilled cutting (97 SD 642921) just north of Sedbergh Station (97 SD 642919) and the A684. We cut across fields to the A 684 just west of Sedbergh Station, now in use by a coal merchant, with its railway origins still obvious if one looked closely. The bridge across (97 SD 643918) the A684 was missing, but a track led up to the embanked line on the southern side of the road. The line crossed the A683 (97 SD 644914) in similar fashion, with the line being used as a gravel store by the council at this point. An embankment took the line across a golf course to a large iron bridge (97 SD 643908) across the River Rawthey. Rawthey Bridge resembled a scaled down version of Waterside Viaduct, with a skewed single iron arch spanning the river between large stone abutments. This time, however, the approach was guarded by galvanised spiky steel security fencing, providing more of a challenge. The bridge was also in use as a support for a gas pipe running over the river, and we guessed that it was fact that had prevented this marvellous bridge from being demolished.

Another scenic and walkable section took us to the A683, where the overbridge (97 SD 630892) was missing. To the south of the road the line entered a cutting that although overgrown remained walkable. At the end of the cutting we left the line for refreshment at The Head Hotel. Being a couple of Motörhead fans, we could not pass up the opportunity of having a pint at a place called "The Head". Needless to say, the cranial reference was more to do with sheep, and heavy rock was not on the menu, but a cheese and onion toastie and beer sufficed.

After a short walk down the A683 we joined the line just south of the site of the long gone Middleton Station (97 SD 626881), at an overbridge crossing the road. An excellent grassy trackbed continued southwards in the now wider Lune Valley. Although often tree-covered, the line passed close to several farms between Middleton and Barbon so caution was required to avoid being seen. A short detour from the line was required on the northern edge of Barbon (97 SD 629827) as the stone bridge crossing Barbon Beck was fenced, tree-covered and appeared to be incorporated into a garden. It was an easy task take a public bridleway that crossed Barbon Beck just east of the line. Barbon Station (97 SD 629824) was unrecognisable, and the line was not accessible at this point so we detoured west through the village stopping to buy sweets in the Post Office shop. The line immediately south of Barbon was very open and difficult to access, forcing us to take a public footpath to a minor road bridge (97 SD 626816) that gave easy access to the trackbed. The line was walkable for about two miles to Casterton, just north of Kirkby Lonsdale where we left the line for an overnight stop at The Pheasant Inn.

**Kirkby Lonsdale to Clapham (9 ¼ miles)**
It was a colder but brighter morning as we rejoined the line where we left off at a bridge (97 SD 627799) over a minor road. The line quickly entered a secluded cutting as it continued past Casterton that was partially infilled with rubble and general rubbish, but was still walkable. A cutting (97 SD 627783) just east of Kirkby Lonsdale was flooded, with a sad looking abandoned overbridge straddling the stagnant pool, but it was easy to skirt round the edge of this obstacle. The cutting gave way to open fields with the line either flat or slightly embanked. There was some new development and a coach park just north of Kirkby Lonsdale Station (97 SD 629774) that was fenced off, so a short cut across an open field to a disused bit (the existing road had been straightened) of the original A65 was required. The uninspiring remains of Kirkby Lonsdale Station consisted of the large station house, now in private use, with few other railway features being visible from the roadside.

Across the road from Kirkby Lonsdale Station, the line entered a damp cutting before running close to the A65 and crossing a delightful five-arched stone viaduct (97 SD 635766) over Leck Beck at Cowan Bridge, that looked resplendent in the autumn sunshine. The line entered Cowan Bridge on an embankment before crossing a minor road via a bridge. Just beyond this bridge a factory blocked the line, so we left the line at the bridge and walked along the A65 for about ½ mile to rejoin the trackbed on the southern side of the road (97 SD 641758). The lay of the land indicated that there once may have been a level crossing but no trace of any crossing remained. The line became thickly wooded before emerging near Low House Farm (97 SD 642755) in open country where the trackbed was used to store black plastic silage bales. After crossing a couple of small iron bridges the embanked line became indistinct due to an infilled cutting near Ireby Hall Farm (97 SD 647751). Fortunately a public footpath enabled us to box round this obstacle, which also housed a few caravans, to rejoin the line via a minor road bridge (97 SD 652747). The countryside was now very open with a dead flat line traversing open fields. There were some large farm buildings built right across the line (97 SD 656742), forcing another detour to the A65. Beyond the buildings the line ran on an embankment visible from the A65, and we were able to join the trackbed via a public footpath (98 SD 661739) that passed under the line. From this point we were afforded a superb view of the flat-topped hill of Ingleborough on the southern edge of the Dales, towering above the village of Ingleton.

Enjoying the view we paused for some lunch above a flooded cutting (98 SD 666737) that was home to a sturdy stone bridge that positively glowed in the low sunlight. Beyond this bridge the cutting was walkable before shortly reaching a minor road in a private garden. A public footpath that ran along the top of the cutting provided an easy escape route to a minor road and another public footpath leading back to the line (98 SD 671736). About 500m of indistinct line with a partially infilled cutting continued to the A65 where the bridge (98 SD 676735) had been demolished. The line, in the form of a clear and high embankment, was clearly visible on the other side of the road. A clear trackbed with plenty of original ballast remaining, provided some excellent walking to the edge of Ingleton, where we parted company from the trackbed at a bridge (98 SD 689734) that marked the boundary of a works yard, which was the site of the former LNWR Ingleton Station. For a few hundred metres we followed a minor road before clambering over a wall and scrambling up the embankment at the western end of the massive eleven-arched Ingleton viaduct (98 SD 692732) that straddled the River Greta. Ingleton Viaduct was fenced off at both ends by spiky galvanised steel fencing. The eastern end of the viaduct emerged in a car park (the former site of the MR station), making a couple of railway walkers climbing over a security fence rather conspicuous. I settled for a quick scout along the top of the viaduct to the eastern end, before backtracking to cross the river via the road. The views across the village of Ingleton from atop of the viaduct were superb. Although the viaduct completely dominates the village, it does not detract from the picturesque setting at all.

From the eastern end of Ingleton Viaduct the line disappeared into new development and playing fields not becoming obvious until just before reaching the A65, where a caravan park completed the obliteration. After a trudge along the A65 we rejoined the line from a minor road (98 SD 702713). We were making good progress on an excellent section of line until we entered a cutting (98 SD 704704). As we reached the cutting's overbridge we spotted a couple of Land Rovers just up ahead. The occupants, who looked like gamekeepers, were milling about near their vehicles and fortunately they did not see us. After a brief pause we set off quickly towards the A65, using the lay of the land and a dry-stonewall for cover. The ground was treeless and boggy and we had to chance a crossing of open country to get back to the line (98 SD 709699) undetected. The line was walkable for about another ½ mile to a cutting which was in use for storing agricultural machines. A short and steep climb to the B6480 took us safely round this obstacle before we rejoined an indistinct trackbed from a gated field (98 SD 722692). From this point the line was in good condition all the way into Clapham with the last ½ mile or so being particularly evocative as the line wound its way into the River Wenning valley before arriving at Clapham Station. With no refreshments being available near the station we headed up to Clapham for a couple of pints in the excellent New Inn.

*The details of a fine overbridge (98 SD 666736) are highlighted in the sunshine. Soot stains from long gone locomotives are still obvious on the bridge's arch.*

*Ingleton Viaduct (98 SD 692732) makes an unusual backdrop for a caravan park.*

# WALK XIX
## The Great Central Railway, Part II
## (Rugby to Belgrave & Birstall)

| Walk Summary | |
|---|---|
| Date walked | November 2004 |
| Line mileage | 22 ¼ |
| OSLR Maps | 140 |
| Opened to Passengers | 15 03 1899 |
| Closed to Passengers | 05 09 1966 |
| PGAG Reference | 10, 16 |
| Pre-Grouping Company | Great Central Railway |

## Walk Highlights

The generally excellent condition of the trackbed and Dunton Bassett Tunnel (aka Ashby Tunnel).

## Public Transport

Rugby and Leicester both have mainline services. The preserved Great Central Railway runs steam trains from Leicester North (formerly Belgrave & Birstall) to Loughborough Central.

## Walk Description

During the planning of this walk I noted a disconcerting feature concerning the proximity of the GCR to the M1. For approximately 10km the GCR is adjacent to the motorway; not exactly everyone's idea of a quite ramble on a rural railway. Observing this stretch of line on the map epitomised the fate of our railways very starkly to me; a mainline railway closed and now all but invisible, whilst a six-lane swath literally roars on, symbolising our transport policy very succinctly.

## Rugby to Belgrave & Birstall (22 ¼ miles)

After our previous experience in Rugby at The Wheeltapper, I chose our overnight B&B with care. In fact, Magnolia House was a splendid place that even had self-catering facilities, so it was homemade curry and a few take-outs in front of Friday night telly, thus avoiding the gauntlet of Rugby town centre.

As it was to be a long day we set off before dawn, walking down to Rugby Station to join the GCR from a bridleway that went under the Oxford Canal straight to the trackbed (140 SP 517765). The line was a permissive path to the M6 (140 SP 532789), where the line ran in a broad deep cutting with the M6 appearing like an earthen rampart directly ahead; another potent symbol of Britain's transport ideology. A short detour via a minor road bridge (140 SP 530790) was required to cross the M6, before walking back down below the M6 embankment to rejoin the line on the northern side. After a few hundred metres the embanked trackbed arrived at the Roman Road of Watling Street, now the A5, where the bridge had been demolished. On the northern side of the A5 the trackbed was walkable but rubble-strewn, before entering a cutting with a graceful but crop-topped overbridge (140 SP 542802) with crudely painted "Private Keep Out" signs. At the end of the cutting, on the edge of Shawell, the way under the minor road was infilled (140 SP 543803), but across the road access was easy via a public footpath running alongside the cutting. Again the cutting was wide and clear with another overbridge and a concrete ganger's hut. A difficult detour was required as the line reached another infilled minor road crossing in an overgrown cutting (140 SP 546815), and as barbed wire fencing and thick blackthorn guarded the line, the escape onto the road was tricky. The cutting on the north side of the road was overgrown, with the line disappearing into open fields close to some farm buildings, forcing us to detour to a nearby public footpath (140 SP 548817) that ran parallel to the M1 motorway. We were forced to follow this footpath for about a mile as the trackbed had completely succumbed to agricultural pressures until reaching the remains of a cutting (140 SP 547830). From this point the line was walkable until reaching the A4303 dual carriageway on the southern edge of Lutterworth, where the bridge was missing. A few motorists gave odd looks as we emerged from the bushes and scrambled down the bank to cross the road. A short overgrown section of line took us to the site of Lutterworth Station (140 SP 548844), where at the site of a split iron overbridge complete with elegant lattice fencing, the line ended abruptly at a garden fence, with the station having been replaced by a housing development. Descending to a public footpath running under the bridge, we saw the bricked up entrance that would have given passengers access to the platforms; a station design typical of the GCR.

Following the public footpath under the bridge towards the M1 we joined a bridleway heading north in close proximity to the built over trackbed, and it was not until we passed the housing estate that we saw the line re-emerge (140 SP 548854), sandwiched between the M1 and some industrial units on the outskirts of Lutterworth. With the oppressive roar of the M1 traffic, we pushed north on a surprisingly walkable trackbed with only a few overgrown or minor blockages until reaching the south portal of Dunton Bassett Tunnel (140 SP 552899), also known as Ashby Tunnel. Dunton Basset Tunnel was short at only 88 yards, and the weathered brick south portal was blocked by tree trunks, branches and a crude wooden and chain link fence that had been forced open at one side. The north portal was blocked by a gated spiky galvanised steel security fence, which was more difficult to get over, making the use of leather gloves and climbing sling essential. The trackbed at the north portal (140 SP 552901) was a wide clear cutting that formed the far end of a timber yard. After proceeding cautiously along the cutting we saw movement in the yard, so we jumped over the fence to walk between the line and the M1 until we rejoined the timber yard's access track that joined a minor road at the site of the obliterated Ashby Magna Station (140 SP 555907). The minor road overbridge at this point was also infilled, but it was a simple task to walk up and over the minor road to rejoin the trackbed.

About ¾ mile up the line from Ashby Magna Station, the trackbed crossed another minor road (140 SP 558914) where the bridge was missing. This was difficult to negotiate as it was impossible to detour via the motorway and the landowner had employed a ridiculous amount of barbed wire fencing in an attempt to block access to the trackbed. Needless to say we overcame the obstacle, and rejoined the trackbed on the other side of the road. The trackbed remained walkable all the way to Cosby (140 SP 550956), passing over and giving a good view of the dismantled Midland Counties Rugby to Leicester Line (140 SP 555938).

From Cosby, the line skirted some playing fields before heading across a golf course on an embankment. The trackbed was more or less intact across the golf course, but it was not a right of way so caution was required to avoid detection from passing golfers.

In fading light we reached the M1 and amazingly the bridge (140 SP 555965) over the motorway was still extant. The next short section of line to Whetstone was overgrown and proved to be a bit of a struggle before we picked up a vestigial stump of trackbed (140 SP 553970) that soon disappeared under a housing development. The site of Whetstone Station (140 SP 554973) had also vanished under the development without trace.

The streets of Whetstone took us to our next major obstacle: the existing Leicester to Nuneaton Line (140 SP 557981). The GCR bridge over the line remained but was heavily fortified by barbed wire and corrugated iron. Over the bridge the line entered the flat land in the River Sence valley, with only a hint of the former Whetstone Junction (140 SP 558983) with the Leicester to Nuneaton Line in evidence. The original bridge across the River Sence was in place but a similar structure a little further north across the Grand Union Canal was missing. Fortunately, just to the west of the trackbed, an arched footbridge was present making the crossing simple. North of the Grand Union Canal the trackbed became lost in a muddy field, and as it was now dark we just took a straight line across the field for a few hundred metres before the trackbed became incorporated into a tarmac cycleway (140 SP 561989) that took us the rest of the way into the centre of Leicester for an overnight stop at a B&B.

The centre of Leicester was once dominated by the GCR's Leicester Central Station and accompanying viaduct. Leicester Central Station had largely disappeared under a car park, and the viaduct remains in chunks forming little islands of the GCR above the busy road network. We did manage to get onto a stretch of the viaduct by scaling the security fence (140 SK 581042) that had once been used as a part of a cycle route but was now closed and covered in graffiti. I have since found out that the council wants to demolish this part of the viaduct rather than pay for maintenance, so I fear that another fragment of our railway history will soon disappear. The trackbed finally became accessible (140 SK

583070) from a side street but unfortunately was in use as the local dog toilet. A walkable trackbed continued for about ¾ mile before being terminated by the A563 dual carriageway (140 SK 586078), with no trace remaining of what would have been a substantial bridge. On the northern side of the A563 the trackbed was once again a cycle route for a few hundred metres before reaching Leicester North Station (140 SK 587082), now the southern terminus of the preserved 'Great Central Railway' (www.gcrailway.co.uk). In GCR days, Leicester North Station was known as Belgrave & Birstall Station, and this was the endpoint of our walk.

Leicester North had been almost entirely rebuilt, and looked sad on a dreary November morning. There was nobody at the station but our luck was in as a steam train pulled in, hauled by 4-6-0 'Ditcheat Manor' no. 7821. Unfortunately this service was being run as a 'Santa special' and was a pre-booked only service, however after a chat with one of the staff he allowed us on in the empty coach behind the loco, which was fine by us. The 7¾ mile trip to Loughborough was very evocative, with the smell of coal smoke and the unmistakeable, hot, musty, aroma unique to old rolling stock. Loughborough Central was delightfully restored with a lot of atmosphere, and it gave us a good idea for what a typical GCR station would have been like. Sitting in the station café by a roaring coal fire sipping a pint was a splendid way to end our explorations of the superb GCR.


**Epilogue**

The Great Central Railway has plans to reconnect their line with the other section of remaining GCR track to Ruddington south of Nottingham, making a route of 16 ¾ miles of the original GCR traversable by train. This would be achieved by re-instating a crossing close to Loughborough Station on the existing line.

*A typical overbridge (140 SP 542802) constructed in blue-brick, straddles the wide trackbed of the GCR. Note the grassy top where the wall is missing.*

*The heavily overgrown and fortified south portal of Dunton Bassett Tunnel (140 SP 552899), guards a largely intact structure.*

# WALK XX
# The Mid-Sussex & Midhurst Junction Railway
## (Pulborough to Petersfield)

| Walk Summary | |
|---|---|
| Date walked | January 2005 |
| Line mileage | 20 ¼ |
| OSLR Maps | 197 |
| Opened to Passengers | *15 10 1859, ♠01 09 1864, ♣15 10 1866 |
| Closed to Passengers | 07 02 1955 |
| PGAG Reference | 4, 5 |
| Pre-Grouping Company | *♣London Brighton & South Coast Railway, ♠London & South Western Railway |

*Hardham Junction to Petworth, ♠ Midhurst to Petersfield, ♣Petworth to Midhurst

## Walk Highlights

Fittleworth Station, Petworth Station, Selham Station, Midhurst Tunnel, and the generally good condition of the trackbed running through picturesque countryside.

## Public Transport

Pulborough is on the London to Arundel line. Petersfield is on the London to Portsmouth line. Midhurst and Chichester are connected by the Stagecoach bus 60. Chichester is on the South Coast Line.

## Background

During many years of living in the south I had eyed the Pulborough to Petersfield Line, which followed the north side of the South Downs in the picturesque Rother Valley, with some curiosity, but I just never seemed to get around to exploring it. Since Chris had moved south and had also spotted this enticing line on the map, it seemed like a good idea to kick off the New Year with a line close to home. The plan was to walk the line in two sections on consecutive days, with Midhurst being the midpoint, returning to Chris's place in between.

This line was essentially two branch lines, connecting at Midhurst run by two competing companies that were eventually joined. Midhurst also had a line running south to Chichester, bestowing the large village some importance in the past, in railway terms at least. For the south east of England a 20 mile dismantled railway is something of a rarity, as this area suffered less than many other parts of the country from rail closures.

## Walk Description

### Pulborough to Midhurst (11 miles)

A grey drizzle awaited our arrival at Pulborough Station. We set off from the station taking the A29 south to a public footpath (197 TQ 042179) that crossed the existing Pulborough Line straight to the site of Hardham Junction (197 TQ 034175), the starting point of the Mid-Sussex & Midhurst Junction Railway. The trackbed was a public footpath heading west from Hardham Junction for about 200m, where the footpath left the trackbed in a south-easterly direction. The wooded trackbed was in excellent condition running on a fine embankment (197 TQ 013174), and we made good progress to the site of Fittleworth Station (197 TQ 008181), well restored in whitewashed splendour and now a private house. The trackbed at Fittleworth Station was in use as a garden, that forced us on a short detour south along the B2138 from the overbridge to a minor road heading west paralleling the line. It was a simple task to cut across a field to a redundant overbridge that straddled a small cutting (197 TQ 005182).

The line from Fittleworth Station became more open, running level close to the River Rother for nearly two miles until reaching a minor road bridge (197 SU 984184). From this bridge the trackbed continued

185

in open country before reaching a strip of woodland (197 SU 982186). Beyond this wood the trackbed became indistinct in open arable fields. Crossing this stretch left us very exposed, and suddenly a pick-up truck appeared on the horizon behind us. The driver must have seen us but did not pursue us, so we just continued walking briskly heading for some woods. In the woodland, the trackbed was again discernible (197 SU 974190) and walkable, running next to the River Rother until reaching the edge of the site of Petworth Station (197 SU 971191). Petworth Station (197 SU 970191) covered an extensive area to which we gained glimpses as we climbed into some woods on the hillside south of the line to the A285. Close to the road bridge a brown tourist accommodation sign: "Old Railway Station" pointed to the beautifully restored Petworth Station; a white timber structure with a slate roof and multiple brick chimneys. From the bridge it was possible to get good views of the station building and surrounding site.

Descending to the trackbed on the western side of the A285 into a deep and overgrown cutting, we got another good view of the trackside of Petworth Station, with its platform and old carriages. Further along the cutting from Petworth Station we found a couple of matt black but rather weathered insulator pots of a type we had never seen before. The cutting gave way to an open trackbed that was in use for vehicle access. After a few hundred metres the line entered another secluded cutting (197 SU 965195). There were recent tyre marks on the well used track, so we proceeded with caution to an ivy covered overbridge (197 SU 962195) where we came upon several four-wheel-drive vehicles. There was no one about but we opted for caution by climbing out of the cutting on the south side. Fortunately for us the line was running through a lovely old wood giving plenty of cover. Beyond the bridge the cutting became an embankment allowing us to walk below the slope out of sight. We started to hear shotgun reports to the north, which confirmed our suspicions regarding the occupants of the four-wheel drive vehicles: fun-killers blasting away at some semi-domestic poultry north of the trackbed and the River Rother. The embankment soon gave way to another short wooded cutting, which housed an old concrete milepost '56', standing quietly complete with its own mossy wig. Leaving the shelter of the cutting we were exposed, as the trackbed was dead straight and flat across open fields, passing close to Cathanger Farmhouse. About 1km east of Selham, a bridleway (197 SU 945203) running adjacent to the line, provided an alternative route if required. After staying on the walkable trackbed we came to the substantial Selham Cutting (197 SU 937205) that was infilled at the eastern end with rubble. It was an easy scramble over the rubble and into the deep sandy cutting that looked like heath land. We exited Selham Cutting on the minor road and walked the short distance to 'The Three Moles' Inn. This lunch stop was one of those wonderful occasions when you feel like an explorer who has just discovered a treasure trove. The Three Moles (built in 1872 as a railway hotel and originally called 'The Railway Inn') was a superb pub specialising in real ales sourced only from micro-breweries, with only the wonderfully named 'Skinners Betty Stogs' being a resident ale. With lots of wood panelling, an open fire and serving no food, we felt at home as we rested our bones and soaked up some atmosphere and ale.

A weak afternoon sun was hanging low in a dramatic winter sky. The bridge across the minor road at Selham was missing, but after a short scramble it was relatively simple to regain the line just west of Selham Station (197 SU 933205). Selham Station, although less substantial than Petworth Station, was a well-preserved timber building with an overgrown platform, and was in use as a private house in a lovely setting. The trackbed just west of Selham Station disappeared into arable fields before entering a partially infilled cutting and passing over an infilled bridge (197 SU 928203) that carried a bridleway. To the west of the bridleway the embanked trackbed had been removed with the line now a close-cropped grassy field. A few hundred metres ahead, a truncated tree- covered embankment was visible on the other side of what appeared to be a polo field. The embankment was in excellent condition; a high level avenue taking the line into a large area of beautiful wooded heath. About half way through the wood we passed under a particularly picturesque overbridge (197 SU 904201), on a trackbed that although not a public right of way was well used by local dog walkers. An excellent trackbed continued across the heath to West Lavington (197 SU 894203) where it disappeared into surrounding fields. Hugging a fence line we regained the line in a rubbish-strewn cutting close to the minor road southwest of West Lavington. To the west of the minor road in a secluded cutting was the eastern portal of Midhurst Tunnel (276 yards long) (197 SU 887203). The narrow single-track portal was a brick structure in a curious egg shape, unlike any that we have previously seen. An easily climbed iron fence provided the eastern portal's only defence. For a short tunnel it was very dark inside as the western portal (197 SU 885205) was boarded up giving the impression of a very long or curved tunnel. The tunnel was dry and in very good condition. There was a small hole in the boards at the western portal that allowed us to escape, only to find ourselves in a housing estate on the edge of Midhurst. Fortunately an electricity sub-station was located close to the western portal thereby helping to mask our exit from the tunnel. The line and the London Brighton & South Coast Railway Midhurst Station (197 SU 884207) to the west of Midhurst Tunnel were obliterated by housing developments. The junction of the LB&SCR Midhurst to Chichester Line (197 SU 882209) was also lost under new houses.


**Midhurst to Petersfield (9 ¼ miles)**
Retracing our steps to Midhurst the following morning, with the weather looking bright and promising, we rejoined the line at Midhurst's other station: The London & South Western Railway Station (197 SU 878212). If this much altered building was not called 'Station House', now in use as offices, one could have been forgiven for missing it. The trackbed from the station disappeared into an industrial estate. To the west of the industrial estate the line disappeared into an old brickworks before we sighted a short embanked section of line running through woodland (197 SU 871207). A few houses had been built where the line emerged from the sand pit on a minor road (197 SU 869206), forcing a short detour via a public footpath to the trackbed a few hundred metres to the west (197 SU 868205).

An excellent trackbed crossed open fields, being frequently wooded and sometimes embanked to the site of Elsted Station (197 SU 834206), now in use as some kind of agricultural supplies yard. The line just east of Elsted Station was lost in the soggy fields so we boxed round the station site by following a stream to a public footpath that took us to the minor road just south of the station site. A house on the western side of the road from Elsted Station made access impossible, but a short detour north on another minor road enabled us to cross an open field to access the line a few hundred metres west (197 SU 831206). Again the line was walkable, traversing more gentle, rolling, countryside.

It was along this section of line that we were spotted by a farmer wandering around in a field carrying a shotgun. Upon seeing us he immediately informed us that we were not on a right of way and was quite hostile, even asking us (pointing at our packs), if we had been "sleeping out". Fortunately we were close to a public footpath that crossed the trackbed, but before we made our escape I decided rather foolishly, to engage him in conversation. After twenty minutes of bizarre 'discussion' I enquired as to the purpose of his shotgun. The farmer said it was for killing moles, at which Chris and I could barely contain ourselves. So there it was: a man in a field claiming he could "hear them moles" before trying to blow the hapless creatures away with a 12-bore. He was obviously quite mad. To cap it all he then invited us to follow the old trackbed west to Nyewood, (although he said that the trackbed was council-owned) having rather quickly forgotten his opening gambit about "rights of way". Taking up on his offer we set off on an overgrown section of line leaving him seeking the principle ingredient of mole pie.

Nyewood was the site of the former Rogate Station (197 SU 805219), now part of a factory complex. Another short detour south via a public footpath was required to get round the station site. Accessing the line west of Nyewood was difficult. In the end we opted for a public footpath (197 SU 802216) before heading north through thick woodland to regain the line close to some pylons. There was a bridge missing across a stream (197 SU 799222) that required some care to get across, but otherwise the trackbed was walkable all the way to a cutting (197 SU 784230) that was partially infilled, but benefited from having a public footpath running along its southern edge to a minor road. To the west of the minor road the line had been consumed by muddy ploughed fields, necessitating some dead reckoning to a public footpath that crossed (197 SU 774230) the River Rother. Following the footpath we re-crossed the Rother where the footpath ran adjacent to a vague trackbed before becoming an embankment (197 SU 767232) that faded away into new houses that had been built over the remainder of the line.

*The magic of the trackbed; a leaf-covered embankment running through an avenue of trees makes for some fine walking.*

*The beautifully preserved timber building at Petworth Station (197 SU 971191) is now home to a hotel and restaurant.*

*The deep cutting (197 SU 937205) (above) at Selham, marks the eastern approach to the delightful timber buildings of Selham Station (197 SU 933205) (below).*

*The unusual narrow 'egg-shape' of Midhurst Tunnel is clearly shown in these pictures.  The top view is of the eastern portal (197 SU 887203) and the boarded-up western portal (197 SU 885205) is shown below.*

*A redundant milepost looks rather comical with a thick cap of moss.*

*A battered concrete gradient marker symbolises the fate of the Mid-Sussex & Midhurst Junction Railway.*

# WALK XXI
## The Waverley Route and Associated Branch Lines
## (Eskbank to Carlisle)

| Walk Summary | |
|---|---|
| Date walked | January 2005, February 2005, September 2005, October 2005 |
| Line mileage | 110 ¼ |
| OSLR Maps | 66, 73, 74, 79, 85, 86 |
| Opened to Passengers | *1901,♦1856,*1862-1864, ♦1831-1862 |
| Closed to Passengers | *12 09 1932, ♦13 08 1948, *15 06 1964, ♦06 01 1969 |
| PGAG Reference | 26, 27, 30, 31 |
| Pre-Grouping Company | North British Railway |

*The Lauder Branch, ♦The Jedburgh Branch, *The Langholm Branch, ♦The Waverley Route

## Walk Highlights

The generally excellent condition of the trackbed and the beautiful scenery, Newbattle Viaduct, Borthwick Bank, Falahill Summit, Heriot Station, Fountainhall Junction, The Lauder Branch as far as Oxton, Stow Station, Bowshank Tunnel, Melrose Station, Kelso Junction, Roxburgh Junction, Ale Water Viaduct, Belses Station, Hassendean Station, Whitrope Summit, Riccarton Junction, Riddings Junction, Liddel Water Viaduct, The Langholm Branch, River Esk Bridge, Scotch Dyke Station, and the River Eden Viaduct.

## Public Transport

Carlisle is on the West Coast Mainline. Edinburgh is on the East Coast Mainline. Edinburgh (bus station) and Carlisle (railway station) are connected by The Waverley Route replacement bus service number 95/X95 operated by First Borders.

# Orientation Map of The Waverley Route, and Principle Branch Lines

*(With the kind permission of Iain Wilkie Logan)*

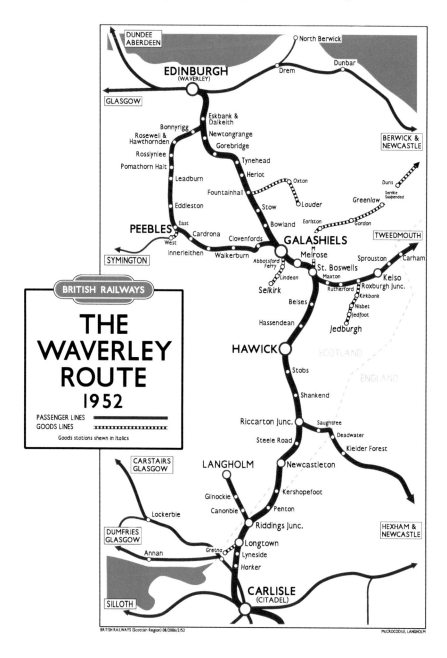

# Background

The Waverley Route was a main line connecting Edinburgh to Carlisle, that ran through the scenic bleakness of The Scottish Borders. This magnificent route was once a vital lifeline to Scottish Border communities such as: Newcastleton, Hawick, Galashiels, and Melrose, just to name the principle centres of population. The Scottish Borders lost a vital artery on the day that The Waverley Route closed, and arguably, the region has suffered economically ever since. As a substitute for trains on The Waverley Route, a 'rail replacement' bus was instigated, which runs to this day, between Carlisle and Edinburgh. Ironically, we would make good use of this service in our explorations of the line. At the time of writing, part of The Waverley Route is due for re-instatement from Edinburgh to Tweedbank, just south of Galashiels. It looks unlikely, however, that the entire route will ever be re-instated, even though there is an arguable passenger demand and a freight demand in the form of logs from the Kielder Forest area, that are currently transported by lorry on unsuitable roads.

Having already walked the Riccarton Junction to Hawick section (see Walk III), we had already experienced a taste of the magic of The Waverley Route. Chris and I had decided that we would have a go at the whole route plus its branch lines. The logistics of such an undertaking were considerable, and we ended up walking the route in four sections, totalling 7 full days of walking. The line from Roxburgh Junction to Coldstream, Alnwick and Alnmouth is not included in this walk, as we considered this to be a 'branch of a branch', and is described as Walk XXII. The branch from St. Boswell's to Reston, a closed station on the existing ECML, is described in Walk XXVIII. The 'Peebles Loop' (Galashiels to Dalkeith via Peebles) is also treated separately in Walk XXIII.

Apart from these exceptions we decided to walk The Waverley Route from north to south, taking in the branch lines on the way. From Edinburgh the first 6 ¼ miles of The Waverley Route is still in use as recently re-instated passenger line to Newcraighall, and beyond Newcraighall the alignment is a freight line to Millerhill Yard, ending just inside the A720 Edinburgh ring road. We decided to pick up the trackbed as close as possible to Millerhill, just west of Dalkeith.

## Walk Description

### Eskbank & Dalkeith to Fountainhall (14 ½ miles)

After an overnight stop at the cheap and cheerful Lugton Inn on the western edge of Dalkeith, we picked up the trackbed just north (66 NT 321678) of the site of Glenesk Junction (66 NT 324671), which connected a short spur from The Waverley Route into Dalkeith itself. Dalkeith Station at the end of the spur was closed in 1943, and the spur itself in 1964. From Glenesk Junction both The Waverley and the Dalkeith Spur were in use as a cycle route, making the start of our journey easy walking, and this was appreciated, as it was still dark on a chilly January morning.

The cycle route ended at the remaining platforms and overbridge of the low-level Eskbank & Dalkeith Station (66 NT 323657) that was situated just north of Hardengreen Junction (66 NT 323659), where the 'Peebles Loop' (walk XXIII) connected with The Waverley Route. Just south of the cutting that housed Eskbank & Dalkeith Station, the line emerged into an open field and quickly came to a roundabout on the A7 (66 NT 323653), where the trackbed had been obliterated, making an early obstacle to any re-instatement plans. On the south side of the A7 we clambered up a tree-covered embankment and quickly came to the fortifications at the northern end of Newbattle Viaduct (66 NT 325649). The fence, looking like a relic of a World War I battlefield, was made up of old sleepers, angle iron topped with barbed wire and even razor wire! Donning leather gloves and summoning some 'bottle', we negotiated the spiky obstacle to find an excellent clear trackbed across the top of the massive 21-arched, 484 yard long, stone and brick viaduct. The southern end of Newbattle Viaduct was similarly fortified but was slightly easier to negotiate. The line was now on a high embankment overlooking a busy road. A few hundred metres south of Newbattle Viaduct were the remains of Newtongrange Station (66 NT 332642), now a fenced off piece of wasteland with some derelict buildings that did not appear to be of railway origin. The shallow cutting of Newtongrange Station was partially infilled with a short section of the trackbed south of the site having been landscaped and converted into a walkway. The trackbed then reverted to a muddy track passing Newtongrange Coal Mining Museum, which looked stark against the bright morning sky. Like The Waverley Route the mining museum was a monument to a similarly once proud heavy industry.

Passing under the B704 the trackbed became a delight to walk as it entered more open country, being populated by saplings with a well-worn path weaving in between. We passed the skeletal remains of a gangers hut as the line continued to climb steeply, with the gradient being more noticeable in the open country. After entering a wood high above the bank of Gore Water, the trackbed became indistinct before emerging at the A7 (66 NT 336616), where the bridge was missing. On the eastern side of the A7 the steeply graded trackbed was easily accessed by a track. Just west of Gorebridge the line entered an overgrown cutting before arriving at the site of Gorebridge Station (66 NT 345613), situated between two overbridges, now in use as offices with some large sheds built right on the trackbed.

From Gorebridge Station the trackbed continued to climb steeply, remaining high above Gore Water. Less than a mile from Gorebridge we entered the cutting of Fushiebridge Station (66 NT 352605). The remains of Fushiebridge Station consisted of one overgrown platform and an overbridge carrying a minor road over the line. Fushiebridge Station marked the start of Borthwick Bank, a very steep four-mile snaking climb, at a gradient of 1 in 70 to Falahill Summit (66 NT 396563), the first major summit on The Waverley Route at an elevation of 880ft. A short distance beyond Fushiebridge the trackbed was infilled at Catcune, forcing us to climb out of the cutting and cross a track before rejoining an excellent trackbed (66 NT 356599), now running on a high embankment in scenic open country. The embankment gave way to a cutting before crossing a minor road to emerge on another embankment at Borthwick Mains. A footbridge marked the start of a three-mile long, deep cutting, that guided the line in a circuitous fashion over Borthwick Bank. After crossing an infilled overbridge (73 NT 391598) in a rather wet section of the cutting, we came to Tynehead Station (73 NT 393592), about halfway along the cutting. The remains of Tynehead Station consisted of overgrown platforms and a stone bridge carrying the B6458 over the line.

The line emerged at the southern end of the long cutting into a stand of pine trees that made progress difficult. We paused, hidden in the pines, to allow some vehicles on a farm track from Cowbraehill to pass by, before picking up an excellent trackbed with quite a lot of original ballast present as the line approached the A7. The countryside was now treeless and bleak as we were in the more hilly terrain. Passing close to the A7 we reached Falahill Summit (73 NT 396563) where the original signalbox was missing but a cottage remained with the trackbed in use as an access road. We passed quietly by and continued to the A7 where the road once crossed the line (73 NT 398555) on a long gone bridge. The trackbed south of the line was vague for a few hundred metres, probably having been obliterated during road works, before becoming obvious again as the line began the descent to Heriot Station (73 NT 403545). Heriot Station was now a private house, with the trackbed on the north side of the site in use as a garden, making a detour through some boggy ground necessary. Heriot Station once had two staggered platforms, one either side of the level crossing of the B709. There seemed to be little trace of the platform on the northern side, but after we skirted the station site we rejoined the trackbed at the southern end of the concrete southern platform, that remained in-situ, and was in good condition.

An excellent trackbed continued to parallel the A7 as we approached a cottage at Stagebank (73 NT 411532). Stagebank was a former surfacemans hut and was now in use as a private house, with the trackbed in use for access. There were people about, so we left the line to join a minor road to the south before cutting across some fields to rejoin the trackbed a short distance further south. The trackbed was in remarkable condition as it crossed Gala Water on a riveted iron girder bridge (73 NT 416526), complete with railings and a painted number '52' on one of the stone pillars. Shortly after the bridge the line ran adjacent to the A7 with the road running high on an embankment for a time before dropping to a similar level with the line. With the line following Gala Water closely in the delightful flat-bottomed valley, the trackbed crossed the river three times in quick succession, on three more iron girder bridges (73 NT 425512, 424508, 423503), taking a straight course across natural bows in the river. A few hundred metres south of the third bridge the line entered a cutting with a footbridge (73 NT 426499) at the southern end. From the cutting the line continued to the site of the level crossing at Fountainhall Station (73 NT 427498). A substantial stone house ('Station House') remained on the southern side of the road with the trackbed being occupied by a large garden. We followed the minor road southwards around Fountainhall Station house before joining a broad grassy section of trackbed just north of Fountainhall Junction (73 NT 428496). Fountainhall Station once had three platforms: an up, a down and a bay platform for the Lauder Branch, but only the down platform remained.


### The Lauder Branch, Fountainhall to Lauder (10 ½ miles)

It was two o'clock when we reached Fountainhall Junction, where The Lauder Branch joined The Waverley Route, and with the sun already low in the sky we realised that we would end up finishing the day in the dark. The junction was quite distinct on the ground, with both lines being on low grassy embankments. The single-track Lauder Branch veered eastwards from The Waverley on a steeply rising tree covered embankment, before crossing Gala Water on a stone bridge (73 NT 432496). Just east of this bridge the bridge crossing the A7 was obliterated. The steeply climbing trackbed hugged the A7 for a few hundred metres before curving sharply north on a dramatic embankment that took the line up into the valley of Nethertown Burn. The surrounding fields were ploughed and treeless, and consequently we were afforded excellent views across the surrounding hills. We passed the substantial farm complex of Middletoun that sat high to the north of the line where the trackbed was in use as a farm track (73 NT 452506). We reached a summit to the northeast of Middletoun where a spring was running, and as we had run out of water some time ago we gratefully took a big drink and refilled our bottles, much as I am sure thirsty track workers would have done in times gone by.

On the descent into the valley of Mean Burn we passed a wooden sleeper-built ganger's hut with a brick chimney. This section of the line was very isolated and with no road being nearby, gave a grand feeling of remoteness. The line did eventually cross a dead-end minor road close to Threeburnford (73 NT 470519) where there was another sleeper built lineside hut, which looked eerie when silhouetted in the low light of a fast dipping sun. A short embankment carried the line to another crossing of the minor road where the bridge (73 NT 472523) was missing. The valley continued to be very scenic with the line now adjacent to the minor road. The grassy trackbed enabled us to make good progress to the village of Oxton, that had the only intermediate station (73 NT 498536) on The Lauder Branch, of which no trace

200

remained. The approach to Oxton was obstructed by houses built on the trackbed, that forced us to detour a short distance to the northeast before walking west right through the village as the trackbed to the south was also built on. We rejoined the line at the southern end of a cutting where the trackbed came very close to the minor road (73 NT 498532). It was now almost dark and we still had some way to go to Lauder. The trackbed was in good condition, running across open fields, until we reached a minor road (73 NT 508514). Beyond this minor road the line crossed a ploughed field (73 NT 511511), where the trackbed was completely obliterated making it very difficult going as it was also now dark. Using torchlight we crossed this muddy obstacle and picked up a reasonable trackbed once more (73 NT 512508), which came as a great relief to our tired limbs. After crossing another minor road (73 NT 517492) the trackbed was a good surfaced track in use as a walkway that ran to the outskirts of Lauder, emerging in an industrial estate (73 NT 522482) that occupied the site of the demolished Lauder Station. We wandered through the industrial estate onto the A68 and into the village of Lauder to The Lauderdale Hotel, where we had a pre-booked room. We had done 25 line miles and about 27 miles of actual walking, and although we were both very tired it had been a magnificent day of railway walking, probably our best yet. A meal and a couple of pints saw us to bed early.


**Fountainhall to Galashiels (11 miles)**
The following morning we took a taxi from Lauder back to Fountainhall, and we accessed the trackbed by re-crossing the bridge (73 NT 432496) to Fountainhall Junction. The trackbed was on a clear low embankment as it proceeded south past the village of Fountainhall. A few hundred metres from the junction there were some new houses being built that looked like that they would eventually encroach onto the trackbed, possibly causing a problem for the future re-instatement of the line. As the line neared a minor road, a clear trackbed entered a buttressed cutting, passing under a delightful brick built bridge (73 NT 439488) that carried a track over the line. The trackbed proceeded in a similar manner to that north of Fountainhall Junction, closely following Gala Water and the A7, being in excellent condition and easily walked. Another bend in Gala Water was traversed by two iron girder bridges in quick succession (73 NT 442484 & 443479), with the latter bridge still

having it's identifying bridge plate '63' in situ, that was very weathered but still legible.

The trackbed remained clear and was pure joy to walk until reaching the outskirts of Stow, where a house had been built right on the trackbed in the shadow of a minor road overbridge (73 NT 455446). This forced us to detour out of the cutting up to the minor road and cross the bridge to skirt round a school and rejoin the line just south of Stow Station (73 NT 456445), a modest single-storey stone house having undergone a lot of alteration as a private dwelling. The line south of Stow Station was in use as a walkway for a short distance, before reverting to its now familiar excellent and walkable trackbed following Gala Water. The line crossed Gala Water once more on a fine example of an iron girder bridge, this time a triple spanned structure (73 NT 448419). At this point the line was adjacent to the A7, before crossing a minor road where the bridge was missing. The trackbed then became a fine clear embankment that was obviously in use for farm access before crossing Gala Water again on a substantial iron bridge (73 NT 453414) complete with diamond lattice fencing on either side standing over six feet high. A short distance south from the bridge was the northern portal of (73 NT 453413) Bowshank Tunnel, a 249-yard long structure taking the line under a steep hill that jutted out into the valley of Gala Water. The trackbed in the tunnel was muddy but the walls were in excellent condition throughout. The south portal (73 NT 454412) was in similarly excellent condition. Just beyond the south portal a high wooden/iron overbridge on brick pillars, in poor condition, straddled the line that made a good frame for photographing the south portal of Bowshank Tunnel.

The trackbed continued as a farm track, quickly crossing Gala Water again, to the site of Bowland Station (73 NT 455402), now demolished where only traces of a platform remained. The line continued its descent to Galashiels, closely following Gala Water unimpeded until reaching the river (73 NT 475378), where the bridge was demolished. At this point the river was too deep to ford, so we were forced to climb up through a steep wooded bank to rejoin the trackbed at a second crossing point (73 NT 475374), where all that remained was a large abutment of the former bridge. The section of trackbed isolated by these missing bridges included the 69 yard long Torwoodlee Tunnel (73 NT 475377), just visible during our climb up through the woods. To access Torwoodlee

Tunnel on foot would have required a long detour, so we decided against this option, promising to come back for a look at a later date.

Just south of the second crossing the trackbed split with a high-level route appearing on the right as we descended towards Galashiels. This trackbed was the Peebles Loop (see walk XXIII) that joined The Waverley Route at Kilnknowe Junction (73 NT 476373), with the site still being obvious on the ground. Not far beyond Kilnknowe Junction the trackbed was tarmaced and in use as a walking and cycleway into the centre of Galashiels. Not much of the railway heritage of Galashiels remained intact. As we followed the trackbed into town we passed under a short tunnel that carried the A7 over the line, and passed by some large brick buttresses before reaching Galashiels Station site (73 NT 494361), now lost completely under a car park and road, although a road overbridge ('Station Bridge') spanning the site remained. After a swift pint at The Abbortsford Inn, we took The Waverley Route rail replacement bus back along the A7 to Edinburgh, which allowed good views of the line that we had just spent two days exploring.

**Galashiels to St. Boswells (7 miles)**
We returned to Galashiels in February for the next leg of The Waverley Route. After an overnight stop at a B&B in Galashiels we rejoined the line at the site of Galashiels Station on a very bright and crisp morning. The surfaced cycle/walkway continued along Gala Water, passing the unrecognisable Selkirk Junction (73 NT 509353) before crossing the River Tweed on a four-arched stone viaduct (73 NT 516353), thus The Waverley was now running in the Tweed Valley. The cycle/walkway veered off to the northeast and the trackbed became indistinct (73 NT 527347) close to where a minor road from Tweedbank joined the A6091 at a roundabout. East of the roundabout the A6091 occupied the trackbed of The Waverley, forming a bypass for the pleasant town of Melrose. Melrose Station, surprisingly, remained intact, sitting rather incongruously next to the main road, with its elegant maroon and cream platform canopy looking like a deluxe bus shelter. Melrose Station sat high above the town and it was still possible to descend the steps from the platform to the town below. A restaurant now occupies most of the wonderful station building.

The line re-appeared from under the road as an overgrown low embankment that ran adjacent to a minor road (73 NT 553340) before skirting around the small settlement of Newstead. We came across a wooden bench on the trackbed with 'Newstead' carved in the shape of a railway station totem, at the site of Newstead Station (73 NT 565341). Other than the bench, there was nothing to be seen of Newstead Station, which was not surprising as the station was only open for two years between 1850 and 1852.

A few hundred metres east of Newstead Station the trackbed once again disappeared under a re-aligned section of the A6091. An embanked trackbed re-appeared on the south side of the road (73 NT 576338). Somewhere close to this point would have been Ravenswood Junction, which took the North British Line to Duns and Reston (see walk XXVIII). The embanked line traversed a ploughed field for a couple of hundred metres before emerging on the A68 (73 NT 578335). The bridge under the A68 was infilled but it was easy to regain the line by climbing over a fence and dropping into a damp and overgrown cutting on the eastern side of the A68. The trackbed ended abruptly (73 NT 577327) at a track running to Monksford, where it had been landscaped out of existence. Shielded by some pines we crossed a grassy field before arriving at the A68 on the edge of Newtown St. Boswells. On the western side of the A68 the line re-appeared, being well walked by the locals, until reaching the main street in Newtown St. Boswells at a car park. St. Boswells Station (73 NT 576316) was now occupied by a fenced off oil depot with what looked like an engine shed and part of a platform as the sole remains of a once large and important junction station.

**Part of The Kelso Branch, St. Boswells to Roxburgh (8 ½ miles)**
Boxing round the oil depot we rejoined the trackbed from a bridge crossing a minor road   (73 NT 577313). We backtracked as far as possible on the trackbed to the perimeter fence of the oil depot for a look at the remains of the station site before continuing south. Not far beyond the bridge the line disappeared into a field, but a convenient path running along the edge of the field to a track enabled us to rejoin the line in a small cutting (73 NT 577312). At the southern end of the cutting was Kelso Junction (73 NT 578309), still remarkably intact and very obvious on the ground, if only vaguely represented on the map.

204

Kelso Junction was where the branch to Roxburgh, Kelso, Coldstream and ultimately Tweedmouth on the ECML joined the Waverley Route. Roxburgh was also the junction for the Jedburgh Branch. Our plan was to take the Kelso Branch to Roxburgh and then onto Jedburgh to complete the day.

From Kelso Junction the line crossed open fields before crossing the A699 (73 NT 581305), where the road bridge had been infilled. The trackbed to the south of the A699 was indistinct with a new house being built to the south overlooking the line. It was a difficult and exposed section, so we followed the road east to a wood where that enabled us to use the trees for cover to access the line at a flooded cutting (73 NT 583304). From the flooded cutting the trackbed became indistinct again before becoming embanked past Mainhill. The bridges across a minor road (73 NT 590301) and the A68 (73 NT 593300) were missing, but the road crossings were simple to negotiate. From the A68 the trackbed, in use for farm access, became wide and a delight to walk on a glorious sunny afternoon. We made good progress to Maxton Station (74 NT 617299), where the iron posts and level crossing gates remained, which were slowly being consumed by vegetation, with Maxton Station House in use as a private dwelling.

East of Maxton Station the line continued to be very walkable, crossing the open arable land of the Tweed Valley. At a small bridge crossing a minor road (74 NT 642308) I found a badly weathered bridge plate (13x7 inches) with a just discernible '73' in white numerals on a black background, which after some renovation would make a nice souvenir. We made quick progress on a good trackbed to Rutherford Halt (74 NT 656308); with its badly overgrown platforms adding a desolate feel to the location. Just west of Roxburgh the trackbed was used to carry a sinister-looking sectioned aluminium pipe of about 4-inch diameter, for a use that remained a mystery.

It was late afternoon when we reached Roxburgh Station (74 NT 697305). Apart from the station house, now in private use, very little remained of Roxburgh Station. We skirted the station site to the south to the minor road that was crossed by two bridges emanating from Roxburgh Junction just east of the Roxburgh Station site. Both bridges had been removed but their abutments remained and the area between had been nicely landscaped with a couple of wooden benches provided for weary walkers.

### The Jedburgh Branch, Roxburgh to Jedburgh (7 miles)

The Jedburgh Branch left the high level Roxburgh Junction and headed abruptly south in the valley of the River Teviot. The trackbed was a wide track in use for vehicle access before becoming a designated walkway (74 NT 696286), providing easy walking which was most welcome due to the fading light and snow flurries. The walkway skirted round the colourful private house that was Kirkbank Station (74 NT 697281), and we made good progress on an excellent trackbed to the B6400. To the west of the B6400 was Nisbet Station (74 NT 673254), that we could only glimpse, and what remained did not look much like an old railway station. We had to cross the Teviot on the B6400 as the railway bridge (74 NT 668250) was missing, before taking the riverside path to the site of the bridge where all that remained was a stone pillar and stone abutments. After some more fine walking on a good trackbed we arrived at the A698 at the site of Jedfoot Station (74 NT 662241), where there were some remains of a platform. As the rail bridge across Jed Water just to the south of Jedfoot Station was missing, we had to cross Jed Water using the A698 bridge. The remains of the rail bridge over Jed Water (74 NT 661238) consisted of staggered cylindrical stone pillars traversing the river and some marshy ground, presumably ground that flooded fairly frequently. The trackbed then followed Jed Water closely running close to some farm buildings (74 NT 658228) before becoming a well-walked footpath that followed the A68 into Jedburgh. Jedburgh Station (74 NT 656215) has been completely obliterated, with the site being occupied by an industrial estate.

As we continued down the road into Jedburgh itself a bizarre thing happened: a double-decker bus pulled over and the driver asked us if we wanted a lift! We took him up on his kind offer, and discovered that the driver, Mark, was driving his bus back to Galashiels, which by coincidence was the service we had planned to take. He even made a special stop right outside our B&B, which was most welcome after a long day on the line.

## St Boswells to Hawick (12 ¼ miles)

The following morning we took the first bus from Galashiels to Newtown St. Boswells, and retraced our steps to Kelso Junction (73 NT 578309). Heading south from Kelso Junction, the trackbed of The Waverley Route soon petered out into a ploughed field. We had little option other than to march right across the field to the A699 (73 NT 578305) where we had to negotiate a thick hedge to get out onto the road. On the south side of the A699 the line entered a cutting that had been planted with pine trees making a formidable obstacle for about a mile, before ending abruptly in open country. Once clear of this arboreal obstacle, the trackbed opened out into a wide track with icy puddles. We reached an overbridge at Greenend (73 NT 587278) that although passable had been partially infilled, requiring a scramble across a 45-degree slope of earth and rubble. The trackbed continued to be clear across Ale Water on a tall stone viaduct (73 NT 583262), before passing close by Belses Mill Farm on an overbridge, and into a cutting (73 NT 581259) that was used for sheep grazing. The line emerged on a high embankment where a bridge had been demolished just north of Belses Station (73 NT 574252). The station house was in use as a private house so we skirted to the west of the site, paralleling the line in an open field. As we were below the embanked line, it was difficult to see the site clearly, but it appeared that some of the platforms remained and a tall narrow building, probably a signal box, was also evident.

After regaining the line just south of Belses Station, the trackbed ended abruptly at a minor road (73 NT 573249) where another bridge had been demolished, that necessitated a scramble down one embankment and up the other. The trackbed was clear and easily walkable until reaching Standhill Farm (73 NT 563233) where farm buildings were present either side of the line. After pausing to assess our options we saw that a detour would be long and difficult, so we marched quickly through the site. Just south of Standhill Farm the line went under a nice stone overbridge, where the trackbed disappeared into a grassy field, with only the redundant bridge remaining as a reminder of the past purpose of the field. The trackbed re-appeared a few hundred metres further south as line crossed an access road for the delightfully named 'Minto Kames', where we paused for lunch sheltering in some pinewoods to escape the biting wind.

Making good, unimpeded progress we reached Hassendean Station (73 NT 548203), a delightful if desolate spot sitting in the shadow of the Minto Hills. The overbridge across the B6405 was intact but was fenced off as the station house was on the other side of the road and in use as a private dwelling. Although the trackbed between the platforms had been infilled and turfed, the vast majority of the station remained intact and sympathetically maintained, with the remains including: the station house, platform canopy, a waiting room and a fine footbridge straddling the turfed trackbed. Hassendean, obviously a large site, was one of those locations where I wondered why on earth it was there at all, as apart from sitting on a road junction it did not seem to serve any significant purpose.

The line continued southwest from Hassendean as an easily walked trackbed, dropping into the valley of the River Teviot, but remaining high above the river itself, giving some lovely views of the surrounding Borders countryside. At a partially infilled cutting we passed under an interesting old footbridge (79 NT 538186) complete with diamond lattice iron fencing atop. The trackbed was walkable until an abrupt ending on the outskirts of Hawick (79 NT 519163) at a minor road. After we meandered across a playing field and past houses the trackbed re-appeared in the form of a tarmaced cycle/walkway that passed a swimming pool (79 NT 505153) that was the site of the completely demolished Hawick Station. Sadly, the massive viaduct carrying the line from the station over the River Teviot and the town was also long gone. Our walk ended in the car park of the Safeway supermarket, where we had left off after our Border Counties Railway Walk (Walk III). This fact meant that we had now walked from Eskbank to Riccarton Junction, a total of 44 ¾ miles of The Waverley Route, leaving 32 ½ miles from Riccarton Junction to Carlisle to be walked.

We were, not surprisingly, in high spirits as we entered Hawick and having plenty of time in hand before the X95 bus back to Edinburgh, we went in search of a pint. On the high street we came across an unassuming bar simply called 'The Waverley Bar', that had 'basic boozer' written all over it, and which seemed the obvious choice to end our endeavours. Like a lot of Scottish bars no real ale was served, but that fact was more than adequately compensated for by the features of the bar itself. The Waverley was busy with Sunday afternoon drinkers, although by the look at some of the characters in the bar we surmised that the days would most likely have melded into one. The atmosphere was smoke-filled and friendly, and a monument to the seventies, with lots of leatherette seating, laminate wall panels and tables. There was a telly with the racing on, but mostly the place was for serious drinking and conversation; a proper pub that made us feel at home. If you ever walk the line through Hawick be sure to stop off at The Waverley Bar for a couple.


## Riccarton Junction to Riddings Junction (18 ¼ miles)

It was a warm Friday evening in September 2005 when we alighted in Hawick from the X95 from Carlisle, and having an hour to kill, we headed straight into The Waverley Bar, where thankfully time had stood still. This time we had a more vociferous welcome from a few after work locals and things could have easily developed into a session if we did not have the delightfully obscure Telfords bus service 128 to catch. The bus stop was less than crowded, and the Telfords 128 service had that kind of vague 'ghostbus' feel to it, where you are only convinced it exists if you see it for yourself. Eventually a young waitress, Anna, turned up who asked *us* if we had seen the 128 bus. When we replied that we hadn't, Anna looked pleased at the fact that she would not need to get an expensive taxi to Newcastleton. During the bus ride we asked Anna about hostelries in Newcastleton and she recommended The Grapes, as she used to work there. Newcastleton was on our route so it was good to have a lunch spot figured out for the next day even before we put a foot on the line.

The bus driver let us off at The Golden Bridge (79 NY 525999). The Golden Bridge looked resplendent with renovated railings and adorned with new bridge plates '200', courtesy of The Waverley Route Heritage Association (www.wrha.org.uk), who have done, and continue to do, a fine job of restoration around the Whitrope area of The Waverley Route. We walked south towards Riccarton Junction passing a few stacks of track lengths that awaited relaying as part of the restoration. During the walk down to Riccarton Junction we passed some excellent replica mileposts '64' & '65' (miles to Edinburgh), that had been placed by the WRHA.

Although it was NEDRAD and not NEDRAT who had returned to Riccarton Junction, the birthplace of NEDRAT (see walk III), our arrival still managed to inspire awe at this most hallowed of dismantled railway locations. Before wandering down to the junction itself we decided to set up at Will's Bothy. From a small sign on the door we learned that the bothy was now in the care of the Mountain Bothies Association (MBA). Although structurally very sound, Will's bothy seemed more spartan than when we last visited, with the Tilley lamp and gas stove gone. There were also fewer utensils, books, and no candles or fuel. It did not take long though to make it home with some food and drink before exploring Riccarton Junction. A lot had changed since our last visit. The generator hut was still there, but there were now a couple of large white on blue 'Riccarton Junction' platform signs, although from my research they were not exact replicas of the original signs. One platform had been excavated with a short length of track having been laid on fresh ballast. Somewhat incongruously a red telephone box had been placed on the platform next to a taped off area, that presumably meant that some reconstruction of the platform buildings was planned. Further south on the site some more track had been laid with a brake van placed by the platform. Without wishing to sound churlish, I felt that the work that had been done looked rather ad-hoc and incomplete, and I feared that some well-meaning types from 'The Friends of Riccarton Junction' (as the site had nothing to do with the WRHA), were eroding the unique qualities of Riccarton Junction.

The morning was bright and had ominous signs of being a blisteringly hot day. Leaving Riccarton Junction (79 NY 540976) we set off at a pace on a gravel forestry road that ran on the trackbed with a noticeable downhill gradient. We soon entered the welcome shade of a cutting in the pine covered hills. The forestry road continued almost to the edge of the plantation (79 NY 532943), before veering due south to a minor road. The trackbed became grassy as it emerged from the forest, giving good views down the valley of Liddel Water. With the sun beating down, we paused in a dilapidated concrete lineside hut, the only shade on the steep descent to Steele Road Station (79 NY 522931). The station was in use as a private house and the garden extended north on the trackbed, so we left the line at a bridge (79 NY 522932) across a minor road. Just south of Steele Road Station it was possible to use the station access track for a closer look at the station remains. There was a derelict platform south of the station house, but not much else. Beyond the platform the line was fenced off and a thick hedge barred access. We struggled through the obstacle, but a better route would have been to access the line via the obvious track that joins the trackbed from the minor road a little further south (79 NY 523930). The trackbed was once again in use as a forestry road to the end of the plantation (79 NY 521919), where the line opened out into a superb grassy trackbed running frequently on an embankment overlooking Liddel Water. Unfortunately for us, the sun was beating down on a very hot and uncomfortable day, making hard work of the still steep downward gradient. The line was clear of obstacles until we reached the B6399, where Hermitage Viaduct (79 NY 496896) had been demolished. It was relatively easy to scramble down the thickly wooded embankment to the road and cross Hermitage Water using the road bridge. The corresponding embankment on the western side of the road was less wooded making an even easier ascent. The trackbed had levelled out noticeably, and running next to the B6357 was well walked and in good condition.

The trackbed skirted the western edge of Newcastleton and was shaded by good tree cover. The once substantial Newcastleton Station (79 NY 481877) had been demolished and a caravan park was occupying most of the site. We left the line and headed for The Grapes, as recommended by Anna, for ice cold lager and sandwiches.

Leaving The Grapes was a struggle as the afternoon was now truly blisteringly hot and airless. Due to a missing bridge (79 NY 480861) across Liddel Water to the south of Newcastleton, we were forced to take the minor road bridge across the river, to join the trackbed at Mangerton (79 NY 480857) that appeared to be a permissive path. The trackbed continued to be excellent passing under a fine stone overbridge (79 NY 476836) sitting close to Liddel Water. A bridge (79 NY 475829) crossing Kershope Burn marked The Waverley's border crossing into England, and a short distance further south was the location of the former level crossing of the small Kershopefoot Station (79 NY 475828), now completely gone. Although the trackbed continued in the same excellent manner we had to remind ourselves that we were now in England, and that greater vigilance was required. From Kershopefoot the trackbed was a gravel track running through mixed woodland latterly emerging in open grassy fields after about 1 ½ miles. The former station site of

Nook Pasture (79 NY 464800) was completely unrecognisable, which was understandable as it only remained open from 1862 to 1873.

Due to houses close to the line, and the consequently usurped trackbed, we left the line (85 NY 442781) to join a minor road that ran next to the line to Penton Station (85 NY 439773), where a very grand station house, now in private use, was visible from the road. No other remains could be seen, but the gateposts at the end of the driveway to Penton Station were decorated with miniature iron signals, presumably as some kind of bizarre monument to The Waverley Route. Accessing the line close to Penton Station was impossible due to the trackbed having been consumed into private grounds or gardens. The first opportunity to get back on the line came at a sharp bend in the minor road (85 NY 436771), where we took a straight line across a field and through a thick hedge to drop into the wonderful and overgrown sanctuary of a cutting. Halfway along the cutting was a tall, 3-arched, overbridge (85 NY 434771) carrying the B6318 over the line. To the south of this bridge the trackbed became boggy and very overgrown with several fallen trees blocking the way. After a few hundred metres things improved as the trackbed was again in vehicular use as we crossed a fence into an estate that was obviously in use by the pheasant-killing fraternity. Aside from the ugly blue pheasant feeding bins this was a beautiful stretch of woodland, with the line providing an excellent route through.

The southern edge of the estate was marked by a fence at an overbridge (85 NY 414755). Here the trackbed was boggy but passable with care, continuing at the edge of a steep wooded embankment before becoming a badly churned up farm track. It was early evening when we reached Riddings Junction (85 NY 410754), where the single-track Langholm Branch headed north from The Waverley Route. Our plan was to end the day here before walking The Langholm Branch the next day. Immediately north of Riddings Junction was the impressive red sandstone Liddel Water Viaduct (85 NY 410755). A barbed-wire fence and the ubiquitous galvanised spiky-steel security fencing, complete with a small British Railways Board sign warning that the viaduct was not "dedicated to the public", dated 1980, guarded the southern entrance to the viaduct. Having a good head for heights I took the easy option and skirted round the fence but Chris, not having a head for heights, had to make a gargantuan effort to get over the spiky obstacle. The top of the viaduct was almost exclusively colonised by Broom, no doubt due to some quirk of soil chemistry and environmental parameters. Being a slightly curved structure the 160 yard long, 9-arched Liddel Water Viaduct offered outstanding views of itself as well as views up and down the river. Crossing the viaduct also meant crossing the border back into Scotland, and we decided to camp immediately as a long hot day had taken its toll. We chose a great spot on the northern bank of Liddel Water almost under the viaduct.

In an attempt at keeping our pack weight to a minimum I had recently invested in a 'basha' to use in place of a tent. A basha is essentially a sheet of green or camouflage waterproof ripstop nylon (designed for use by armed forces around the world) about 2.5m x 2.5m, with loops for pegging or tying. This rudimentary, but versatile shelter, weighs about 600g and can be pitched anywhere where it is possible to tie some 'Paracord' to trees, fence posts etc., giving protection from the worst of the elements. Once the basha is pitched you then just get a sleeping mat/bag out and sleep underneath. It is advisable to also use a waterproof bivvy bag to cover your sleeping bag; as if it is wet and windy some rain will inevitably get under the basha. The other huge advantage of using a basha instead of a tent is it can be pitched very low making it very difficult to spot.

From our idyllic campsite the full glory of the elegant viaduct could be studied. The pillars of the arches were offset at a diagonal to the top of the structure, with an intricate spiral effect in the apex of each arch. The contours of the structure and the deep colour of the red sandstone looked spectacular in the dipping sunlight. As the light faded a warm breeze got up and soothed two tired bodies into much needed sleep.

**The Langholm Branch, Riddings Junction to Langholm (7 miles)**
After a late start caused by the effects of the previous days long walk and subsequent dehydration, we slowly clambered up the high embankment to regain the trackbed, with the morning bringing no relief from the heat. Just north of the overbridge at Rowanburnfoot (85 NY 411758) the trackbed became a permissive path through a pinewood. Leaving the pinewood a narrow but good trackbed opened out into grassy fields before ending abruptly at an overgrown and infilled crossing (85 NY

407770) of the B6357, that was now home to a shed. After crossing the B6357 we skirted Canonbie Station (85 NY 40777), now in use as a private house with the trackbed forming a garden, on a track before dropping into a clear cutting just north of the station site. From the cutting it was possible to see the remaining overgrown platform of Canonbie Station. The line emerged from the cutting on a low embankment but soon became indistinct as it traversed a field to a minor road (85 NY 401774). Across the road the trackbed was vague before dropping into a thickly-wooded cutting with an overbridge carrying an access road to a house that was guarded by fences cameras and warning signs. As we slipped quietly by, we surmised that somebody either paranoid, important or both resided behind this technological shield. The line dipped into an overgrown deep cutting to emerge at a junction of a minor road with an access track (85 NY 397783) on the edge of the steep, wooded valley of Byre Burn. The viaduct across Byre Burn had been demolished, forcing us to take the steeply descending minor road across the stream. A convenient track (85 NY 397785) allowed us to contour along the valley to the location of the former viaduct. The remains of the viaduct were difficult to find, as the steep hillside was heavily overgrown, but perseverance paid off as we found tell-tale piles of rubble during our ascent of the slope. Back at the top of the valley the line quickly emerged from the woods to cross some open ground to the minor road at the site of Gilnockie Station (85 NY 392784). The single-story stone station house was now a private residence with the overgrown platform still present and the trackbed running past as a well used vehicle access.

A good walkable trackbed continued to the minor road at Upper Mumbie (79 NY 382800), where the trackbed disappeared into an open field. Fortunately a partially infilled overbridge (79 NY 381802) gave a good marker of the line's course. North of this bridge the trackbed continued on an open embankment with only a missing culvert bridge (79 NY 381806) providing a minor obstacle. The embankment continued to the B6318 at Tarras Water where once again the viaduct had been demolished, forcing us to cross the river on the nearby road bridge. From the road bridge we followed a rough, wooded path running westwards along Tarras Water, before climbing out of the valley to join the trackbed that traversed open fields and contoured round the scenic valley of the River Esk. The bridge across the B6318 (79 NY

214

377822) was missing, but to the north of the road crossing the trackbed became a permissive path running through scenic woodland to the edge of Langholm.  Due to a house on the trackbed (79 NY 371838) we had to leave the line, dropping down to the A7.  Langholm Station (79 NY 365843) was completely demolished and had sadly been replaced by a car park.  After a pie and pint in Langholm we took the now familiar X95 bus back to Carlisle for the train home.


**Riddings Junction to Carlisle (14 ¼ miles)**
It was October 2005 when we returned for the last leg of The Waverley Route.  After an early start we left my van in Canonbie to rejoin the trackbed at dawn from the overbridge at Rowanburnfoot (85 NY 411758) before crossing Liddel Water Viaduct to return to Riddings Junction (85 NY 410754).  The station of Riddings Junction lies about 500m south of the junction itself, with the extensive site having been consumed by Riddings Farm (85 NY 407751).  Following the wide muddy trackbed we proceeded with caution until the numerous buildings of Riddings Farm came into view.  We knew that the site of Riddings Farm was lived in so we dropped off of the embanked trackbed to a farm track running parallel on the northern side of the line.  Fortunately all of the farm buildings were located to the south of the trackbed with the embankment completely screening us from view.  As we proceeded slowly along the track some cows appeared from an overbridge, wandering slowly towards the field.  We feared that a farmer might be close behind so we dashed back over the fence and up the embankment back to the trackbed. Finding ourselves behind a large stack of silage bales we felt relatively secure.  This feeling was shattered when suddenly I came face to face with a large dog that greeted me with bared teeth and a low, menacing growl.  In what must have been a comical scene, Chris walked into the back of me as I had stopped dead.  Amazingly the dog did not attack or start barking, so we backed away steadily from the canine threat, trying not to show any fear.  It was only when we got back down the embankment that the beast started barking, forcing us to head down the minimal cover of a hedgerow towards the river.


After walking in a large loop we rejoined the line (85 NY 403744) close to where Liddel Water ran adjacent to the trackbed.  The trackbed

215

was damp, sandwiched between the steep hillside and Liddel Water for about a mile, and we passed a couple of concrete lineside huts, one very overgrown and dilapidated and one in reasonable condition. Leaving the wooded hillside the line pushed out across the open floodplain of the River Esk. The bridge (85 NY 391729) across the Esk was an impressive iron girder structure known at Thistle Viaduct, and was a larger version of the bridges that we had seen crossing Gala Water. It had four stone pillars with five rusty low riveted iron arched girders that resembled a military pontoon bridge. It was fortunate that this excellent bridge remained in place, for a detour at this point would have been a real headache. The line crossed the floodplain of the western bank of the Esk before arriving at Scotch Dyke Station (85 NY 387723). The level crossing was gone but the platform and single-story red sandstone station house remained as a private house. Rather quaintly, a sign stating "Speed and Comfort by Rail" adorned the station canopy. The trackbed seemed to be an access track so we just walked quietly past the station to a gate. The wooded trackbed, sometimes overgrown, ran adjacent to the A7 for nearly two miles before curving away to follow the Esk, where the trackbed soon became a public footpath crossing open fields, apart from a short section, to the edge of Longtown (85 NY 376689). Longtown Station (85 NY 376690) and the former junction (85 NY 376688) of the line to Gretna have been totally demolished and replaced with a trucking yard and industrial estate. The viaduct (85 NY 376687) across the Esk for The Waverley was also demolished. Crossing the Esk on A7 road bridge we joined the riverside path, which part way along, had a sign detailing some local history including a picture of the former railway viaduct.

The riverside path bisected the truncated line (85 NY 377685), allowing easy access to the overgrown embankment. The trackbed crossed some open fields before entering a very boggy and impassable cutting (85 NY 377675) that forced us to climb out of the cutting and join a minor road that bridged (85 NY 378672) the line at the southern end of the cutting. Just as we joined the trackbed on the south side of the road we heard a lot of activity out of sight but just ahead. Beating a hasty retreat to the road we saw that a group of farm workers were busy on and around the trackbed, leaving us no alternative but to follow the minor road to rejoin the line at a former level crossing (85 NY 382661). At this point the trackbed became Sustrans Route 7, to run across the floodplain of the River Lyne for about 1 ½ miles to the site of Lyneside Station (85 NY 387644). Lyneside Station remained as a two-storey house but the platforms and level crossing had disappeared. To the south of Lyneside Station the line looked like Steptoe's Yard, with all manner of rubbish turning the trackbed into a linear junkyard. We proceeded with caution past wrecked vehicles, sofas, fridges, sheds, and piles of rubble before crossing a fence that marked the southern boundary of the awful mess. A small missing culvert bridge (85 NY 321628) across a stream proved to be a trickier obstacle that it looked, with both of us narrowly avoiding wet feet. The trackbed improved and became a farm track close to Newtown of Rockcliffe passing a concrete lineside hut and overbridge (85 NY 392625). Just south of the overbridge we were caught out in the open with a tractor coming right at us. We had no option but to proceed on, armed only with a smile. Unexpectedly, the farmer greeted us with a friendly: "Lost are yer?" and after a brief, chat he said that we could follow the line towards Harker but that a bridge (85 NY 389617) across a stream was missing up ahead. The bridge was indeed missing, but a short detour westwards took us to an alternative bridge used for farm vehicles. The line, running across flat open fields was vague until we reached a wood (85 NY 387612) north of Low Harker.

Harker Station (85 NY 386609) was screened from view by a high wooden fence and evergreen trees. The obvious detour was to climb over a fence to our left into the neighbouring field, east of the station site, and parallel the trackbed to a minor road overbridge just south of the station. Harker Station was difficult to see in its entirety, but we had a reasonable view from the overbridge. The station house was in use as a private dwelling and the platforms had been landscaped, with what appeared to be the remains of a signalbox just visible through the trees. To the south of Harker Station the trackbed had been developed for at least one new house, making a detour to the minor road bridge (85 NY 382609) crossing the A74 inevitable. After following the minor road running adjacent to the A74 we joined an overgrown trackbed (85 NY 385603) at the site of an overbridge, on the edge of an industrial estate. After a few hundred metres the trackbed became easily walkable and was possibly a permissive path until reaching an industrial estate access road (85 NY 385591). Just across the road it was possible to skirt the perimeter fence of some industrial units. At this point The Waverley remained in use as a siding on an embankment, giving access to a rail freight distribution depot. We pushed on to join a public footpath (85 NY 385587) that formed the boundary of Kingmoor Nature Reserve. The public footpath ended at a minor road (85 NY 385582), next to where the rail siding crossed the road on an overbridge. It was impossible to follow the existing railway any further, so we walked under the rail overbridge and followed the minor road bridge (85 NY 382583) over the WCML.

Once across the WCML we turned south on a minor road where we could see a vestige of The Waverley Route crossing the WCML on Kingmoor Yard Bridge (85 NY 383581), before closely paralleling the road on a high embankment. The single-track siding ended at a 'head-shunt' that ultimately allowed rail access to Kingmoor Yard on a truncated embankment (85 NY 382572) with a buffer stop symbolically marking the end of the line. Across the road from the buffer stop the line was lost in an open field, re-appearing as a cutting, which we accessed from a public footpath that crossed the cutting on an overbridge (85 NY 382569). The cutting was partly infilled with overgrown rubble but was navigable with care, ending in dramatic form at the 6-arched stone viaduct (85 NY 383565) crossing the River Eden. Although in reasonable condition, the Eden Viaduct had lost some of its topside walling. The southern end of the viaduct had the remains of galvanised spiky steel security fencing, with more holes than slats, and was easily passable, and the trackbed on the south side of the River Eden was in use as a path for a short distance. The Waverley Route officially ended at Canal Junction (85 NY 386563) where the North British Metals joined Caledonian Metals to give access to Carlisle Citadel Station. The exact site of Canal Junction was difficult to discern on the ground, but it was of no consequence as we were in high spirits, having just completed The Waverley Route in its entirety. In a bit of an anti-climax to such a magnificent route, the line petered out in some derelict land and we just meandered through the streets of Carlisle to the Railway Station for the X 95 to Canonbie.

*Newbattle Viaduct (66 NT 325649) today has more traffic passing under than over.*

*This view looking north along the trackbed from the southern end of Heriot Station (73 NT 403545) clearly shows the southbound platform.*

*Fountainhall Junction (73 NT 428496) is still clearly visible on the ground. This view was taken looking west from the trackbed of The Lauder Branch with the trackbed of The Waverley Route in shadow.*

*A very weathered bridge-plate adorns a bridge in the valley of Gala Water.*

*Between Falahill Summit and Galashiels, Gala Water is crossed numerous times by The Waverley Route on sturdy iron bridges.*

*Two views of the impressive iron lattice bridge (73 NT 453414) just to the north of Bowshank Tunnel.*

*The north portal (above) of Bowshank Tunnel (73 NT 453413) is clear and dry, in contrast to the damp south portal (below). The slender legs of an access bridge are just visible from the inside the south portal.*

*Melrose Station (73 NT 547339) survives remarkably intact and is now home to a restaurant. The ornate canopy sits next to the A6091.*

*The crossing gates at Maxton Station (74 NT 617299) have seen better days. Maxton Station is on the Kelso branch.*

*Staggered bridge supports (74 NT 661238) across the marshy ground at Jed Water are all that remain of this bridge on The Jedburgh Branch.*

*The trackbed at the isolated Hassendean Station (73 NT 548203) is now a lawn, but the footbridge survives as a splendid reminder of the past.*

225

*Riccarton Junction Station has been 'improved' by the addition of: some track, station signs, a brake van, and a phone box....*

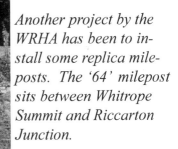

Bridge '200' - The Golden Bridge
(79 NY 525999) - has been lovingly
restored by The Waverley Route
Heritage Association (WRHA).

Another project by the
WRHA has been to in-
stall some replica mile-
posts. The '64' milepost
sits between Whitrope
Summit and Riccarton
Junction.

When looking north on
the trackbed at the
southern end of Steele
Road Station (79 NY
522931), one can see the
plaform remains.

Some superb trackbed north of Steele Road.

*The magnificent skew arches of Liddel Water Viaduct (85 NY 410754)*
*mark the start of The Langholm Branch.*

*A walker's view of Liddel Water Viaduct.*

*A very grand house at Penton Station (85 NY 439773) is guarded by 'Private' signs and minature signals.*

*A halo of light guides the railway walker under a fine overbridge south (85 NY 434771) of Penton Station.*

*The five spans of Thistle Viaduct (85 NY 391729) are still giving good service to those that care to cross.*

*A cheery sign at Scotch Dyke Station (85 NY 387723) still offers 'Speed and Comfort By Rail'.*

*Eden Viaduct (85 NY 383565) is the last significant structure on the line before entering Carlisle.*

231

# WALK XXII
## Part of The Kelso Branch (Roxburgh Junction to Coldstream), The Cornhill Branch (Coldstream to Alnwick), & The Alnwick Branch (Alnwick to Alnmouth)

| Walk Summary | |
|---|---|
| **Date walked** | April/May 2005 |
| **Line mileage** | 51 ¾ |
| **OSLR Maps** | 74, 75, 81 |
| **Opened to Passengers** | ♠1850 & 1851, ✦08 1850, *09 1887 |
| **Closed to Passengers** | *22 09 1930, ♠15 06 1964, ✦29 01 1968 |
| **PGAG Reference** | 31 |
| **Pre-Grouping Company** | ♠1North British Railway, *♠2✦North Eastern Railway |

*Coldstream to Alnwick, ♠Roxburgh Junction to Coldstream, ✦Alnwick to Alnmouth
1Roxburgh Junction to Sprouston Junction, 2Sprouston Junction to Coldstream

## Walk Highlights

Roxburgh Viaduct, Sunilaws Station, Willow Burn and Duddo Burn Viaducts, Akeld Station, Haugh Head Signal Box, Ilderton Station, Glanton Station, Whittingham Station, Hillhead Tunnel, Edlingham Viaduct, the dramatic trackbed crossing Alnwick Moor, Alnwick Station, and Cawledge Viaduct.

## Public Transport

Berwick-Upon-Tweed and Alnmouth are on the ECML. Bus service number 23 from Berwick Railway Station runs direct to Kelso. Bus service number 60 from Berwick Railway Station runs to Duns, to change for bus service number 82 from Duns to Kelso.

232

## Walk Description

### Roxburgh Junction to Mindrum Station (16 ¾ miles)

After getting the bus from Berwick Railway Station to Kelso we walked down the scenic River Teviot riverside path (part of the Border's Abbey's Way) to the village of Roxburgh. Our access point was Roxburgh Junction (74 NT 697305) (see Walk XXI); this time taking the eastern branch from the junction. It was a warm sun dappled evening as we walked along a high, grassy, embankment that after a few hundred metres crossed the River Teviot on Roxburgh Viaduct (74 NT 702304), an impressive curved stone structure that was unimpeded. Not far along the line we entered a boggy and overgrown cutting (74 NT 706306) before the trackbed opened out to contour high above the River Teviot.

A little over a mile from Roxburgh Viaduct we set up our basha in a copse of trees for an overnight stop. The chilly night gave way to a bright morning, and that fact along with some strong coffee helped us onto the line early. The line was easily walkable until it approached the A698 (74 NT 721325), where the trackbed was planted with trees, but an access track veered round to join a minor road/A698 junction at the site of the former Wallace Nick Station (74 NT 723326). There was no trace of Wallace Nick Station that closed in 1851, which was understandable since this station was only a temporary terminus until the extension to Kelso Station (74 NT 731330) was constructed in 1851. From Wallace Nick Station site the trackbed was now utilised by the A698, completely obliterating Kelso Station. With Kelso occupying the northern bank of the River Tweed, Kelso Station in its day was not conveniently located to serve the town.

After about a mile along the A698, the road veered away from the trackbed into Kelso, with the truncated line (74 NT 736337) being clearly visible on an embankment. From this point the trackbed was in use as a permissive path. Some fine railway walking took us past the unrecognisable site of Sprouston Junction (74 NT 744345), the point at which The North British Railway, coming from the west joined The North Eastern Railway coming from the east. The well-preserved Sprouston Station (74 NT 759353) was now a private single-storey stone cottage, but no trace of the level crossing remained. Across the minor road from Sprouston Station the trackbed became a farm track,

233

periodically shielded by trees providing some splendid walking to Carham Station (74 NT 791371). Carham Station looked more like a Halt, as the location was miles from any centre of population, and all that remained was an overgrown platform with some concrete posts and wire fencing. Carham was also the site of a long gone level crossing.

The farm track continued from Carham Station for about 1 ½ miles before reverting back to a grassy trackbed, meandering along the scenic open country of the Tweed Valley, and running through the occasional cutting or along an embankment. Sunilaws Station (74 NT 826374) and associated cottages was a thriving if ramshackle settlement. The two-storey stone station house, sitting on the north side of the line was in good condition and in use as a private house. The most remarkable feature of Sunilaws Station House was the presence of the 'N.E.R.' station clock, still resident in the wall of the house. At the roadside there was an original post from the level crossing gates and east of the crossing were the overgrown platforms. A couple of residents observed our passing with a cheery wave and a "Good Morning".

The trackbed east of Sunilaws was a farm track to a point just north (74 NT 846379) of the hamlet of West Learmouth, where it reverted to footpath on a grassy embankment leading to the 5-arched stone Willow Burn Viaduct (74 NT 851379) that took the line across a minor road and Willow Burn. Only a few hundred metres further down the line was the equally impressive 7-arched viaduct (74 NT 855379) across Duddo Burn. Just over a mile of splendid trackbed took us to the junction (74 NT 863388) of The Cornhill Branch. The junction was obvious on the ground, but we could not see The Cornhill Branch Line until we were right at the junction, as both lines emerged from a cutting at the junction. We headed south on The Cornhill Branch trackbed and the single-track line was a footpath to a minor road (74 NT 865377), where the bridge was missing. After an easy scramble up the embankment on the south side of the road, we found ourselves on a delightful birch covered high embankment. An occasionally overgrown trackbed crossing open country took us to a field where the line disappeared (74 NT 856346), forcing a detour round the edge of the field to a minor road. A short walk took us to a riveted iron road bridge (74 NT 854343) that overlooked Mindrum Station (74 NT 856339). The view from the bridge was one of a wide rubble-strewn trackbed leading to an old engine shed at Mindrum

Station. Mindrum Station, now a private house, was not visible from the bridge, but a reasonable view of the rather grand house could be had from the minor road south of the bridge.

It was impossible to access the trackbed close to Mindrum Station. A few hundred metres south, the line went under the B6396 (74 NT 856336), where it was possible to scramble down the bank to the overgrown trackbed on the south side of the road. The line continued for a few hundred metres to a stream in the valley of Bowmont Water where the stone overbridge was partially demolished, with half an arch remaining that looked like some kind of ancient monument. This obstacle forced us to follow the stream eastwards back to the B6396. The line across the valley of Bowmont Water was indistinct, with the only remains being the bridge abutments (74 NT 858333) of the demolished bridge across Bowmont Water. It was early evening and the abutment on the south side of Bowmont Water provided a good location for us to set up the basha for an overnight stop.

## Mindrum Station to Hedgeley Station (18 ½ miles)
A mild night had given way to a breezy morning with heavy showers. Fortunately we had pitched our basha to keep the worst of the rain off, with only the bottom of our Gore-Tex bivvy bags exposed. It was with a certain cosy smugness that we listened to the rain lashing on the basha whilst watching the water droplets beading together on the bottom of our bivvy bags like aqueous gemstones.

With the trackbed being obliterated we backtracked to the B6352 before crossing Bowmont Water on the road bridge (74 NT 874333). At the site of a former level crossing (74 NT 874332) the house was in use with a paddock occupying the trackbed to the east, forcing us to detour on the road to access the line a few hundred metres east (74 NT 876332). A low grassy embankment with trees on either side ran right next to Bowmont Water to the B6352 (74 NT 884327) and the hamlet of Kilham. Again there was a private house at the former crossing that required a short detour to the east. An overgrown trackbed quickly arrived at a burn (74 NT 886326) where the bridge was missing. From here the line became sandwiched between the steep, wooded hillside and Bowmont Water, which required several short cuttings and bridges to carry the trackbed through the topography to a splendid three-arched stone overbridge (74 NT 899318) that carried a track to Canno Mill. South of the bridge the line was damp underfoot and overgrown with trees for a few hundred metres before emerging in more open country on a good trackbed. The bridge across a deep, fast flowing College Burn (74 NT 908304) was missing making a considerable obstacle, and it was only just possible to ford the burn close to where it drained into the River Glen.

Kirknewton Station house and platform (74 NT 910304) remained in use as a substantial, single-storey private house, looking totally over-specified for such a small community. As we were to later find out, the stations along The Cornhill Branch were all similarly grand affairs, which were obviously built in a vane hope of a considerable passenger traffic that never materialised. The trackbed east of Kirknewton disappeared into ploughed fields on the floodplain of the River Glen. We left the vague trackbed at a minor road (74 NT 915304) for the B6351, to box round an obliterated section of line.

Skirting a field we rejoined the trackbed at the western end of a cutting (74 NT 924306) where we startled a stoat that had just taken a young rabbit. A good trackbed continued to a minor road (74 NT 938305) where a short detour from the trackbed was required to avoid houses and gardens on either side of the road. The trackbed to the east of the minor road appeared to be in use for some kind of equestrian activity, but using the screen of a high hedge, we successfully passed by un-noticed to rejoin a wooded trackbed that was walkable until the A697 (74 NT 956300), where the bridge was demolished. A short distance east of the A697 was Akeld Station (74 NT 956299). The trackbed at the station was in use as a garden, but it was possible to follow the fence line to the north to garner a good view of this most impressive and well restored structure. The two-storey stone house had a long wooden and glass veranda painted in maroon and cream on the platform, which presumably functioned as various passenger waiting rooms. Like Kirknewton and Mindrum, the grand station at Akeld appeared over-specified for the job. Under a dark and thundery looking sky we continued to the small settlement of Bendor (74 NT 965297) where a private house, probably of railway origin occupied the trackbed. A detour across a field up to the A697 took us to a minor road that enabled us to continue on the line east of Bendor. Our return to the line was greeted by a long threatened thunderclap and torrential downpour, which continued for the rest of the way into Wooler, where the trackbed (75 NT 993287) was in use as a cattle market. Wooler Station (75 NT 994285), another large structure, was occupied as a very grand private house.

Lunch in the Ryecroft Hotel was a leisurely affair as we gazed out of the window to see the roads turn into rivers as the heavy downpour continued. At the first sign of the rain easing, we set off through the streets of Wooler to join the trackbed out of town where the line ran under the A697 (75 NT 997272). The trackbed from the A697 was flat, sometimes disappearing into open fields before becoming wooded as it ran into the small settlement of Haugh Head. Haugh Head had no station but it was the site of a level crossing (75 NU 001260), and a well maintained signal box called "The Crossing" sat at the bottom of a garden like a Victorian folly. Beyond Haugh Head a wooded trackbed, ran closely parallel with the A697 and continued southeast until reaching a house built on the trackbed (75 NU 004254) that required a short detour south. With the line leaving the valley of Wooler Water, the trackbed traversed some open country of ploughed fields that looked like some kind of smoking volcanic waste as the strong sunshine caused rapid evaporation of the recent heavy rainfall.

A spectacular high embankment (75 NU 015237) guided the trackbed into the broad valley of Lilburn Burn. The high bridge across Lilburn Burn (75 NU 017236) had been removed. In its place there were a couple of taught cables straddling the burn, from which three panels of wooden fencing were precariously suspended. The burn was too fast and deep to ford, and with the lack of a decent crossing point nearby, we had little choice other than too scramble across on the cables, with the prospect of a soaking if one were to fall. On the southern bank of Lilburn Burn a high bridge abutment led to another bridge over a path before the line reached Ilderton Station (75 NU 019236). Ilderton Station was similar in construction to Akeld Station and was also beautifully restored as a private house and offices for a mail order company. More information about Ilderton station can be found at: http://home.clara. net/iwf/ildertonstation/index.html. As the station sat in a half-cutting on the north side we followed the fence line to the top of the cutting side to avoid the garden and to get a better look over the extensive site.

The former crossing across the A697 at Ilderton was obliterated, necessitating a short walk along the roadside. Just past a house at the head of a minor road we moved quickly across an open field to a wooded trackbed (75 NU 023234) where it was possible to walk until the farm at Lilburn Glebe (75 NU 033224), where another detour to the A697 was required. With the trackbed very overgrown and adjacent to the road, we opted for an easy walk along the tarmac until reaching a bridleway that crossed the line (75 NU 037217). At the crossing point there was a fine, small, signal box that appeared to be in use as a garden shed. A good trackbed running close to the B6346 continued to the site of Wooperton Station (75 NU 048201), with the grand station house now part of a large sawmill. Due to large buildings and piles of logs, the trackbed was unwalkable from Wooperton Station, so it was back to the A697 for about half a mile before a public footpath (81 NU 053194) allowed access the trackbed. The trackbed was not in good condition at this point, with a large chunk of embankment having been dug out at the site of a stream. Across the stream the line was wooded for a short distance before crossing open fields and a small bridge before becoming a farm track. Two-thirds of the way along a long cutting the trackbed passed under a minor road overbridge (81 NU 059177) to become an access road for Breamish Gravel Works. A muddy trackbed stopped at the north shore of the River Breamish (81 NU 060171) where only the bridge abutments remained.

Having already decided that it was time to camp, we were following the boggy bank of the River Breamish to the A697 when we came across a small concrete WWII pillbox (81 NU 059171) that once guarded the A697 road bridge across the river. Apart from some plant debris the pillbox was dry and in excellent condition, giving us a perfect location for an overnight stop. The pillbox was just big enough for the two of us plus our gear, and once the stove was going we made it cosy in no time. A few hundred metres south of the River Breamish was Hedgeley Station (81 NU 060169), which was rather curiously named, as the closest village was Powburn a short distance further south.

**Hedgeley to Alnmouth (16 ½ miles)**
The trackbed south of the River Breamish was inaccessible as it ran to Hedgeley Station, now a private house, so we followed the road towards

Powburn and stocked up on supplies at the well-stocked petrol station. A public footpath (81 NU 062165) gave easy access to a well-walked trackbed, where the line climbed on a steep gradient and entered thick woodland to become a forest track. The trackbed was occasionally overgrown but generally walkable to Glanton Station (81 NU 081147); another grand structure and now a private house. To detour round the trackbed running past the station house we had to clamber east out of the muddy, overgrown cutting that was made very slippery by the downpour that had just started. At the southern end of Glanton Station some coal drops remained by a badly overgrown trackbed.

A wooded, often overgrown, and wet trackbed ended at an access road for Low Barton (81 NU 088127). The access road continued towards the River Aln but it was obvious from the map that the railway bridge across the river was missing. Our only option was to take the public footpath to the A697 to cross the river. From the road it was possible to see that the trackbed had disappeared into the fields on both sides of the River Aln. A short walk to a minor road bridge gave us an excellent view of Whittingham Station (81 NU 089122). Whittingham Station was a different design from previous stations in that it had a large island platform complete with elegant iron canopy, although the glass panes were missing. The large station site had a goods shed, station cottages, and a Station Master's House. Although a different design to previous stations that we had passed, Whittingham Station was equally impressive and relatively well preserved.

It was possible to scramble down into the cutting on the south side of the road bridge overlooking Whittingham Station to an overgrown and boggy trackbed. At the edge of a wood the trackbed emerged to cross open fields past Lowfield Farm, and with people about we moved quickly along a muddy trackbed that had been badly churned up by cattle. A high embankment took the line over Coe Burn (81 NU 099112) to a track with permissive access (81 NU 101112). To the east of the track there was a house, probably of railway origin, right on the trackbed barring the way to Hillhead Tunnel (81 NU 106111). A short box round to the south of the house across open fields enabled us to access the trackbed in a wood that lead into the cutting of the western portal of Hillhead Tunnel. The stone portal was guarded by a wooden and barbed wire fence with a sigh reading: "DANGER KEEP OUT –

Lemmington Estate". Hillhead Tunnel (aka Edlingham Tunnel) at 351 yards long ran under a low hill to emerge in the valley of Edlingham Burn. The inside of the tunnel was in good condition with the trackbed only becoming damp at the eastern portal (81 NU 108108). The eastern portal of Hillhead Tunnel was rather more overgrown with the trackbed heading away in a wet cutting.

A splendid section of line took us to Edlingham Viaduct (81 NU 117093), a magnificent 5-arched stone structure built on a curve, which guided The Cornhill Branch high over Edlingham Burn. With the sun now shining strongly, we descended down the steep bank to have lunch under one of the graceful arches; it felt like we were dining in an open-air cathedral. The trackbed beyond the viaduct, on a steep gradient, curved very sharply northwards to form the eastern side of a horseshoe. We passed Edlingham Halt (81 NU 122092) that sported a fine house and signal box perched next to the line as a splendid and broad trackbed left the woods to reveal superb views across the surrounding countryside. The trackbed became lined with the bright yellow blooms of gorse bushes as several rock-hewn cuttings and high embankments guided the line on its convoluted course towards a summit, making it probably the best, uninterrupted section of line that we had walked since leaving Roxburgh Junction. Unfortunately the long summit cutting (81 NU 147122) was boggy and impassable. Therefore, we had to skirt the edge of the cutting, passing the summit cottages to the B6341 bridge (81 NU 157118), before it was possible to regain the trackbed. From the B6341 a rapidly descending and walkable trackbed lead to the south-western edge of the historic town of Alnwick, where the line disappeared under new housing and a caravan site (81 NU 189121).

Since we had previously visited the magnificent Alnwick Station (81 NU 192129), now home to the excellent bookshop of 'Barter Books', we detoured past a cricket ground and through an industrial estate to the A1 (81 NU 200123) dual carriageway. I would, however, strongly recommend a visit to Alnwick Station, as it is not often that you can look round or have a rest in a wonderfully atmospheric waiting room of an old railway station. One can also get a cup of coffee whilst browsing the extensive range of second hand books, including an excellent railway section.

The 3-mile branch from Alnwick to Alnmouth Station provided a link from The Cornhill Branch to the ECML, with Alnwick Station being the terminus 'in-out' station for both branches. In fact the station that is now home to Barter Books was the second station built in Alnwick, replacing an earlier station in 1887 when The Cornhill Branch was opened. This short branch line outlived The Cornhill Branch by 38 years, falling belatedly to Beeching's Axe in 1968. Today, The Aln Valley Railway Society (www.avrs.co.uk) is trying to get the Alnwick branch line re-opened, and there are also rumours that the council may have a competing plan to turn the trackbed into a public footpath.

Taking our lives in our hands we scurried across the A1 to pick up an excellent and well-walked trackbed (81 NU 201123). The line was carried over Cawledge Burn, a tributary draining into the River Aln, on the splendid stone Cawledge Viaduct (81 NU 213115). About a mile from the Cawledge Viaduct the trackbed swung to the south to run alongside the ECML to the former junction (81 NU 228114) north of Alnmouth Station. It was possible walk along a track next to the ECML for a few hundred metres onto the platform at Alnmouth Station, to provide a fitting end to a long and excellent walk.

*Only an overgrown platform and some fencing remain at Carham Station (74 NT 791371) on The Kelso Branch.*

*A substantial house remains in use at Sunilaws Station (74 NT 826374) on The Kelso Branch. The inset shows the 'N.E.R.' clock that still can be seen in the wall to the right of the porch.*

*A close-up of Willow Burn Viaduct (74 NT 851379) on The Kelso Branch.*

*The delightful house at Mindrum Station (74 NT 856339). This was the first stop on The Cornhill Branch after leaving Coldstream.*

243

*The Cornhill Branch must take the title for the grandest stations on a rural branch line.  Akeld Station (74 NT 956299) (above) and Ilderton Station (75 NU 019236) (below) are particularly fine, and wonderfully restored examples.*

*Trackbed does not get much better than this section near Ilderton.*

*Signal Box (74 NU 037217) in use as a garden shed.*

*The engine shed and station building with ornate canopy on the island platform at Whittingham Station (74 NU 089122), are of an unusual design for The Cornhill Branch. The buildings remain in private use today.*

*Two ends of the same tunnel. The above left picture shows the western portal of Hillhead Tunnel (81 NU 106111), and the above right picture shows the overgrown and boggy eastern portal.*

*The clear trackbed of Edlingham Viaduct (81 NU 117093) is now providing good service as a farm track.*

*Edlingham Viaduct passes high over Edlingham Burn at a point where The Cornhill Branch starts a severe horseshoe curve.*

# WALK XXIII
## The Peebles Loop (Kilnknowe Junction, Galashiels to Hardengreen Junction, Eskbank via Peebles)

| Walk Summary | |
|---|---|
| Date walked | October 2005 |
| Line mileage | 37 ½ |
| OSLR Maps | 66, 73 |
| Opened to Passengers | *04 07 1855, ✦01 02 1864 |
| Closed to Passengers | *05 02 1962, ✦10 09 1962 |
| PGAG Reference | 30 |
| Pre-Grouping Company | North British Railway |

*Hardengreen Junction to Rosewell & Hawthornden, ✦Rosewell & Hawthornden to Galashiels (Kilnknowe Junction), ✦Hardengreen Junction to Peebles, ✦Peebles to Galashiels (Kilnknowe Junction)

## Walk Highlights

Walkerburn Station, Innerleithen Bridge and Station, Cardrona Bridge and Station, Tunnel under A72 at Peebles, and Leadburn Station.

## Public Transport

Galashiels can be reached from Edinburgh or Carlisle on The Waverley Route replacement bus service number 95/X95 operated by First Borders. Carlisle is on the WCML. Edinburgh is on the ECML. Dalkeith is well connected to Edinburgh by several bus services.

## Walk Description

Preliminary planning for this walk had revealed two major bridges missing across the River Tweed, and this would mean enormous detours if we were to successfully walk all of the trackbed. After considerable

248

thought the only real option was to cross the river by boat. We opted to buy a rubber dinghy for the crossings, and the craft would have to be substantial enough to carry Chris and myself plus all our gear. I purchased a 'Sevylor Caravelle 3-person dinghy' that seemed to suffice, but added about 6 Kg to our packs, not to mention the bulk. It had been a very dry summer and early autumn, so we thought that the Tweed would be very low making the crossings simple; an assumption that we would later regret.

### Galashiels to Peebles (18 ½ miles)
It had been raining heavily during our Friday night trip down from Edinburgh to Galashiels on the X95 service. The Abbotsford Hotel was conveniently situated next to Galashiels Bus Station, but it was overpriced for what it offered. The torrential rain had continued all night and when we left the hotel we were in full raingear. Rejoining the cycle route, we retraced our steps northwards (see Walk XXI) along The Waverley Route to Kilnknowe Junction (73 NT 476373). It was on this short section that we got our first idea of how much water was in the local rivers, as Gala Water was a gravy brown turbulent spate.

From Kilnknowe Junction the trackbed was walkable, climbing through woods to the A72 (73 NT 470377), where the line disappeared. The rain continued to pour down heavily as we trudged along the A72 with short sections of boggy, unwalkable trackbed appearing on the right hand side of the road. It had not been a good start to the day. Upon reaching Clovenfords we found that the station (73 NT 451366) had been incorporated into a housing development with only the single-storey station house remaining. Following the A72 through Clovenfords, we found a poorly defined trackbed through a gate in an open field (73 NT 446361). The trackbed looked as if it had been infilled and it was not until we reached a bend (73 NT 447356) in the line that the trackbed became truly recognisable with a partially infilled bridge/cutting. A few hundred metres further on and a cutting had obviously been infilled, that meant a muddy trek across a field as the line swung into the valley of the River Tweed. Just beyond the infilled cutting (73 NT 446352) the trackbed became clear and walkable, running high above the Tweed. It was at this point that we realised the folly of our dinghy. The Tweed looked more like the Zambezi as it writhed through the valley; an angry-looking, foaming morass of chocolate-brown flood water. The weight of the dinghy in my sodden pack seemed to double at this realisation. We passed a telegraph pole adorned with several intact white insulators (73 NT 442352) before reaching the crossing point of the A72, where the bridge was demolished (73 NT 436352). Due to the flooded river we had to quickly change our plans, and we opted to cross the Tweed at a minor road bridge (73 NT 438351), and continue along the minor road on the south bank. From the bridge we gained a full appreciation of the amount of water hammering down the valley at an incredible rate with whole trees being tossed about like matchsticks.

Walking on the minor road allowed us to get good views of the trackbed on the north side of the river. Through binoculars I could just make out the remains of Thornielee Station (73 NT 412362), which appeared intact and in use as a private house. Leaving the minor road we headed down a steep wooded bank to the first crossing point of the Tweed (73 NT 398366), where all that remained was a rusty fence post. With the rain easing slightly we followed an excellent trackbed that hugged the river, passing an interesting brick buttress (73 NT 387374) that shored up a section of the wooded bank on the left hand side of the trackbed. Close to Walkerburn, the river had burst its banks and the trackbed became a causeway through the flood; a credit to the engineers and men who had built the line, and who obviously had full knowledge of the Tweed's capabilities. A small culvert bridge (73 NT 364369) was missing and the flood waters made what would have normally been a simple crossing impossible. We had to make a wet and muddy detour south along the culvert to the minor road to rejoin the line at the former level crossing at Walkerburn Station (73 NT 361368). Walkerburn Station house was now a B&B, with flood water from the Tweed lapping at the walls. Skirting south, we followed the fence that enclosed the station site, where there appeared to be an engine shed in use as part of an engineering company's yard.

The trackbed became grassy and indistinct before running adjacent to a minor road (73 NT 355368), where due to the weather conditions it was easier to walk along the road for about a mile to a point where the line and road parted company. This was the next crossing point of the Tweed, and according to the map the bridge (73 NT 341366) was present. The bridge, an impressive five-span riveted iron girder structure was indeed in-situ, but it was crawling with engineers in hard hats and fluorescent yellow jackets. Taking this to be an ominous sign I gingerly ventured out onto the bridge to see if it was okay to cross. The engineers were in the middle of renovating the bridge as part of a cycleway from Innerleithen, when the swollen Tweed had washed away most of their scaffolding. Even though I had given them a sob story about Chris having a bad blister they said it was too dangerous to cross, thus forcing us to take a significant detour on the minor road into Innerleithen. What should have been a simple, if long detour, turned out to be an epic struggle as flood water from the Tweed had flooded the minor road to a depth of about half a metre. To get round this obstacle and keep our feet dry we had to scramble up the steep wooded bank and skirt the flooded section. It was with some relief that we found food and tea at a café in Innerleithen, which gave us a chance to rest and dry out.

Retracing our steps we regained the line opposite Innerleithen Station (73 NT 332363), where the two-storey station house still had a platform and wooden canopy in a good state of repair. The trackbed, accessed through a gate, west of Innerleithen Station was well-walked and easy to follow as it hugged the northern bank of the Tweed. Under a leaden sky we reached the third crossing point of the Tweed (73 NT 308380), and the second without a bridge. No trace of a bridge could be seen, and we left the trackbed to walk along the A72 once more for about 1 ½ miles to the turn off (73 NT 299392) for Cardrona. The area around Cardrona had been developed as a golf resort complete with an ugly hotel, but the weather made sure that the golfers were well and truly confined to the 19th hole. The single-storey, wood and brick structure of Cardrona Station (73 NT 301391) had been elegantly restored in cream and maroon and was in use as the village store. Just west of Cardrona Station the line crossed the Tweed for a fourth time, and this time the bridge was present and easily accessible, being another five-span riveted iron girder bridge that was in use as part of the access road for the golf course. A flat and easily walked line continued from Cardrona Bridge for just over 2 miles, hugging the north bank to the site of the former gasworks (73 NT 272397) on the outskirts of Peebles. With the light fading we explored the remains of the gasworks with its large brick buildings still present, before regaining the trackbed just north of the site. The muddy trackbed went through some woods to a tunnel portal (73 NT 271398) that would have originally gone under the A72. The rather eerie tunnel was rubble and rubbish strewn and completely blocked after about 25 metres that forced us to backtrack and climb out onto the A72. The remaining trackbed was largely built on as we walked along the A72 into Peebles, but with short detours on side roads it was possible to see traces of the line paralleling on the north side of the A72.

It was dark when we reached The Cross Keys Hotel in the centre of Peebles; a nice old hotel full of wonky angles and creaky floorboards, that was allegedly haunted by a former landlady. After turning our room into a drying room we spent a wonderful evening in The Bridge Inn, which apart from serving some excellent ale had a remarkably extravagant Victorian Gents toilet. In fact, The Bridge Inn was probably the best pub that we had visited north of the border.

### Peebles to Eskbank (Hardengreen Junction) (19 miles)
The morning was dry as we waited for the Post Office to open. I had decided, rather than hauling the dinghy any further, to post it home which gave us a significant reduction in pack weight.

The North British Station in Peebles (73 NT 253407) was absent having been replaced by the A703. After wandering through residential streets we found the trackbed on the northern edge of Peebles (73 NT 248413). The line, now heading north, followed the scenic valley of Eddleston Water. After passing the remains of a concrete line-side hut we came to a crossing point of Eddleston Water (73 NT 246422) where the bridge was missing. Under normal circumstances we would probably have been able to ford the stream but after all the recent rain this was impossible, so we were forced to follow the eastern bank to a minor road. On the other side of the road the trackbed was in use as access to Kidston Mill, (73 NT 243428) with the original rail bridge having been replaced by a new wooden bridge. The track to Kidston Mill branched sharp left with the trackbed continuing northwards through some trees.

An excellent trackbed passed under a twin-span iron overbridge (73 NT 237445) and over Eddleston Water on a single-span iron bridge (73 NT 238465), before coming to Eddleston. The approach to Eddleston Station

(73 NT 241470) was barred by a fence, where the trackbed was in use as a garden. We boxed round the remaining single-story station building to the road, picking up a wet trackbed that was sandwiched between a track and a wood on the north side of Eddleston (73 NT 242472). The line continued northwards now on the eastern bank of Eddleston Water. Passing a house (73 NT 242489) we were somewhat amused to see an old home-signal in the garden with a TV aerial perched on top. It was just as well that there were no trains anymore as any upward movement of the signal arm would have severely interrupted TV reception.

The line again crossed Eddleston Water (73 NT 243500) on an iron girder bridge to emerge in the yard of an abandoned gravel pit, just south of the site of Earlyvale Gate Station (73 NT 243507), of which we saw no trace. The trackbed was overgrown at the station site and crossed an overbridge before running on an embankment that ended abruptly at Waterheads (73 NT 242510) in a stable complex where the original bridge over the stream was gone having been replaced by a metal bridge that was accessible by clambering down the embankment. The line from Waterheads veered away from the road and stream, and began climbing steeply across some open ground, past some huge poultry sheds (73 NT 235529) that belonged to Millennium Farm, where the trackbed had been infilled. The line continued to climb across open country giving some splendid views before entering a wood (73 NT 235543) to reach Leadburn Junction (73 NT 235549) where the former NBR branch to Dolphinton (See Walk XXXI) joined the Peebles Loop. The junction was clearly visible on the ground with the trackbed covered in rough grass, and the line to Dolphinton looked a tempting prospect.

The bridge across the A703 to Leadburn Station (73 NT 235554) was missing and access to the line on the north side of the road was difficult so we opted to walk to the crossroads and walk along the A6094 to Leadburn Station. The station site was now a pleasant picnic area with both platforms remaining. A short distance north along the A6094 the trackbed was easily accessed via a farm gate, where it continued across open fields to a crossing cottage (73 NT 242571), that required a short detour through some trees to access the minor road. The line was a delight to walk with some great views from this point. Just as we were enjoying the scenery a 4x4 pick-up truck came hurtling across some stubble fields from our left straight towards us. The driver was a gamekeeper, no doubt doing his master's bidding, and he said that he would have to stop us going on as he "had a line of beaters coming across the fields towards us". The deerstalker-wearing idiot also had to get the obligatory jibe in about us "having disturbed some game already", which was nonsense, as was his story about the non-existent beaters. He knew, of course, that with access rights in Scotland he could not just forbid us to carry on but instead he had to dream up some rubbish about beaters i.e. a 'legitimate activity' taking place where we may have to alter our route to avoid any interference. After managing not to lose our cool we fobbed him off with an agreement to detour to the road. After he had gone we made a short box round, which would have been necessary anyway as there was a substantial bridge missing (73 NT 242578) across Black Burn, before immediately returning to the trackbed.

The trackbed continued to be excellent to Pomathorn Station and goods yard (73 NT 242593), that once rather inconveniently served the town of Penicuik. The station house was a private dwelling with a remaining overgrown platform. A good trackbed enabled us to make good progress to the B7026 where it was once crossed via a level crossing. Although the crossing itself was long gone, the crossing keeper's cottage (66 NT 248599) remained, and was lived in by a friendly old couple who were happy for me to take a picture and chat about the old line. The line now veered northeast passing Rosslynlee Hospital that once had its own timber-platformed halt (66 NT 268613), of which no trace remained. The trackbed although walkable along this section was frequently muddy until reaching a minor road and the site of Rosslynlee Station (66 NT 273618), now a private house. The trackbed from Rosslynlee Station was flooded and overgrown making it unwalkable, but it was possible to shadow the line by following the thick hedge growing alongside the trackbed. About ¾ mile from Rosslynlee Station the trackbed disappeared into an open and grassy field, that made a straight line heading for Rosewell the only option. Whilst traversing the field we could see cyclists coming in from our left on the old Penicuik Branch, now a cycleway, that joined the Peebles Loop at Hawthornden Junction (66 NT 286630). From Hawthornden Junction to Hardengreen Junction (about 3 ½ miles) the Peebles Loop was now a surfaced cycleway, with platforms remaining at Rosewell & Hawthornden (66 NT 288631) and Bonnyrigg (66 NT 310648) Stations.

*The River Tweed makes its presence felt. This view shows the site of a missing culvert bridge close to Walkerburn where the flood waters have rushed through. Weather conditions on the day were atrocious.*

*The quaint house at Walkerburn Station (73 NT 361368) is now in use as a B&B.*

*Engineers renovating Innerleithen Bridge (73 NT 341366) for use as a cyclepath had most of their scaffolding washed away in the floods.*

*The platform and canopy are still present at Innerleithen Station (73 NT 332363).*

*Cardrona Bridge (73 NT 299391) is a similar structure to Innerleithen Bridge, and is now used as an access road for the golf course.*

*Flood debris has attached itself to this fine old single-span iron bridge (73 NT 238465) across Eddleston Water.*

257

*Signal post as TV aerial (73 NT 242489).*

*Missing Bridge across Black Burn (73 NT 242578).*

# WALK XXIV
## The Allendale Railway (Allendale to Hexham)

| Walk Summary | |
|---|---|
| Date walked | October 2005 |
| Line mileage | 13 ½ |
| OSLR Maps | 87 |
| Opened to Passengers | 01 03 1869 |
| Closed to Passengers | 22 09 1930 |
| PGAG Reference | 27 |
| Pre-Grouping Company | North Eastern Railway |

## Walk Highlights

Staward Halt, Langley Station, Elrington Station, the surrounding scenery and a very walkable trackbed.

## Public Transport

Hexham is on the Newcastle to Carlisle Line. Newcastle is on the ECML and Carlisle is on the WCML. Allendale Town is connected to Hexham Railway Station via bus service 688.

## Walk Description

It was a fresh blustery autumn morning when we arrived in Allendale Town. Allendale Station sat about a mile north of Allendale Town itself in the valley of the River East Allen (87 NY 831571) and was in use as a caravan park, with the trackbed well colonised by caravans. Due to the occupation of the line by the two-wheeled invaders, we joined the trackbed from a byway (87 NY 828573) that crossed the line at the boundary of the caravan park. The embanked trackbed soon entered a couple of short overgrown cuttings before opening out, contouring

259

along the hillside with good views across the valley westwards. After just over a mile of slightly overgrown trackbed the line was joined from the south by a vehicle track, making the trackbed very easy walking to a minor road where the bridge was missing (87 NY 810579). On the northern side of the road the trackbed reverted to a grassy path, again with some dramatic views made more intense by looming rain clouds partially obscuring the low sun.

The line veered northeast as it left of the East Allen Valley above the confluence of the River West and East Allen to run adjacent to the A686. After a short distance next to the main road, we had to leave the line at an overbridge, as the trackbed was in use as a garden at Staward Halt (87 NY 806596). Staward Halt, now a private house, had a well preserved timber building on the platform, which was easily viewed from the overbridge. After following the A686 for a few hundred metres it was simple to regain the line across open fields, with the trackbed being walkable to the B6305 (87 NY 818604). A farmer tearing about on a quad bike prevented us form accessing the line on the other side of the B6305, so we followed the road and a public footpath to the village of Langley. Arriving in Langley we found the cutting on the western side of the road partially infilled, with the bridge across the road missing. Langley Station (87 NY 828613), however, remained in a delightful condition and was the highlight of the line. The station, now called 'The Garden Station', was home to a garden centre for the sale of plants with a sideline of gardening and arts courses. The original timber station buildings remained on the platform surrounded by many potted plants. An interesting feature was 'The Leaning Shed', an old shed on the platform at a less than perpendicular angle which looked as if it had been damaged in a storm. The trackbed was accessible to the public and just up the line in a colourful autumnal wood were two overbridges in quick succession. One bridge was built to carry a huge chimney flue across the line that once carried fumes away from a nearby lead smelter. With unusual sculptures and much vegetation this section of line running through the woods was a pure joy to walk.

Upon leaving the woods of The Langley Estate the rain came down hard as we traversed the open country of the South Tyne Valley. The trackbed was largely walkable to Elrington Station (87 NY 863633), the last intermediate station on the branch before Hexham, which was now a private house with grassy trackbed and a fenced off platform. From Elrington Station an excellent trackbed, becoming a forestry road (87 NY 869653) took us through more scenic woodland to the A69(T). The line, running adjacent on the south side of the A69(T), was inaccessible for about 500 metres before crossing to the north side of the road. The exact crossing point was impossible to see, with no trace remaining of the bridge, and the trackbed had been absorbed into a field on the north side of the road due to infilling. An overbridge (87 NY 902656), looking more like a wall in a field due to the arch being almost completely infilled was a good marker, and our access point for the continuing trackbed. From the bridge a thickly wooded line crossed Darden Burn on a fine bridge before opening out into a muddy field where the line ended at a minor road overbridge (87 NY 909654).

A gate in the corner of a field provided an easy escape route to the A69 where the alignment of the dual carriageway had obliterated the trackbed. After an unpleasant walk along the hard shoulder we regained an overgrown line (87 NY 917653) that continued for a few hundred metres to the site of the junction (87 NY 921653) with the existing Newcastle to Carlisle Line. A short backtrack down the line allowed us to access a footpath that crossed a golf course on the outskirts of Hexham. With a low autumn sun now shining we ambled into Hexham for the bus back to Allendale Town.

*A dramatic autumn sky brings to life an otherwise annonymous shallow cutting north of Allendale Town.*

NORTH EASTERN RAILWAY.
PUBLIC WARNING.
PERSONS ARE WARNED NOT TO TRESPASS
ON THIS RAILWAY, OR ON ANY OF THE
LINES, STATIONS, WORKS, OR PREMISES
CONNECTED THEREWITH.
ANY PERSON SO TRESPASSING IS LIABLE
TO A PENALTY OF FORTY SHILLINGS.
R.F. DUNNELL,
SECRETARY.

*Views from the
idyllic site of
Langley Station
(87 NY 806596)*

# WALK XXV
## The Rothbury Branch
## (Scot's Gap to Rothbury)

| Walk Summary | |
|---|---|
| Date walked | January 2006 |
| Line mileage | 13 |
| OSLR Maps | 81 |
| Opened to Passengers | 01 11 1870 |
| Closed to Passengers | 15 09 1952 |
| PGAG Reference | 27, 31 |
| Pre-Grouping Company | North British Railway |

## Walk Highlights

Bridge over Delf Burn, Longwitton Station, Ewesley Station, Fontburn Viaduct, Crook Crossing, Brinkburn Station, cutting near Rothbury and an excellent trackbed through some superb scenery.

## Public Transport

Scot's Gap can be reached from Morpeth Bus Station by services (infrequent) 340 and 819. Rothbury is connected to Morpeth via bus services 416, 516, and 817. Morpeth is on the ECML and is served by local trains and limited Inter-City services from Newcastle and Edinburgh.

## Walk Description

This single track branch was originally intended to run from Scot's Gap, on The Wansbeck Railway (see walk XII), to Coldstream (see walk XXII), but due to financial problems the line ended up terminating at Rothbury. The lack of a northern extension and a very sparse population of the area inevitably lead to an early closure of this picturesque branch line.

Due to a lack of public transport between Morpeth and Scot's Gap on Sundays, we travelled up to the start of the walk on Saturday with the aim of camping out ready for the walk on Sunday. It was one of those very bright, dry and wonderfully clear winter days as we joined the permissive path on the trackbed at Scot's Gap, just north of the station site (81 NZ 039864), now in use by an agricultural supplies company. With the winter sun dipping fast, we crossed Hart Burn looking for a spot to camp, and with the night set to be very cold we were looking for a sheltered spot with a good wood supply. A shallow cutting just north of Hart Burn (81 NZ 033875) seemed to fit the bill, and we had our basha and bivvy bags set up in no time. With a frost already forming on the grass and dead nettle stalks, we frenetically gathered wood for a camp fire that was soon giving essential warmth and the evocative smell of wood smoke. Only the crackle of the fire and the hiss of the occasional ring pull broke the absolute silence of the cutting.

Overnight the temperature had fallen to at least -5°C. Peeping gingerly out of our synthetic cocoons the world had turned white and brittle. The clear skies of yesterday had turned a smoky grey with a damp mist swirling in a cold breeze. The basha was frozen solid, and it was only the call of nature and the sound of a nearby quad bike that forced us out of our sleeping bags. Our equipment resisted being stuffed into our rucksacks as the cold had transformed once pliable fabrics into stubborn fold-resistant puzzles that proved a real challenge for numb fingers.

The line continued due north to Delf Burn (81 NZ 034886), where the permissive path left the trackbed to follow the burn westwards. The bridge across Delf Burn was more of an impressive short stone tunnel and on the far side of the bridge was a fence and bridle gate with a sign saying that the land ahead belonged to The National Trust. As the line curved to the northeast we had a good view of the trackbed running on a high embankment. A wonderfully clear and grassy trackbed passed under a substantial stone bridge (81 NZ 037897) that carried the B6342 over the line. The next stone overbridge (81 NZ 038902) that conveyed a minor road was a skewed stone arch structure with the trackbed under its arch being flooded, that necessitated a short detour up and over the road. Beyond the bridge the line entered a deep rocky cutting that was made easier to negotiate due to the frozen ground. With the line once again going under the B6342 we arrived at Longwitton Station (81 NZ 045907) to find a low timber platform quietly decaying among mossy trees and fallen leaves. The trackbed at the northern end of the platform was obstructed by rubble and a fence but it was a simple job to access a public bridleway that utilised the trackbed northwards for a few hundred metres. A short distance along the line we passed a lineside hut as we progressed along the muddy trackbed, until the bridleway veered away from the line to the southeast, where the trackbed ahead was in use for farm access.

The site of a missing bridge (81 NZ 059916) marked the spot where a public bridleway crossed the line. From this point to the next crossing of the B6342 (81 NZ 059926) (bridge missing) the embanked trackbed was signed as a 'Countryside Commission' bridleway. A sign at the B6342 informed us that a Countryside Stewardship Scheme was in operation to the west of the road, which probably meant a subsidy for the local landowner to do something for 'conservation', with the quid-pro-quo for the public being a permissive path running north along the trackbed for a few hundred metres. Of course unless you happen to walk past this sign, you would be very unlikely to even know of its existence, as these schemes are not detailed on OS maps.

Ewesley Station (81 NZ 058926) sat on the western side of the B6342, where the single-storey brick house was in use as a private dwelling. An overgrown derelict timber platform, similar to the platform at Longwitton Station also remained. A wet trackbed headed northwest from Ewesley Station past a plantation to a public footpath (81 NZ 055930). The line immediately entered a shallow and muddy cutting before opening out into the valley of the River Font. At the site of a former bridge (81 NZ 053933) part of the embankment had been excavated, with a weathered sign warning the walker that the whole valley was likely to sudden flooding from overspill from the nearby Fontburn Waterworks and Reservoir. This explained the large marker poles that we had noticed scattered throughout the valley. The trackbed was briefly interrupted by a tarmac access road (81 NZ 052935) for Fontburn Reservoir, before resuming in a partially infilled and wet cutting.

Pushing through a thick growth of saplings we arrived at the southern end (81 NZ 052936) of Fontburn Viaduct, which sat high above Fontburn Waterworks. Screened by the trees we managed to scale an awkward chain-link fence topped with barbed wire to access the trackbed on the viaduct. The fence at the northern end was simpler to negotiate by going round instead of over, but a good head for heights was required. From the northern end we had a good view back along the viaduct; an elegant 12-arched stone structure. The embanked trackbed to the north of the viaduct was planted with pine trees and very difficult to negotiate, forcing us to traverse along the slope of the embankment to the end of the wood (81 NZ 051941). Beyond the wood the trackbed became a dirt access road to Fontburn Halt (81 NZ 051942), where only a few concrete fence posts remained. Just north along the trackbed was a house and an old lineside hut that was in use as a shed. The line north of Fontburn Halt snaked through a couple of clear cuttings to a point (81 NZ 054954) where the trackbed was in use as a dirt access road to a couple of isolated private houses. Close to Forest Burn (81 NZ 059959) the access road left the line as the trackbed continued on an embankment that ended abruptly at Forest Burn, as a section had been excavated. The embankment resumed on the northern bank of Forest Burn and soon levelled out to run next to the private access road again for a short distance before crossing (81 NZ 062963) with the trackbed being wet and overgrown but walkable with care. The line crossed under the B6342 for the fourth time (81 NZ 065966) on a damp section of trackbed. A drier grassy trackbed continued from the bridge, to run across open country before becoming a badly churned up farm track to a public bridleway at Crook Crossing (81 NZ 069973). The crossing cottage at Crook was a fine single storey cottage with a replica crossing gate bedecked with some cast iron signs, including a whimsical warning: "Penalty for Neglect £2".

North of Crook Crossing the trackbed was a very muddy track running flat across an open field until reaching a secluded bridge (81 NZ 068977) over a burn. In a cutting north of the bridge were the skeletal remains of a lineside hut on a particularly pretty section of line. Apart from a wet cutting under a minor road (81 NZ 076983) the trackbed was easy walking, contouring round the hillside to Brinkburn Station (81 NZ 087995). Brinkburn Station, the last intermediate stop before Rothbury, was a single storey red brick building and was in use as a holiday home.

Brinkburn Station marked the start of a permissive path that occupied the trackbed for the rest of the way into Rothbury.

The last few miles into Rothbury were excellent walking with fine views across the the River Coquet Valley, and included a dramatic rock-hewn cutting with some brick buttressing. Our arrival into Rothbury was a bit of an anti-climax as Rothbury Station (81 NU 063016) was sadly, completely lost under an industrial estate.

*A sturdy but rather irregular looking overbridge (87 NZ 038902).*

*The platform at Longwitton Station (87 NZ 045907) decays quietly.*

*The dilapidated platform of Ewesley Station (81 NZ 058926).*

*Fontburn Viaduct
(81 NZ 052936) towers above
the River Font close to the foot
of Fontburn Reservoir.*

269

# WALK XXVI
## The Wick & Lybster Light Railway
## (Wick to Lybster)

| Walk Summary | |
|---|---|
| **Date walked** | January 2006 |
| **Line mileage** | 13 ½ |
| **OSLR Maps** | 11, 12 |
| **Opened to Passengers** | 01 07 1903 |
| **Closed to Passengers** | 01 04 1944 |
| **PGAG Reference** | 38 |
| **Pre-Grouping Company** | The Wick & Lybster Light Railway |

## Walk Highlights

Thrumster station, Ulbster station, Mid Clyth Station, Roster Road Halt, Occumster Station, and Lybster Station.

## Public Transport

Wick is a terminus of the North of Scotland Line and is served by trains from Inverness. Inverness is served by trains from Edinburgh and The Caledonian Sleeper service form London Euston. Lybster is connected to Wick via Rapsons bus service 75.

## Background

The Wick & Lybster Light Railway (W&LLR) has the honour of being the UK's most northerly dismantled railway line, and although it was classed as a light railway, it was constructed and operated using standard gauge. It turned out that the planning for this walk was to be more arduous than the walk itself, as Wick really is an outpost of the rail network. In the end it took us four days to get to Wick, walk the line and

270

get home; all for 13 miles of dismantled railway line.

I had travelled south from Darlington to meet Chris in The Full Head of Steam outside Euston Station, as we were booked on The Caledonian Sleeper to Inverness, at the incredible price of £19 each. Although the sleeper was an efficient use of time we only really used it to utilize this excellent service. The sleeper service only runs to Inverness, where a change is required for Wick, still 4 ½ hours away in a miserable class 158 unit.

## Walk Description

The short lived W&LLR was primarily constructed to serve the once thriving fishing industry by transporting herring from Lybster to Wick, although at the time of the line's construction the fishing industry was already in decline. It would have been impossible for passenger revenues alone to sustain a railway in such a sparsely populated part of the country.

On a very grey day we accessed the line at the point where it crossed (12 ND 354508) the A882(T), where no trace of the level crossing remained. The trackbed was indistinct for a few hundred metres and very quickly we had to cross a ditch where the bridge was missing. We spotted a small overbridge (12 ND 353504) where the trackbed became more distinct, and was in use by farm vehicles. Upon crossing a minor road (12 ND 353501) the line had been usurped into a garden forcing us to follow a burn on the opposite bank to the line. After a couple of hundred metres we managed to cross the burn to follow a very vague trackbed across open fields, with barely a tree in sight. After crossing numerous farm tracks that crossed the trackbed in about 1 ½ miles, the line skirted Loch Hempriggs, running on a very low embankment dotted with gorse just above the water level of the loch. Not far from the southern end of Loch Hempriggs, the trackbed disappeared completely into the surrounding fields, and it was very difficult to see where it reappeared. After traversing several fields we could see a short section of embankment running towards the A9(T) on the outskirts of the small settlement of Thrumster. The line disappeared at the edge of Thrumster, and after a short walk along the main road we came to Thrumster

Station (12 ND 336451). The stone station house was present, but the highlight of Thrumster Station was undoubtedly the slate-roofed, timber waiting-shed that sat next to the main road. It was remarkable that this structure remained at all, let alone in a reasonable if somewhat weathered condition, with the peeling and oxidised white paint looking like a scaly skin. A notable feature was the housing for the station clock that had been blanked off by a rusty circle of metal.

The trackbed south of Thrumster Station was either built on or overgrown, until reaching a minor road (12 ND 333447) where it was possible to regain the line behind a private house. A clear trackbed either flat or on a low embankment climbed to the site of a quarry. The water filled quarry workings (12 ND 325433) had extended to completely remove the trackbed for about a hundred metres or so, but it was a simple task to walk round the edge of the workings to join the trackbed on the south side.

An unremarkable trackbed continued past the site of Welsh's Crossing Halt (12 ND 324418) that had completely vanished, with short sections of line blocked by thick stands of gorse that were easier to bypass than walk through. Being a light railway, the earthworks of the line were minimal, but a notable engineering feature were the characteristic culvert bridges built to a set design with stone abutments with a concrete span straddling the mid-section. At the southern tip of Loch Watenan a house had been built on the trackbed that required a short detour via the loch-side path before we regained the line at Ulbster Station (12 ND 318407). Ulbster Station House was a single-storey stone cottage now in private use, and of similar construction to Thrumster. The line from Ulbster continued in a similar unremarkable vane, being largely accessible with few earthworks and sporadic colonisation by gorse until reaching Mid Clyth Station (11 ND 298383). Mid Clyth Station had been extended, painted white and was in use as 'Station House' B&B. The lady owner was in the garden, and seeing us taking an interest in her house stopped for a chat about the old line and some of the other local antiquities in the area worth a visit.

Across the road from Mid Clyth Station the trackbed was in use as a private drive to a house, so we detoured north through a couple of fields to access the line a short distance further south. In less than a mile, we arrived at Roster Road Halt (11 ND 292374), now a private house which was of the same design as the previous station houses. Leaving the line at the access track to the house at Torranreach (11 ND 287366) we shadowed the line by walking beside the A9(T) for about a half a mile as the trackbed was in use for storing silage bales. A short hop across a field enabled us to regain the line as it veered away from the main road (11 ND 271362), and after about another half a mile we arrived at Occumster Station (11 ND 264363). Occumster Station was another well kept stone cottage, again identical to the previous station cottages, but no trace of the original level crossing remained.

A muddy but walkable trackbed continued for another mile or so, with the only significant impediment being a large bull on the line, to which we gave a wide berth, until we reached the A9(T) where the line became indistinct at Parkside. A railway cottage remained at the site of Parkside Halt (11 ND 251364) next to the A9(T). On the south side of the road the trackbed was in use as a private driveway, therefore we headed about 100 metres east and through some thick woods (11 ND 252364) to see the trackbed emerging from a house to our right. Crossing an open field in the fast fading light, we were able to regain the trackbed on the edge of Lybster Golf Course and after a few hundred metres we arrived at Lybster Station (11 ND 249358). Lybster Station House, unlike the previous stations, was a two-storey house with a landscaped grassy platform and was in private use. Lybster's timber waiting shed had been painted dark green and was now used as the club house for Lybster Golf Club. It was a short walk from Lybster Station to the wide, dead straight and austere looking central boulevard of Lybster. Lybster Harbour is worth a visit, but the fact that it was almost dark, and with a bus to Wick due in a few minutes we opted for a post-line pint in Wick.

*This concrete mid-section culvert bridge is typical of the type used on the Wick & Lybster Light Railway.*

*The weathered but largely intact timber building at Thrumster Station (12 ND 336451) is undoubtedly the highlight of the line.*

*The house at Mid Clyth Station has been extended for use as a B&B.*

*Lybster Station (11 ND 249358) is now home to golfers rather than rail passengers.*

# WALK XXVII
## Branches Around Weymouth
## (The Bridport & West Bay Branch, The Abbotsbury Branch, and The Portland Branch)

| Walk Summary | |
|---|---|
| Date walked | February 2006 |
| Line mileage | *11 ¼, ♣6, ♠8 ½ |
| OSLR Maps | 193, 194 |
| Opened to Passengers | *12 11 1857[2] & 31 03 1884[1], ♣1885, ♠16 10 1865[5] & 01 08 1902[6] |
| Closed to Passengers | *22 09 1930[1] & 1975[2], ♣01 12 1952, ♠03 03 1952[3] & 14 09 1959[4] |
| PGAG Reference | 3 |
| Pre-Grouping Company | ♣♠Great Western Railway, ♠London & South Western & Great Western Joint Railway |

*The Bridport & West Bay Branch, ♣The Abbotsbury Branch, ♠The Portland Branch, [1]Bridport to Bridport, West Bay, [2]Bridport to Maiden Newton, [3]Melcombe Regis to Easton, [4]Weymouth Junction to Melcombe Regis, [5]Weymouth to Portland, [6]Portland to Easton


## Walk Highlights

*The Bridport and West Bay Branch:* West Bay Station, Powerstock Station, and the excellent trackbed.
*The Abbotsbury Branch:* Portesham Station, engine shed at Abbotsbury Station, and the pleasant downland scenery.
*The Portland Branch:* Rodwell Tunnel and Station, the trackbed skirting Portland Harbour and the unique landscape of the Isle of Portland.


## Public Transport

Weymouth is served by trains from London and east and west coast services. Bridport and Abbotsbury are connected to Weymouth by

Firstbus service X53. Upwey is one stop up the line from Weymouth. Maiden Newton is a few stops up the line on the Weymouth to Bristol Line. Easton is connected to Weymouth by very frequent Firstbus services.

## Background

After walking the northern most dismantled line at Wick we decided on a walk at the opposite end of the country, to keep things varied a little. Weymouth was an ideal location to explore three former branch lines that served destinations on the south west 'excursion' coast, with two branches radiating north and south from or close to Weymouth. The third, The Bridport and West Bay Branch, was a short distance along the existing Weymouth to Bristol Line. Weymouth once had two stations: Town and Quay, with only Town station still in use. The Quay Station, which once connected trains with ferries to the Channel Islands is disused, but the unusual street level track to the quay is still present and runs for one mile and 31 chains through the streets of Weymouth from Weymouth Quay junction just north of the Town Station. Although we walked this interesting short spur of line, we decided that it did not qualify as dismantled railway as the track remained in-situ. Although the three branches detailed here share a close proximity they could not be more different in character and landscape.

## Walk Description

### The Bridport & West Bay Branch (West bay to Maiden Newton) (11 ¼ miles)

Because the train service from Weymouth to Maiden Newton did not provide a frequent service, we decided to walk this branch line from the terminus station of West Bay Bridport to the junction at Maiden Newton. The bus service from Weymouth was good and we alighted right outside West Bay Bridport Station (193 SY 465904) on an unseasonably warm day, to find a well preserved station building complete with canopy, in use as a restaurant: 'The Station Diner'. Along the platform there was also a large weathered dark blue enamel station sign reading 'WEST BAY BRIDPORT', and a couple of old Mark-I coaches in use by the

277

restaurant on a short section of track next to the platform. From the northern end of the platform, the trackbed was a compacted gravel cycle path as far as the B3157 (193 SY 466914), where the trackbed disappeared into some private gardens. The B3517 joined the busy A35 at a roundabout with the A-road being built over the trackbed as far as Bridport East Street Station (193 SY 471927), of which there was no trace as the site was occupied by industrial units. Bridport Station (193 SY 474934) was also a disappointment with no trace remaining, but just beyond the station site, traces of the trackbed emerged as the line veered to the northeast away from the A3066 along the valley of the Mangerton River.

We followed a footpath that ran along the river to a minor road at Bradpole (193 SY 481939), where the trackbed became visible but was difficult to access, forcing a detour along a public footpath up a hill before descending past a private house to the obliterated trackbed (193 SY 484941). Following the stream east, it was not until reaching the outskirts of the village of Loders did we see any real remains of a walkable trackbed (194 SY 493941), that ran along the base of the hill overlooking Loders. We quickly came to the first iron bridge in Loders that crossed a minor road (194 SY 496941) only to find that the trackbed beyond the bridge had been melded into the gardens of the village. Our escape from the bridge was hampered by a polite, but obviously miffed woman, who had spotted us from her garden, which resulted in a scramble down the bridge abutment on the south side through the brambles to the minor road. Fortunately a public footpath crossed a small field to the trackbed on the eastern side of Loders where we accessed the trackbed in a leafy cutting (194 SY 498942).

East of Loders the line became an absolute joy, as its grassy trackbed winding out into open country took us to Powerstock Station (194 SY 522953). The overbridge to Powerstock Station, now a private house with a remaining platform, was inaccessible but a track left the line for the road and a public footpath on the opposite side of the road climbed back up to the trackbed north of the station site. A short overgrown section of line became a farm track passing under an isolated stone overbridge (194 SY 523955) that carried a public footpath over the line. The next overbridge (194 SY 528961) that carried a minor road over the line was an iron span on brick abutments, its sharp angles contrasting with the more graceful arch of the previous stone bridge. With the line climbing to the thickly forested Powerstock Common, we were treated to another stone overbridge straddling a cutting (194 SY 533966), which conveyed a public bridleway across the trackbed. As the line emerged from the woods it became a fine gently sloped cutting (194 SY 538975) with a grassy trackbed and a few birch trees. Close to a minor road the trackbed levelled out in a field, and became muddy before crossing a minor road on a very overgrown bridge (194 SY 547974).

Towards the Roman-named village of Toller Porcorum (meaning 'valley of the pigs') the trackbed became a permissive path covered by a Countryside Stewardship Scheme, until reaching a public footpath (194 SY 558979) where the public access on the trackbed ceased. A wooded cutting guided the line into Toller Porcorum where we had to leave the trackbed (194 SY 561979) just west of the twin span iron road bridge as the line was occupied by private gardens. It was an easy detour through the village to Toller Porcorum Station (194 SY 563978), that had a heavily overgrown platform and a private house that was difficult to see from the trackbed. We left Toller Porcorum via the minor road heading east before accessing the trackbed via a track (194 SY 565979) to a barn where the line was a well walked track. A short way along we chatted to a couple of friendly locals, who were out with their dogs and binoculars. One of the old boys said he counted forty seven roe deer that afternoon. He also told us about an enormous badger set further up the line and informed us that the local farmer was relaxed about people walking across his land on the trackbed.

With a full moon rising we crossed a substantial bridge over the River Hooke (194 SY 571977) as the line followed the river's valley down to Tollerford. The only notable obstacle before reaching Tollerford was an overgrown bridge across a minor road (194 SY 580976). Tollerford was notable for having three overbridges across the line in quick succession, with the first one under the A356 being clear, the second under a minor road being partially blocked (deliberately) by garden refuse and the third impassable just beyond the bridge. It was a difficult clamber out of the cutting past the third bridge to an allotment where we met another old chap who told us, in his splendid West Country accent, that the man who throws his garden rubbish into the cutting gets very irate if he sees anyone in the cutting, even though the cutting was not on his property.

By the wry smile on his face we deduced that this old chap did not care too much for the garden refuse-dumper.

It was a simple task to regain the well-walked trackbed east of Tollerford, where after crossing high over the River Frome, the line veered sharply south, becoming a public path passing under two more minor roads before running right up to Maiden Newton Station platform.

### The Abbotsbury Branch (Upwey to Abbotsbury) (6 miles)

Catching the first London-bound train out of Weymouth on Sunday morning we arrived at a wet and windswept Upwey Station, the weather having taken a turn for the worse since the previous day's glorious sunshine. We found no trace of the line from Upwey Junction due to housing developments until we reached the old Upwey Station (194 SY 667835), which was now a builders yard. Taking a minor road we accessed the line at a stone bridge (194 SY 666836) finding an overgrown trackbed that quickly disappeared into a wet and muddy field. From the bridge the line was obliterated until we reached a farm track (194 SY 649843), and we had a very difficult time traversing arable fields, ditches, hedges and fences until reaching this point. Anyone attempting this section of line would be well advised to take public footpaths to a point where they cross the trackbed (194 SY 643844) and start the walk from there, as apart from the stone bridge very little remains of the line.

From the farm track, a dead straight trackbed ran across open fields with overgrown sections, occasional fences, and hedges that required negotiation before the line emerged on a minor road at the now unrecognisable site of Coryates Halt (194 SY 628847). With the trackbed beyond the road being impenetrable with thorny plants we regained the line via a public footpath (194 SY 626847) only to find a totally overgrown trackbed that forced us to shadow the line on the northern side by walking in the fields. The trackbed became clearer at a point where it was crossed by another public footpath (194 SY 619852) before entering a cutting just east of Portesham, where the western end of the cutting was occupied by sheds and stables. After a thorny scramble out of the cutting, we walked into Portesham on the B3157, where it was possible to see Portesham Station (194 SY 604855) via a public footpath. Portesham Station was in good condition consisting of a platform and small single-storey stone building (now in private use) with three tall chimneys that looked out of scale with the house. The trackbed provided access to the sheds and stables that we had seen from the other end of the cutting.

On the opposite side of the road from Portesham Station a caravan site nestled behind the embankment making access to the line difficult, so we followed the road round to the far side of Portesham village to pick up the trackbed via a public bridleway (194 SY 597855). From this point the trackbed was a muddy public bridleway forming part of the designated 'Abbotsbury Round Walk' for the remainder of the line into Abbotsbury. Abbotsbury Station was a rather non-descript private house, but an interesting stone engine shed remained (194 SY 582853) that was in use by the local farmer to store farm equipment.

The village of Abbotsbury was a pretty place to wait for the bus back to Weymouth, and with the bus stopping right outside The Ilchester Arms it was not hard to figure out what we would do for an hour. Over a pint we reflected on the six miles of The Abbotsbury Branch, and we decided that it had been tough going as it really was only walkable for the last half, probably as a result of the lines early closure due to poor passenger numbers and the faltering iron-ore mining industry.


**The Portland Branch (Melcombe Regis to Easton) (8 ½ miles)**
Fresh from our struggles on the Abbotsbury Branch we were plunged into the altogether different environment of The Portland Branch. The purpose of this railway was transport of both passengers, and the famous Portland Stone; the white oolitic limestone that adorns many famous buildings such as St. Paul's cathedral.

The Portland Branch left the existing but disused Weymouth Quay line close to the long gone Melcombe Regis Station (194 SY 677795) crossing Weymouth Harbour on a demolished viaduct that is now a road bridge (194 SY 676794) carrying the A353. We joined the trackbed close to the site of Westham Halt (194 SY 676792) where only a platform remained, at the start of The Rodwell Trail; a tarmac cycle/walkway running from the centre of Weymouth for about 2 ½ miles to the southern tip of land at the causeway at the end of the shingle embankment of Chesil Beach. The cycleway passed through the now illuminated, 51-yard long Rodwell Tunnel (194 SY 674785) and Rodwell Station (194 SY 674784) before passing the obliterated remains of Sandsfoot Castle Halt (194 SY 675775) and Wyke Regis Halt (194 SY 669765), before coming to an abrupt end at the site of a demolished viaduct (194 SY 668762) on the western edge of Portland Harbour. After a short walk along the A354, on the causeway that joins the Isle of Portland to the mainland, the trackbed re-appeared in the form of a low embankment (194 SY 668758) adjacent to the road.

As we ambled along the embankment, The Isle of Portland appeared as a steep and austere looking rock jutting out of the sea, with HMS Osprey, a naval base casting a dark grey shadow at the base to the rock and the stark looking Portland Prison crowning the cliff top. To the east we could see the breakwaters that formed the seaward defences of Portland Harbour, which may have calmed the excesses of the sea but not the wind that made us don woolly hats and gloves. As the line reached the Isle of Portland a large oil storage depot occupied the site of Portland Station (194 SY 678746). A cycleway wove its way around the depot and through a new yachting complex, arriving at Fortuneswell close to the entrance of the naval base and some vast, sinister-looking, disused buildings. Since the line disappeared into the naval base we had little option other than to climb the steep hill on a public footpath (194 SY 685742) into a housing estate.

On top of the hill we had excellent view across Portland Harbour as we followed another public footpath that skirted an old cemetery below the cliffs and prison. The path ended abruptly at a fence that seemed to form the perimeter of an older military installation. There was a large hole in the fence so we ventured inside to find all manner of derelict old military structures including gun emplacements. I cannot be sure of the route we took through the derelict complex, as it was tortuous with many obstacles, but we eventually worked our way down the steep hillside to pick up the trackbed running on a steep gradient (194 SY 699737) overlooking the sea. We continued past a timber yard and a derelict site full of all kinds of waste, with the landscape looking scarred from years of human activity. Another prison, this time a young offender's institution, came into view sitting directly above the line on top of more cliffs. We continued on a walkable trackbed (194 SY 698713) to a point where a once deep cutting and overbridge had been infilled forming a track up to a minor road. The landscape with its quarry workings had a blasted look about it, as white dust coated the surrounding debris. The trackbed re-appeared in a very wet and muddy cutting (194 SY 694713), and the mud clung to our boots like white glue, as we trudged under an overbridge (194 SY 693713). The mud eased as the trackbed became drier and full of rubble in a steep sided cutting at the southern edge of Easton (194 SY 691716). The remaining short section of trackbed running to Easton Station (194 SY 690718) was largely built on with the Easton Station site being occupied by a residential home.

*A weathered enamel station sign still adorns the platform at West Bay Bridport Station (193 SY 465904).*

*Splendid walking on a clear trackbed across Powerstock Common on the Bridport & West Bay Branch.*

*Waymark on
The Abbotsbury
Branch.*

*Portesham Station (194 SY 604855).*

*The 51-yard long Rodwell Tunnel (194 SY 674785) is now part of a
cycleway on The Portland Branch.*

# WALK XXVIII
## The Berwickshire Railway (St. Boswells - Ravenswood Junction to Reston) and part of The Kelso Branch (Tweedmouth to Coldstream)

| Walk Summary | |
|---|---|
| Date walked | March 2006 |
| Line mileage | *12 ¼, ♠30 ¾ |
| OSLR Maps | 67, 74, 75 |
| Opened to Passengers | *27 07 1849, ♠13 08 1849[1], ♠16 11 1863[2], ♠02 10 1865[3] |
| Closed to Passengers | *15 06 1964, ♠10 09 1951[1], ♠13 08 1948[4], ♠02 07 1949[5] |
| PGAG Reference | 31 |
| Pre-grouping Company | * North Eastern Railway, ♠North British Railway |

*The Kelso Branch, ♠The Berwickshire Railway, [1]Reston to Duns, [2]Duns to Earlston , [3]Earlston to Ravenswood Junction, [4]Duns to Greenlaw, [5]Duns to St. Boswells

## Walk Highlights

*The Kelso Branch:* Norham Station Museum, West Newbiggin Viaduct, and Twizell Viaduct.
*The Berwickshire Railway:* Leaderfoot Viaduct, Greenlaw Station, Marchmont Station, Edrom Station, Chirnside Station and a generally good trackbed.

## Public Transport

Berwick-Upon-Tweed is on the ECML. Coldstream and Kelso/St. Boswells/Melrose are connected by Firstbus services 67 and 68. Reston and Berwick-Upon-Tweed are connected by Perrymans Buses service 253.

286

**Walk Description**

**Part of The Kelso Branch (Tweedmouth to Coldstream, 12 ¼ miles)**

Having taken the train to Berwick-Upon-Tweed, we walked back across the River Tweed on the road bridge (75 NT 993533), which was a good vantage point for views of the magnificent Royal Border Bridge, which is actually a massive and spectacular viaduct still carrying ECML trains high over the Tweed. Upon reaching the site of the junction of the Kelso Branch with the ECML (75 NT 994520) we found the way onto the embankment barred by a padlocked gate, and due to the proximity of houses it was impossible to gain access to the trackbed, at or close to the junction. After about ¾ mile we accessed the trackbed via a public footpath at the site of an infilled bridge (75 NT 986517), where a grassy trackbed ran for a few hundred metres to a roundabout on the A698. From this point the A698 utilized the trackbed until reaching another roundabout at the A1(T), where after a scramble thorough some undergrowth on an embankment (75 NT 975514), we were able to join a good walkable trackbed that crossed grazing land. We quickly passed under a redundant stone overbridge (75 NT 968512) that had had its walls removed, with tufts of grass appearing like eyebrows just above the bridge's arch. A splendid trackbed continued, rising on an embankment to a minor road (75 NT 958508) where the bridge had been demolished. On the western side of the road the embankment had been completely removed, having been replaced by an arable field. After a short detour along the minor road, we regained the trackbed by following a hedgerow to a clear cutting (75 NT 950506) that soon passed under a minor road bridge. The cutting gave way to a clear and tree-covered embankment crossing more arable land until coming to an abrupt halt (75 NT 946495) in more arable fields with a new crop just sprouting, forcing us to follow a field margin to the A698.

After a brisk walk down the road we soon came to Velvet Hall Station (75 NT 944491), where the substantial two-storey station house was in private use. Just along the road from the station, a stand of pines growing on the trackbed shielded our progress along a short section of line to a minor road (75 NT 942488) where the bridge had been demolished. A convenient farm track led back up an embankment onto the line before ending in a muddy and flooded cutting. We were forced to climb out of the cutting close to an overbridge (75 NT 937485), as the flood water trapped by a wall of earth beyond the bridge, was too deep to negotiate. The cutting soon gave way to an embankment, where we were able to access the trackbed that was occasionally overgrown and impassable (but easily bypassed in adjacent fields) to a splendid sandstone bridge (75 NT 915469) at the B6470. A good tracked resumed from the bridge and soon became a high wooded embankment to a minor road and the site of Norham Station (75 NT 907467), where the overbridge had been demolished.

Norham Station is both a private residence and a museum, open only on bank holidays or by special appointment by prior arrangement (Tel. 01289 382217). The road the back of the station house and buildings, some coal drops and an engine shed can be clearly seen from the road. Close to the gate a nice NER 'Public Warning' sign remained warning all comers about trespassing on railway property. A subsequent visit to Norham Station on Good Friday 2006 revealed a quirky but excellent museum full of curios and railwayana, from The Kelso Branch. The elderly couple who own the station, Peter and Katherine Short, had purchased the station and surrounding land when Norham was closed. Peter being the last Station Master at Norham, was ideally placed to purchase the property. On my trip Katherine acted as museum guide, regaling many fascinating stories of the station's history, but sadly she was concerned that as a couple now well into their seventies, they would soon no longer be able to maintain the museum as a going concern. For me the highlights of the museum were the signalbox and the wonderfully musty ticket office, both festooned with Norham Station, NER, and other railwayana.

Skirting Norham Station in the adjacent field to the north, we passed the tall brick signal box with the sun shining through the aspect glasses of the adjacent signal like a kaleidoscope. At the western perimeter of Norham Station the trackbed was completely obliterated having been lost in a ploughed field. This obstacle set us on a tortuous detour following field margins in an attempt to regain the line as soon as possible, but the lay of the land prevented us from seeing any re-emergence of the line as recognisable trackbed. The trackbed eventually re-appeared as an embankment (74 NT 899462) just prior to the viaduct across Newbiggin Dean. In hindsight it would have been easier to walk into Norham and follow the footpath heading south from the village to eventually pass under the viaduct. The Newbiggin Dean Viaduct (74 NT 899460) was a substantial stone structure with six arches and a clear trackbed, that became a permissive path under a Countryside Stewardship Scheme at the southern end. The permissive path continued from the viaduct across the minor road as a muddy but easily walked track to a public footpath (74 NT 888446) close to Tilmouth Farm. Upon reaching the footpath the trackbed once again disappeared into another ploughed field, and a quick assessment revealed very little in the way of available detours. We could see the line resuming a few hundred metres away in a shallow cutting with trees on the other side of the field, so we had a long walk round the field edge to rejoin the trackbed.

The line resumed (74 NT 885445) as a farm track, and was an excellent walk to the delightfully named Twizell Station (74 NT 876437) where precious little remained apart from a small section of overgrown platform and what appeared to be a few railway cottages. The trackbed continued as an excellent cinder track beyond Twizell Station as a permissive path that ran across the spectacular 6-arched, 130 yard long Twizell Viaduct (74 NT 873430), that straddled the beautiful wooded valley of the River Till just above it's confluence with the Tweed. The permissive path turned sharp right at the southern end of Twizell Viaduct to join up with a public footpath running way below along the bank of the Till. The trackbed south disappeared into the edge of a ploughed field, however this time no major detours were required as it was a simple task to follow the field edge to a gate at a track close to St. Cuthberts (74 NT 873424). This track seemed to provide vehicular access in preference to the stone bridge that straddled the line in front of us. Passing under the bridge, a good trackbed that was well used by local dog walkers, continued to a public footpath (74 NT 867413) at the point where the line once again had succumbed to the plough. It was an easy box round along the footpath to the A698 to another public footpath that crossed the line (74 NT 867410) at the site of what appeared to be an area being turned into a garden with a house yet to be built. The line continued in the cleared cutting under the A698 before reaching a flooded and badly overgrown cutting (74 NT 868405), which forced us out into the adjacent field to skirt the line until we reached an access track just north of the site of Coldstream Station (74 NT 863395). Coldstream Station, originally known more appropriately as Cornhill due to its location in the village of Cornhill-On-Tweed, was now a small development houses right up to the remaining bridge abutment on the A697. In glorious evening sunshine we crossed the road to pick up the last short section of line, that was a public footpath, through a lovely stand of glistening birch trees, to the junction (See Walk XXII) with The Cornhill Branch (74 NT 863388).

After an interminable walk for nearly two miles along the road, we crossed the border into Scotland and the pleasant town of Coldstream, famous for being home to The Coldstream Guards. The bus to Melrose, the destination of our overnight stop, stopped right outside The Besom Inn, so we had time for a couple of pints of Caledonian Deucars IPA, an excellent Edinburgh brew that had established itself as a favourite on our previous walks in The Borders.

## The Berwickshire Railway (St. Boswells, Ravenswood Junction to Greenlaw, 14 ½ miles)

After a two mile walk from Melrose we accessed the line via an impressive three-arched stone overbridge (74 NT 574342), that took a track over a wooded cutting just north of the site of Ravenswood Junction. Ravenswood Junction (74 NT 575339) was where The Berwickshire Railway joined The Waverley Route (see Walk XXI) and was now lost under the A6091, making the start of The Berwickshire railway an embankment by the road. Passing back under the three-arched overbridge the trackbed soon emerged from the cutting to cross open fields that formed the approach to the Leaderfoot Viaduct (74 NT 574347), which is undoubtedly one of the wonders of the dismantled railway network of The Scottish Borders. Straddling the River Tweed close to the confluence with Leader Water, Leaderfoot Viaduct had 19 graceful red brick arches spanning 302 yards, and at a lofty 130 feet high gave a fantastic exposed feeling of a path in the sky; not a place for vertigo sufferers. Access to the ballasted trackbed across the viaduct was simple with only small security fences at either end.

The northern end of Leaderfoot Viaduct emerged on a high embankment that was very muddy and smothered in cattle dung as it was occupied by a large silage feeder and a huddle of cattle happily munching away. After skirting this morass by sliding down the side of the embankment, we rejoined the line in a waterlogged cutting that ended abruptly in a pile of rubble at the A68 (74 NT 574355). From this point to the village of Earlston, about two miles of the trackbed had been largely occupied by an 'improved' A68, although it was possible to follow parts of the old road that still remained as secluded lay-bys, making the walk bearable.

The former rail bridge (74 NT 573383) across Leader Water to Earlston was demolished, with the embankment still clearly visible on the northern bank, making the A68 road bridge the only viable crossing point, as the overnight rain had swollen the river to a swirling muddy torrent. After a brief stop at the Co-op we went in search of Earlston Station (74 NT 576383), only to find some new buildings and wasteland. The line turned sharply east at Earlston, and following the largely obliterated trackbed was difficult due to a school and industrial units occupying the trackbed. After a tricky crossing of a rain-swollen ditch on a weir (74 NT 582386) we found the trackbed just before it disappeared into a freshly ploughed field, with the only evidence of the line being a black shadow clearly visible across the field. We skirted the field margin to join the trackbed where it appeared in a stand of pines (74 NT 587388), as a reasonably clear trackbed before ending at a fenced-off ploughed field (74 NT 592391), that meant a short detour onto the B6397. The trackbed became visible again adjacent to the road on the right hand side before crossing over at a sharp bend at the site of a demolished overbridge (74 NT 602394), that provided easy access to a clear embankment. The grassy trackbed soon entered a cutting and rather curiously some old railway sleepers had been placed about 3 metres apart on the trackbed, that served no obvious purpose. After passing under a minor road overbridge (74 NT 603397) the line was infilled, but it was a simple task to follow a well walked field margin to a wood and a wild fowl pond. The trackbed re-appeared running dead straight across some flat open country, and although occasionally wooded the line looked, and felt very desolate.

The broad and easily walked trackbed came to Hareford Burn that marked the western boundary of the Gordon Moss Wildlife Reserve (74 NT 632423), where the bridge was missing. The Burn was very full owing to the heavy overnight rain, and what would probably have been an easily fordable stream, now became a major obstacle with no signs of a bridge in the vicinity and no easy alternative routes round.

After about half an hour of scouting around the Burn we came across an old five-bar gate laying discarded close to the bank. With some difficulty we managed to heave the gate into the water and wedge it rather precariously on the tufted grass on either side of the bank, as it was only just long enough to straddle the burn. As I gingerly walked out onto the gate it bowed alarmingly with my feet dipping to ankle depth into the water, with only my gaiters preventing me from getting wet feet. Once across I found an old sleeper, and after some difficult man handling, I managed to get the sleeper into the burn with the idea being to place the gate on top to minimise the disconcerting flexing. Chris navigated our re-enforced bridge successfully, and we proceeded into the woods in search of the line as we were some way down stream from the original crossing point.

The line emerged from the Gordon Moss Wildlife Reserve at a gate into an open field where the trackbed was obliterated until a high embankment appeared at the former crossing point of the A6105, (74 NT 639427) close to the Gothic-looking Greenknowe Tower, where only the bridge abutments remained. A thickly-wooded trackbed continued from the road skirting the village of Gordon in a cutting, which formed part of a right of way, to the partially infilled A6098 bridge (74 NT 647437) with the platform of Gordon Station (74 NT 648437) being clearly visible under the bridge. The right of way was stepped up to the A6089 and a convenient public track continued on the eastern side of the road, running past the two-storey red stone Gordon Station House and yard that was now in use for coal and agricultural supplies. It was a simple task to rejoin the line just east of Gordon Station on an easily walked clear trackbed across more open country to Eden Water (74 NT 658441) where the bridge was missing. Although the swollen stream was not fordable we managed to just get across by taking a running jump, using the advantage of a slightly higher western bank. From Eden Water the line took a direct route through some lovely woods to arrive at an infilled bridge at a minor road (74 NT 667443). On the eastern side of the minor road, the line continued dead straight as far as the eye could see, looking more like a Roman road than a railway. At this point we found what looked to be an original and well restored "BEWARE of the TRAINS" sign, with raised black lettering on a sky blue background, placed rather enigmatically on the boundary fence. An unimpeded trackbed made an excellent walk for nearly three miles to Greenlaw Station (74 NT

708455), where the extensive yard was filled with heavy good vehicles, sheds, and stored fairground rides. We could not see an easy way round the yard, but all was quiet so we decided to slip quickly and quietly through the site, which worked until the resident Jack Russell came out of nowhere to attack my ankles! He was only doing his job, I reasoned, as we beat a hasty retreat to the road past Greenlaw Station House, now a private residence. Apart form the red stone house, very little seemed to remain of Greenlaw Station, and the original road bridge had also vanished.

The village of Greenlaw stands on the fantastically named river of Blackadder Water, and it was only appropriate that our overnight stop was at The Blackadder Inn. It was the first night of the smoking ban in Scotland and the jovial landlord of The Blackadder was less that impressed at his sudden downturn in customers. We did our best at keeping his place afloat by eating, supping, and playing a few games of pool in the unusual silence of the empty bar.

### Greenlaw to Reston (16 ¼ miles)

The rail bridge across Blackadder Water (74 NT 717460) was missing so we accessed the line via a track to a waterworks (74 NT 720462). An excellent embanked trackbed followed the gentle scenery of The Blackadder's valley to a minor road where the overbridge (74 NT 736466) was infilled. Although there was no station or halt at this point there was a platform on the eastern side of the road that looked like some kind of freight loading facility. The line passed under an ornate overbridge (74 NT 737469) as it veered out of the valley of Blackadder Water into the narrower valley of Howe Burn. The trackbed entered a short scenic cutting (74 NT 739476) as the land narrowed before curving round on a low embankment that traversed a beautiful open valley below the Marchmont House Nursing Home, situated high above to the west. A truckers yard (74 NT 752488) occupied the trackbed on the approach to Marchmont Station (74 NT 753489), but a farm track paralleled the trackbed to the minor road making an easy detour. Marchmont Station was a single-storey stone house in private use with the platform and trackbed being used for car parking. It was a simple task to box round the station on the minor road before descending a track to the line, where it was in the form of a clear, grassy trackbed that meandered along a lush valley.

A clear trackbed passed under an iron overbridge (74 NT 773504) that carried a minor road, and soon became a muddy and overgrown cutting, that forced us off the trackbed into the adjacent field to the north. At the end of another overgrown cutting, the line ended abruptly in a ploughed field (74 NT 778511). From this point we could not see where the trackbed re-emerged, as the line curved sharply north with all traces having been removed by the plough. After a circuitous route following the edges of arable fields we found the trackbed at the site of a demolished bridge (74 NT 779515) across a stream. A walkable line continued for about half a mile, passing under a minor road, before ending abruptly at the cliff-like bank of Langton Burn (74 NT 779520). It was this bridge across Langton Burn that sealed the fate of The Berwickshire Railway, as during the serious flooding of 12th August 1948 the bridge was washed away, severing the line and ending the passenger service between St. Boswells and Duns on 13th August 1948, as the bridge was never repaired. Other damage to the line caused by the same floods between Duns and Reston was repaired and the passenger service was restored between these stations, only to last for three more years.

We followed the minor road northwest for a few hundred metres where we crossed Langton Burn on a foot/cycle bridge (74 NT 777522), as the road crossed the burn via a ford. Once across Langton Burn we accessed the embanked line via a grazing field. The embankment soon ended, however, as another substantial section of line had been ploughed up, and we had to follow a fence that more or less followed the alignment of the former trackbed to a cutting (74 NT 782527) that again ended in another ploughed field. We exited the line onto a minor road at an overbridge (74 NT 783529) close to some large farm buildings. The line on the northern side of the road was completely obliterated, once again having been ploughed, but it was possible to follow a field margin to the southern edge of Duns on some wasteland next to a recycling plant.

Duns Station (74 NT 788532) was once a thriving station with a large goods yard and a couple of platforms. The large station house remained as a private house and the yard area and shed were in use by a timber and building supplies company. We followed the industrial estate access road round the station site to access the line at a well walked trackbed

(74 NT 792532). Some easy walking for about 1 ½ miles took us to a point where the trackbed disappeared into a field (74 NT 811535) next to the A6105, that meant a detour along the road for about half a mile before regaining the line in a wooded cutting (74 NT 817542). An excellent trackbed continued from the cutting to an overbridge at Edrom Station (74 NT 833550), with the small station house, now in private use, being situated on the eastern side of the bridge. Edrom Station still had its platform and the trackbed continued unobstructed, obviously in regular use by farm vehicles. An infilled overbridge (74 NT 839553) marked the start of an obliterated section of trackbed that traversed a field close to the sheds of a whisky maltings, before passing under a partially infilled bridge to cross an open field to a thin plantation of pines planted on the trackbed (74 NT 846557). As we entered the pines our nostrils were accosted by a foul smell, emanating from some kind of effluent that was tricking down the trackbed in a series of overflow weirs constructed out of plywood that formed a series of lagoons. Apart from the awful smell we noticed a distinct lack of anything green, or indeed anything living in the effluent. We wondered if the effluent was coming from the maltings, and if so was it a legal practice?

The effluent disappeared underground at the site of an infilled bridge of the A6105, where some steps gave easy passage to the road. On the northern side of the road the trackbed had been consumed by the large Ahlstrom medical device plant (74 NT 850563), making access impossible. Nestled inside the plant was the viaduct over Whiteadder Water (74 NT 850563), which we could just about see as we skirted the site through some woods to the east. Our detour round the steaming plant lead us to a rubble strewn trackbed at the B6355 (74 NT 851565) where the bridge had been removed. After a few hundred metres we arrived at Chirnside Station (74 NT 853567); a delightful station complete with house, platform, and green wooden waiting shed, that was in use by an agricultural supplies company. Walking past the waiting shed perched on the platform we struggled through the undergrowth past a large shed built partially on the line before emerging onto an open trackbed. An excellent section of line took us to a minor road (74 NT 858593) where the bridge had been demolished. To the north of the road the trackbed had been ploughed up, but a wide field margin with the stubbly remains of a decaying crop smelling like rotting cabbage, enabled us to reach a cutting that passed under the B6437 where a good trackbed re-appeared

(67 NT 861600).

From the B6437 an excellent, clear trackbed ran through two cuttings and under three fine overbridges in a little under two miles to reach Reston (67 NT 878619) and the junction with the ECML. Although there were buildings around the junction we could not make out any remains of Reston Station. Our exit from the line was via a farm track that crossed the ECML via an underpass (67 NT 879619) into the small village of Reston, where as it was four o'clock we arrived just in time for The Wheatsheaf Hotel to open for a swift pint, while we waited for the bus back to Berwick.

*The splendid museum at Norham Station (75 NT 907467) is full of interesting railwayana and other exhibits. Although it has limited opening times it is definitely worth making the effort to visit.*

*The towering signal box at Norham Station remains unchanged since its closure. This photograph was taken from the adjacent field.*

*The trackbed across Twizell Viaduct (74 NT 873430) is now a permissive path.*

*The impressive overbridge (74 NT 574342) close to the start of The Berwickshire Railway.*

*The view from the clear, ballasted, trackbed on Leaderfoot Viaduct (74 NT 574347) is breathaking if you have a head for heights.*

*Leaderfoot Viaduct must be one of the most outstanding disused railway viaducts in the country. To walk over this magnificent structure is a rare treat indeed.*

*The trackbed has been landscaped at Gordon Station (74 NT 648437), but the platform end can still be seen.*

*A well restored but enigmatic sign guards a superb section of clear trackbed (74 NT 667443).*

*Edrom Station (74 NT 833550).*

*Chirnside Station (74 NT 853567) is in good shape and in use as an office.*

# WALK XXIX
## The Somerset & Dorset Joint Railway (Bournemouth West to Bath Green Park)

| Walk Summary | |
|---|---|
| **Date walked** | April 2006 |
| **Line mileage** | 71 ½ |
| **OSLR Maps** | 172, 183, 194, 195, |
| **Opened to Passengers** | [1]20 07 1874, [2]20 07 1874, [3]03 02 1862, [4]31 08 1863, [5]1860, [6]14 12 1865, [7]31 08 1863, [8]15 06 1874 |
| **Closed to Passengers** | [9]07 03 1966, [10]04 10 1965 |
| **PGAG Reference** | 3 |
| **Pre-grouping Company** | The Somerset & Dorset Joint Railway (S&DJR) |

[1]Bath to Bath Junction, [2]Bath Junction to Evercreech Junction, [3]Evercreech Junction to Templecombe, [4]Templecombe to Blandford, [5]Blandford to Corfe Mullen Junction, [6]Corfe Mullen Junction to Broadstone, [7]Broadstone to Poole, [8]Poole to Bournemouth West, [9]Bath Green Park to Poole, [10]Branksome to Bournemouth West

## Walk Highlights

Charlton Marshall Halt, Stourpaine & Durweston Halt, Shillingstone Station, Charlton Road Viaduct (Shepton Mallet), Bath Road Viaduct, Windsor Hill Tunnel, Ham Wood Viaduct, Masbury Halt, Chilcompton Tunnel, Midsomer Norton Station, Wellow Station, Midford Viaduct, Tucking Mill Viaduct, Combe Down Tunnel and Bath Green Park Station. The S&DJR traverses some lovely countryside, often with fine views. The trackbed varies from easily walkable to totally overgrown and impenetrable, but there are usually easy detours around the overgrown sections.

302

## Public Transport

Bournemouth and Poole are served by trains from London Waterloo and services east and west along the south coast. Bath Spa is served by trains from London Paddington and Bristol.

## Background

It is arguable that The Somerset & Dorset Joint Railway (S&DJR) was *the* quintessential example of the English country railway, serving a sparse rural population and running through some beautiful countryside, including the traverse of the picturesque Mendip Hills. It is also arguable that the closure of the S&DJR was a classic example of the folly of the Beeching Closures, with the line being closed almost exactly three years after the release of Beeching's Report. The S&DJR would have been an extremely route useful if it had remained open today. One could even argue that the S&DJR was 'The Waverley Route' of the south with regards to its function and fate. The 'Slow & Dirty' as the route was sometimes harshly called, has generated a plethora of literature detailing the lines history and operation, making even the most obscure facts about the S&DJR readily attainable. Of all the books written about the line, a special mention must be made of the fine study of the route by Mac Hawkins, entitled 'The Somerset and Dorset, Then and Now'; truly an invaluable source of material for the dismantled railway walker.

The S&DJR network consisted of a main trunk running between Bournemouth West and Bath Green Park, with western branches to Burnham that had subsequent branches to Wells and Bridgewater. We decided to explore the main trunk from Bournemouth West to Bath Green Park of the S&DJR, as this is arguably the 'classic' route of 'The S&D'.

## Walk Description

### Bournemouth West to Poole (4 ½ miles)

Bournemouth West Station was long gone, with the whole area having been re-developed. A short 70-chain spur of the line from Branksome

Junction (195 SZ 058919) was still in use as a depot and sidings for units serving the South Western Region. The line from Branksome to Poole is still in use. A short section of line from Poole Station to Holes Bay Junction (195 SZ 010920) also remains in use, making this the real starting point of the walk.

## Poole to Spetisbury (11 miles)

A short walk north from Poole Station along a minor road took us to the site of Holes Bay Junction (195 SZ 010920), with all trace having disappeared under an industrial estate. We had to walk for about a mile past the industrial estate to where a huge B&Q superstore and car park had been built across the trackbed (195 SZ 008929). To the north of the B&Q car park, the trackbed now occupied by the A349 passed under the A35. The A349 was equipped with a cycle lane that made the walk along the busy road bearable, but it was not for another mile or so until reaching a point at, or close to, the original junction with Clay Siding (195 SY 998947) did we set foot on a recognisable trackbed that was in use as a cycle/walkway. The cycleway ran for about ¾ mile passing under the B3074 to a sports centre (195 SZ 004959), where a barely recognisable vestige of trackbed was in use as a public footpath. Just north of the sports centre was the site of Broadstone Station (195 SZ 005962) that had completely vanished. The footpath continued to the site of Broadstone Junction (195 SZ 005963), where it veered east to follow the trackbed of the dismantled Southampton & Dorchester Line towards Wimbourne and Ringwood. The S&DJR trackbed was not a public footpath, and the trackbed had been incorporated into Broadstone Golf Club complete with 'Private' signs and fences acting as a deterrent to the dismantled railway walker. Fortunately, just east of the trackbed and the golf club, there was a large piece of open heath land that allowed us to shadow the line before climbing over the fence a few hundred metres further along using the cover of the trees growing on the embanked trackbed. Bizarrely, we noticed that there was a public footpath coming in from the west that terminated in a cutting (195 SZ 003972) right in the middle of the golf course. We proceeded north into the clear cutting and narrowly avoided being seen by a green keeper on a sit-on mower. From the northern end of the cutting it was only about 150 metres of open ground before the northern perimeter of the course, and we proceeded briskly to a sandy ditch with a scrappy fence of corrugated iron that had 'PRIVATE KEEP OUT', crudely daubed on in white paint.

With the adrenalin rush over we now started to enjoy the gloriously sunny morning following a pleasant wooded trackbed that even had a wooden walkway crossing a boggy section to a three-arched brick overbridge (195 SY 999979). A few hundred metres further on a walkable trackbed, we arrived at an overbridge and infilled cutting at the site of Corfe Mullen Halt (195 SY 996983). The bridge carried a bridleway across the cutting thus allowing for an easy means of skirting the site of Corfe Mullen Halt, now occupied by a large new house and immaculately landscaped garden, which was well screened by evergreen trees. Just across the road from the Halt site was a development of houses in a cul-de-sac named 'Corfe Halt Close' that occupied the trackbed completely. A public footpath provided an easy route round the housing development and across an open field to an overbridge (195 SY 991985) that straddled an impassable, flooded cutting. Taking the footpath to a minor road we could hear an ominous metallic clanking of what was obviously some heavy machinery at work. A short distance further along the road was a metal reclamation plant, situated right on the line (195 SY 988986), with a gargantuan monster of a machine spewing out shards of metal at a frenetic rate into an enormous glistening pile.

Once round this obstacle we regained the line where two trackbeds ran side-by-side towards Corfe Mullen Junction (195 SY 978983), where a branch from the S&DJR left to join the Southampton & Dorchester Line at Wimbourne Junction (195 SZ 018989). The approach to Corfe Mullen Junction was a broad grassy trackbed straddled by an overbridge carrying the B3074. Just beyond the overbridge the trackbed was occupied by the garden of Corfe Mullen Crossing Cottage (195 SY 976983), where we had to cross a stream on a flimsy plank to get out onto the road. The crossing cottage was in use as a private house with the original and very nicely restored crossing gates still in place. Opposite the crossing gates, a rather battered fence and gate allowed easy access to a continuing clear grassy trackbed that passed quickly under another overbridge (195 SY 974983) before arriving at the A31 at the site of Bailey Gate Crossing (195 SY 969985). A modern looking house stood on the site of the original signalbox, with no trace of the crossing remaining.

The busy A31 was no place to dwell, so we moved quickly across to join a rough grass trackbed running across open flat country in the valley of the River Stour. The line continued more or less unobstructed to the outskirts of Sturminster Marshall, where some large sheds had been built on the trackbed (195 SY 952993), forcing us to take a track designated as a 'byway open to all traffic' round the sheds to the north into the village. Being a warm afternoon we could not walk past The Churchill Arms without a pause for a swift pint, before heading off in search of Bailey Gate Station (195 SY 949995). Unfortunately all traces off the station were gone, having disappeared under Bailey Gate Industrial Estate that had previously blocked our progress. The station actually served Sturminster Marshall, so we wondered why the station was named Bailey Gate as there appeared to be no point of reference for this name in the vicinity.

Opposite the Bailey Gate Industrial Estate, the line continued as 'Railway Drive' (195 SY 947995) which was undergoing a further development of houses known as 'The Sidings'. Railway Drive was designated a public footpath with the tarmac giving way to an embanked trackbed that continued as a public footpath to a minor road (195 SY 945998) where the bridge had been demolished. It was straightforward to rejoin the line on the other side of the road on an embankment that quickly gave way to an overgrown cutting. At the western end of the cutting a public bridleway came in from the right, running parallel with the trackbed, before taking an abrupt left turn at a private house to the A350. The trackbed beyond the private house was busy with kids messing about with air rifles, and as we were also being eyed suspiciously by the house owners we followed the bridleway out to the road. After a few hundred metres the line crossed the A350 (195 ST 934009) with no trace of the crossing remaining. It was late afternoon and we needed somewhere to bivvy for the night, but sites on or close to the line did not look promising. Following a public footpath we headed for Westley Wood (195 ST 925004) where we found a nice spot to camp among the trees.

A beautifully bright and frosty morning had us up early, and we took public footpaths across country to join the line where it became a permissive path; part of the North Dorset Trailway, (195 ST 918017) at the site of a demolished overbridge. The trackbed was a splendid leafy walk running past Spetisbury Halt (195 ST 913022), where only the overgrown platforms remained.

## Spetisbury to Sturminster Newton (11 ¾ miles)

From Spetisbury Halt the line was a delight to walk. Some of the early morning local dog walkers using the line looked bemused as we wandered along carrying large backpacks. Charlton Marshall Halt (195 ST 898040), a further two miles up the line also had its two platforms remaining, but unlike Spetisbury it also had an overbridge taking a minor road over the line. Close to Charlton Marshall we also saw a concrete gradient marker indicating 'level' and '129'; a nice reminder of the trailway's heritage. The trailway ended at Charlton Marshall Halt, but we continued along the trackbed that was well used by farm vehicles. The line came to an abrupt end at a gate to a ploughed field (195 ST 892048), leaving us no option other than to skirt the edge of the field to emerge at a gate onto a public bridleway (194 ST 889051) to the village of Lower Blandford St. Mary as the trackbed ahead was obliterated.

The remainder of the line into the pleasant market town of Blandford Forum had disappeared, so we followed the road into the town, pausing for a lungful of malt and yeast aromas emanating from the independent Hall & Woodhouse Brewery (194 ST 886058), where the well known Badger and Tanglefoot Ales are produced.

Another short section of the North Dorset Trailway appeared in the centre of Blandford Forum at the site of Blandford Station (194 ST 888066), that had been completely redeveloped as housing. The start of the trail, however, was marked with a buffer stop on a short piece of track sitting under an iron footbridge. The trailway through Blandford Forum only ran for about 1km, before reaching a tangled mass of wood and barbed wire across the trackbed (194 ST 881073) where a public footpath crossed the line. An overgrown trackbed, still with plenty of original ballast remaining, continued to a large shed situated next to an underpass at the A350 (194 ST 880081) where, once under the road, the trackbed became a clear farm track. After a few hundred metres the farm track turned sharp right and the line disappeared into a field on the other side of an easily scalable fence (194 ST 875083). A faint outline of the trackbed could be just made out as we proceeded along the Stour Valley contouring around the hillside to rejoin at the A350 (194 ST 868082).

Due to the trackbed being obliterated, we followed the A350 to the junction with the A357, to access the line via a very difficult descent down an overgrown bank (194 ST 863088) to an infilled cutting topped with much tree debris. The elongated bridge that resembled a short tunnel under the A350 was open, and with hindsight it would have been easier to access the line on the other side of the road by cutting across the field to go under the road. The cutting soon gave way to a good trackbed on a clear embankment to Stourpaine & Durweston Halt (194 ST 861091), which consisted of a single stilted concrete platform that looked rather forlorn with various concrete slabs being either fractured or missing. Although the trackbed heading north from the halt looked clear, we had noted that a major bridge across the Stour was missing about ¾ mile up the line, so we opted to cross the river via the picturesque footbridge and weir at Durweston Mill (194 ST 859090), and follow the A357 to pick up the line on the other side of the river (194 ST 850099). An easily walked trackbed continued to an infilled bridge (194 ST 844102) that once straddled a deep cutting that was now completely infilled with rubble. The infill sloped away steeply just north of the infilled bridge to the original level of the trackbed and another section of the North Dorset Trailway resumed, creating an easy walk through pleasant countryside to Shillingstone.

Upon arrival at Shillingstone Station (194 ST 825116) we were amazed to see that some major restoration work was underway by The Shillingstone Station Project (http://www.digitalfox.co.uk/shillingstonestation/index. htm). The trackbed had been cleared and ballasted, and the station building with its splendid wooden canopy had been renovated. Although the wooden shed on the 'down' platform was absent, a sign pinned to the fence indicated plans to rebuild the structure. At the northern end of the station site a partially restored locomotive, 9F 92207 "Morning Star", a class once seen on the S&DJR sat proudly on a track panel. According to their website, The Shillingstone Station project wants to restore Shillingstone Station to the period of the early sixties, whilst simultaneously making the station a museum. At a previous visit to Shillingstone in 1999, I had remembered a pub near the station with the evocative name of 'The Silent Whistle'. After a brief search and enquiry at a local car dealership, we found that the pub had sadly been re-developed into 'executive homes'.

Beyond Shillingstone Station the line ended at an overbridge (194 ST 822120), but a public bridleway provided an easy access to the line (194 ST 821123) via a farm track. The farm track continued along the trackbed to a minor road, where the overbridge (194 ST 814136) was infilled, blocking the way to the overgrown cutting on the northern side of the road. A reasonable trackbed became a public bridleway (194 ST 808137) to the site of a demolished bridge (194 ST 801138) across the River Stour, where the abutments and pillars remained. The bridleway continued to the picturesque Fiddleford Mill, crossing the river on a footbridge before regaining the trackbed at the northern side of the demolished bridge, where it became a public footpath into Sturminster Newton. No trace remained of Sturminster Newton Station (194 ST 788142), as it had been replaced by a car park and commercial developments. In an infilled cutting, now a park opposite the station site, however, there was a commemorative plaque stating: "Here once passed the engines and men of the Somerset & Dorset Joint Railway, closed 6 March 1966", screwed onto a gatepost sporting S&DJR commemorative gates. It was late afternoon, so we decided to call it a day and get a room in The Swan Inn, which was well stocked with Hall & Woodhouse beers from just down the line at Blandford.

## Sturminster Newton to Wincanton (10 ¾ miles)

Before setting off we had an excellent breakfast at the 'Poet's Corner' Café. The proprietor was a friendly and well travelled Turkish guy, who found himself in living in Sturminster Newton as a result of a holiday romance. We did not enquire about the current status of his relationship, but from some of the things he said we figured that he wanted to swap his apron for a backpack sometime soon.

We knew that a major bridge (194 ST 783144) across The River Stour to the north west was demolished, so we opted to cross the river via a footbridge (194 ST 783143). From the footbridge we had a good view of the partially demolished rail bridge, which consisted only of the twin-arched masonry abutments as the iron-latticed mid-section had been removed. Rejoining the line via the embankment of the western abutment, we found a good walkable trackbed that was in use as a farm track. The line crossed the River Divelish (183 ST 777151) close to where it joined the River Stour, and the trackbed became overgrown and impenetrable at this point. It was, however, straightforward to shadow the line in the adjacent fields until we reached a point (183 ST 774154) where the trackbed disappeared into the surrounding field. After a struggle through some thick hedges, we picked up a re-emerging trackbed a few hundred metres further north until reaching an infilled minor road overbridge (183 ST 769161) that once straddled the now overgrown cutting. Once across the road, we followed a track that joined the line at the far end of the cutting, where the line ran across open country to the River Lydden, where the bridge (183 ST 763165) had also been demolished. All that remained of the bridge were the brick-built pillars and abutments. Fortunately, a sturdy metal footbridge present close to the site, facilitated a simple crossing of the Lydden.

A good clear trackbed continued across open fields to a minor road overbridge (183 ST 758168), where the trackbed became very overgrown. After a thorny scramble over the embanked road, it was possible to rejoin the line after a few hundred metres where the trackbed became a public footpath (183 ST 753170) for about 300 metres before it veered away from the line to the Stalbridge road. An unremarkable trackbed continued across open fields into an industrial estate on the outskirts of Stalbridge, with the trackbed becoming a public bridleway to the site of Stalbridge Station (183 ST 739181). Nothing remained of the station site or line, with the whole area now in use by a large steel mill. We skirted the perimeter fence of the steel mill, walking across a muddy field to a public footpath (183 ST 738183) where there was no trace of the line. An overgrown trackbed re-appeared at a former level crossing on a minor road (183 ST 737184) that forced us to shadow the line in adjacent fields for a few hundred metres before it became walkable again to the site of an another overgrown minor road overbridge (183 ST 731192).

The line crossed a track and another minor road, both locations of level crossings with some original artefacts such as gateposts remaining in-situ, before reaching Henstridge Station (183 ST 726201). Henstridge Station also had a level crossing, but that had disappeared along with the station site under a housing estate where only a fraction of the trackbed remained as a landscaped footpath that ended at the embankment of the A30 (183 ST 725203). We had to go up and over the A30 to join the trackbed that had been recently cleared by machine to the minor road and level crossing site that marked the southern terminus of the Gartell Light Railway (183 ST 721211). Although the tracks of the Gartell Light Railway (www.glr-online.co.uk) did not cross the road, a nice crossing gate complete with red waning disc hung from original gateposts.

The Gartell Light Railway is a 2ft narrow gauge line that runs for about ¾ mile between two minor roads, and is named after the family who own the line. The southern end consisted of a low platform with a single track and run-round loop, and a lever rack for points. Judging by the rust, the line had obviously not been used for some time, so we set off to walk along the edge of the ballast. We arrived at the northern end of the line to find an impressive array of signals and another platform. There was a 'No Admittance' sign next to the line, so we left the line to walk in the adjacent field for the remaining short distance to the road. The trackbed (183 ST 717217) littered with old narrow gauge rails and farm equipment continued north towards Templecombe, only to disappear into the surrounding fields. Arriving at a minor road overbridge in Templecombe (183 ST 713224) we opted to detour into the village rather than struggle through the extensive undergrowth. Templecombe seemed to be taking a siesta with the Post Office shop and 'The Royal Wessex' pub both being shut. We decided to have a picnic lunch on the platform of the delightful Templecombe Station that boasts an interesting art-deco ticket office where passengers still have to go upstairs to buy tickets.

Templecombe was once a complicated rail junction where the Salisbury to Exeter Line intersected with the S&DJR. The existing station was formerly known as 'Templecombe Upper', and was originally operated the London & South Western Railway (L&SWR), with 'Templecombe Lower' (183 ST 709227) being the S&DJR station. The S&DJR passed under the L&SWR (183 ST 711226) with two junctions to the north of this bridge giving access both east and west from the S&DJR along the L&SWR. Only a bridge abutment remains (183 ST 709226) of the spur from the S&DJR that headed west into Templecombe Upper. The trackbed to the north and Templecombe Lower had been occupied by an

311

access road and an extensive marine equipment factory.

It was very difficult to skirt the factory site as we had to cross several fences, trudge along the edge of a very muddy field, and battle with extensive undergrowth to access the line at the site of a public footpath (183 ST 709231). I would advise anyone attempting this to just take the footpath out of Templecombe and save a lot of hassle. Once back on the trackbed the going was straightforward to Horsington where the trackbed became a well used farm track passing under a fine twin-arched overbridge (183 ST 709243). An excellent trackbed continued to the crossing point of the Monarch's Way (183 ST 709254), where due to the proximity of Maltkiln Hill Farm and the need to find a bivvy site, we opted to follow the path round the farm. After a brief reconnoitre of nearby woods we decided to push on as no decent bivvy site was forthcoming in the damp and boggy woodland.

Leaving the Monarch's Way we rejoined the line at an overbridge (183 ST 711262) close to Grove Farm, where the trackbed was vague but it was straightforward to follow the alignment. When the trackbed re-appeared it was quite overgrown but a narrow path wound its way through the vegetation. Seeing no decent sites for a bivvy we decided to push on into Wincanton for a B&B. The trackbed stopped abruptly on an embankment (183 ST 711277) at the A303 dual carriageway. The way was also barred by a deep drainage ditch that we had to follow east to the River Cale that ran in a steeply sloping concrete culvert under the A303. Fortunately the river was running low, allowing us to ford with ease and join the Monarch's Way into the inevitable edge-of town-industrial estate. Wincanton Station (183 ST 710283), once the dropping of point for horses going to the Wincanton Races, was long gone with the site now used by local industry. Wandering into town on a hot afternoon we found a no frills B&B at The Bear for £17.50; it was nice to see a sub-twenty pounds B&B still in existence.

**Wincanton to Winsor Hill Tunnel (About 14 miles)**
Little did we realise at the time, but our early night in Wincanton would serve us well as this stretch of line would be the most problematic due to detours and obstacles that we were to encounter. After going the wrong way out of Wincanton, due to my usual miserable standard of 'urban'

navigation, we ended up on top of Windmill Hill, which however, allowed good views across the countryside as a consolation.

Our first glimpse of the line came at the site of a demolished bridge (183 ST 709291), where just the ivy covered abutments remained. Judging by the map this was probably the first part of line to the north of Wincanton that was intact. The trackbed on either side of the bridge was in private use, so we continued along the minor road to a public footpath that crossed the trackbed via a bridge (183 ST 708291), which gave easy access to a cutting. The cutting ended after a few hundred metres, where the line continued to run level across open fields, skirting the hill below Wincanton Race Course. The trackbed turned into a farm track that headed straight into Moorhayes Farm (183 ST 699301), and with no easy box round option, or cover, we had to detour via the minor road, to rejoin the trackbed about two hundred metres up the line from the farm buildings. The level trackbed became overgrown and rubble strewn in places forcing frequent detours into neighbouring fields before it disappeared altogether (183 ST 691310). Feeling very exposed, we took a direct line across open fields to a culvert bridge and embankment (183 ST 688313) that was littered with an old boxcar, a rusty old Land Rover and assorted old farm machines. The embankment quickly entered a wet and shady cutting that was home to a notable and very high twin-arched overbridge (183 ST 687316) that carried the minor road from Shepton Montague. A good section of trackbed that became a high embankment skirted Shepton Montague before running adjacent to a minor road with a curious corrugated iron fence between the trackbed and the road.

The bridge across the A359 (183 ST 676325) was missing, with the vacant ground on the south side home to a couple of travellers' vans. To the north of the A359 the trackbed was easily walkable through a good cutting before opening out again on an embankment sitting above the village of Pitcombe. The overbridges that take the line over a couple of minor roads in Pitcombe remained in-situ with the southern-most being easily negotiated. The northern-most bridge (183 ST 673332), however, was fenced off and the trackbed was very overgrown. The approach to the bridge also leaves the walker in full view of houses on the eastern side of the trackbed and we were spotted by a bemused looking woman in a garden below. The overgrown trackbed continued into what was obviously an infilled cutting where we had to climb up a earth and rubble slope and bash through more thick vegetation to emerge at a minor road (183 ST 672334) on the edge of Cole village, where only a tell-tale bridge wall indicated the presence of the S&DJR.

The trackbed had been built over to the north, so we followed the road round to Cole Station (183 ST 671336), where the fine single-storey stone station building and the equally fine two-storey red brick Station Master's House still stood as private residences. Cole was a notable location on the S&DJR, for it was close to the point at which two railway companies, namely The Dorset Central and The Somerset Central, joined in 1862 to form the S&DJR.

The line was inaccessible at or close to the station, but a short walk north along the road took us to the site of a missing bridge (183 ST 670337) where it was possible to regain the line running on a high embankment. In just a few metres the line ended abruptly on a high wooded embankment overlooking the River Brue at the site of the demolished Cole Viaduct that once carried the S&DJR across the river.

Crossing under the Great Western Mainline (the S&DJR bridge - 183 ST 668339 - having been demolished) on the minor road running north out of Cole, we could see that the line had been obliterated by ploughed fields, until it reappeared at a redundant bridge (183 ST 662341) south of the village of Wyke Champflower. The trackbed from the bridge into Wyke Champflower was landscaped and the bridge (183 ST 661344) was infilled with the trackbed in use as a garden. We continued to walk along the road to access the line from a public footpath (183 ST 661344) that ran north across open fields from the village. The line was impenetrable from Wyke Champflower, and when we arrived at a byway (183 ST 658349) we could find no trace of the line in the surrounding ploughed field. This forced us on a long and tedious detour via road and public footpath to a point where a footpath crossed under the line in a shady underbridge (183 ST 644362). The trackbed was completely overgrown, so we shadowed the embankment on the western side taking the footbridge across the River Altham, before accessing a clear but muddy trackbed that ended at a gate onto the A371 (183 ST 640365). With The Natterjack Inn directly opposite, we could not miss the chance of a lunchtime pie and pint and a well earned rest after the morning's struggles.

After a leisurely lunch we walked a short distance north from The Natterjack to the unforgettable and evocatively named Evercreech Junction Station (183 ST 639366). It was difficult to get a good view of the station as the site was occupied by light industrial units and was fenced off, with the station buildings having been converted into private dwellings. My research also indicates that some of the station buildings have been demolished. Evercreech Junction Station sits about ½ mile south of the actual junction (183 ST 636371), where the branch line to Burnham joined the main trunk of the S&DJR. The trackbed from the station was inaccessible so we headed north along the A371 to a public footpath (183 ST 639369) and access road to a waste reclamation plant. Once round the waste, plant we had to use dead-reckoning to find the trackbed as the whole area was unrecognisable as a former railway with huge piles of rubble scarring the landscape. In one large pile of rubble there was the rather amusing sight of a 'Double Diamond' road tanker half buried; a symbolic and fitting end for a particularly awful brand of beer.

Eventually we came to the actual site of Evercreech Junction, which was a sad sight indeed. The trackbed of the branch to Burnham was completely lost under a ploughed field, eventually becoming visible in the distance in a clump of trees (183 ST 635376). The main line was gated and a grassy trackbed proceeded in a shallow cutting where there was a retaining wall still present. The cutting turned into a stinking quagmire, filled with foul smelling slurry at the site of an overbridge (183 ST 638374) and farm building. It would have been impossible to get through the mess with dry feet without wearing gaiters. From the cutting the line became a farm track and we arrived at the demolished bridge across the A371, where the remaining abutments (183 ST 639375) looked rather like a castle. The line was easily accessed on the other side of the road via gate and a path up onto the embankment, where a well used grassy trackbed ran into the village of Evercreech (183 ST 644383). We opted to walk into Evercreech as the trackbed north was inaccessible, and we saw no trace of Evercreech New Station (183 ST 645386) as the site had been used for housing. The bridge (183 ST 645388) and trackbed north of the station site had suffered a similar fate with just the abutments visible. The recent long section of relatively flat countryside began to peter out, with Evercreech marking the beginning of long and steep climb over the Mendip Hills.

After a short pause to by supplies at the Evercreech Co-op, we took the B3081 north out of the village to the point where the S&DJR crossed (183 ST 644394). The bridge was missing and the remaining embankment was home to an inexplicable large white crucifix; too large to be some melancholy reminder of a road crash victim, so I wondered if the monument was the work of a sentimental rail enthusiast living in Evercreech?

A trail of false hope led us into a veritable jungle up the embankment on the other side of the road. Detouring was difficult due to numerous fences and spiky hedges to a minor road (183 ST 636406) that was once crossed by Prestleigh Viaduct. No trace of Prestleigh Viaduct remained, as the 11-arched, 187 yard long stone structure was demolished in January 1993, and the resulting gap meant a considerable hike to cross the valley. Just north of the viaduct site, the trackbed once again yielded to ploughed fields, requiring another detour round field margins until we were able to join a farm track (183 ST 632410) that ran more or less on the trackbed. With a tractor working in a field close by, we made an undetected hasty retreat to the A371 via a byway (183 ST 629414).

As we progressed northwards along the busy and narrow road (no walkway) we could see that the trackbed to our right, once a cutting, had been completely infilled. The point at where the Witham to Yatton Line crossed over the S&DJR (183 ST 629426) on the outskirts of Shepton Mallet was just recognisable to the east at the edge of a factory site, but was completely lost under the industrial estate to the west. Further industrial units had also been built on the site of Shepton Mallet, Charlton Road Station (183 ST 629430) with no trace of the station remaining. It was a shame to see so many architectural features and so much trackbed obliterated on the run into Shepton Mallet. This was more than made up for, however, by the superb Charlton Road Viaduct (183 ST 628435). This magnificent 27-arched, 317 yard long structure, one half constructed in stone and one half in brick, presumably a feature of when the line was doubled, strode proudly across the valley taking the S&DJR around the eastern side of Shepton Mallet. A short climb up the embankment at the southern end of Charlton Road Viaduct revealed a well restored tarmac surfaced trackbed with considerable fortifications in the form of a double fence and loads of razor wire to deter the dismantled railway walker. We opted not to scale the fence on this occasion, as it was late in the day and exposed; besides I had already been across the viaduct some years previous which would enable me to sleep at night safe in the knowledge that it was 'in the bag'!

Charlton Road Viaduct ran onto an embankment on the northern side of the valley, which in turn ended at the A37 at the site of a demolished bridge (183 ST 627438). The line across the A37 was easily accessed by a public footpath, and the trackbed itself, thick with conifers, soon became the public footpath for a few hundred metres. Where the footpath left the line the trackbed remained easy to follow to the southern end of Bath Road Viaduct (183 ST 620442), where some razor wire topped fencing and thick vegetation made the option of crossing of the viaduct very difficult. Like Charlton Viaduct I had been over the 6-arched, 118 yard long Bath Road Viaduct previously, so was not too concerned at the lengthy detour required. At the base of the viaduct by the road side there was a stone plaque commemorating the reconstruction of the viaduct in 1946 (it had partially collapsed in a gale in February 1946). We regained the line to the north of the viaduct via public footpaths (183 ST 620443) that turned onto the trackbed close to an interesting iron overbridge, and ran as far as a minor road (183 ST 616448) at the site of a missing bridge. The trackbed from the road was well used by local dog walkers and was a delight to walk in the evening sunlight to the southern portal of Winsor Hill Tunnel (183 ST 615450). Winsor Hill Tunnel actually consists of two single bore tunnels with the original 'down' tunnel at 242 yards long, and the 'up' tunnel added during the doubling of the line in 1892, at 132 yards. Both tunnels were open, and we walked the 'down' tunnel which was slightly curved, that gave an impression of a much longer tunnel.

It was seven o'clock when we emerged from Winsor Hill Tunnel and it had been a long day on the line, so finding a place to bivvy was now a priority. The trackbed opened out after the north portal of Winsor Hill Tunnel (183 ST 614451) as there was once a stone signal box, quarry sidings, and associated buildings here. We managed to get our basha set up amongst the thickly wooded ruins of the quarry sidings, and once we got a fire going, the beers that I had lugged from Evercreech Co-op helped sooth away our aches and pains.

### Winsor Hill Tunnel to Midsomer Norton (About 7 miles)

We slowly emerged from our bivvy bags, as the fine weather of the previous day had turned overcast and cold. After a swift breakfast we ventured a few hundred metres up the line to the brick 6-arched Ham Wood Viaduct (183 ST 610454), which was difficult to see and photograph because of the dense growth of the surrounding trees. Close to the northern end of Ham Wood Viaduct a ramshackle fence barred the trackbed with a 'Private' sign attached. North of the fence a good trackbed soon opened out into a well used farm track climbing towards Masbury Summit, where we walked briskly along as we were rather exposed in the open countryside. A short embankment terminated at a public footpath (183 ST 605464), as the small bridge had been removed. The grassy embankment continued north from the path for about 50 metres before reaching a minor road where the overbridge had also been removed. For convenience we used the path to get to the road, and rejoined the line on a thickly wooded embankment. The wooded trackbed was obstructed by a fence with 'Private' signs that marked the southern boundary of Masbury Station (183 ST 604473), now a private house. We detoured to the west of the station through the woods to a minor road where it was possible to view the remains Masbury Station from the extant overbridge (183 ST 604473). Both platforms were present along with the substantial station house and platform buildings, probably a waiting room and ticket office.

Upon leaving Masbury Station, we followed a minor road north running adjacent to the line to avoid a private house built on the trackbed. At a point where the trackbed, now in a cutting, veered away from the road it was possible to cut across a field and drop into the cutting where the trackbed was clear and a joy to walk. The northern end of the cutting marked the spot of Masbury Summit (811 ft) (183 ST 609477); the crossing point of the Mendip Hills and the highest point on the S&DJR. The northern end of the summit cutting was infilled where the bridge carrying the B3135 had once been. A rough trackbed continued northwards from the B3135 on an embankment that soon ended at a pheasant enclosure (183 ST 611488), with the line that once curved gracefully towards Binegar being totally obliterated under the fields. We took a dead-reckoning course across the fields, using Binegar Church as a reference point to enter Binegar north of the original station site. Binegar Station House (183 ST 616492) was divided into two private dwellings: 'Station Cottage' and 'Station Masters House', with the house signs being in the form of steam engines on the stone window lintels. The goods shed had been renovated and was in use as offices.

The bridge (183 ST 617492) across Station Road in Binegar was demolished with only the stone abutments remaining, but a convenient gate allowed us to rejoin the line from Station Road, with a vague trackbed following a fence and a tree line before crossing a minor road on an overgrown bridge (183 ST 621497). A few hundred metres of overgrown trackbed ended abruptly at the site of a missing bridge that once straddled a staggered crossroads of minor roads (183 ST 621502). It was easy to get off the line by descending on the embankment to the left but rejoining the line to the north was more difficult due to substantial vegetation and fencing. An excellent ballasted, clear trackbed rewarded our struggle, but after about one hundred metres a substantial fence topped with coils of razor wire barred the line. This was the boundary (183 ST 621504) of Emborough Quarry, and judging by the signs hanging off the fence, the owners were definitely not keen on anyone walking the line. A quick reconnoitre revealed steep ground falling away on either side of the line into the quarry, and the thick growth of brambles complimented the razor wire to create a formidable obstacle. With some careful footwork through the brambles it was just possible to go round the fence on the left hand side and rejoin a wonderfully clear trackbed. Although we could hear some vehicles moving around in the quarry we were invisible due to good tree cover and the fact that the depth of the quarry excavations had effectively turned this section of the S&DJR into a high causeway. Our reward for the struggle lay in the shape of a magnificent seven arched viaduct (183 ST 622507) that straddled an access road that joined the two halves of the quarry. At the northern end of the viaduct the trackbed was crossed by an access road that descended to the quarry, so we passed quickly and quietly across a gate into a field just east of the access road. A very overgrown trackbed ended at the A37 (183 ST 626509) where the bridge had been demolished, that forced us to shadow the line in the adjacent field to the road before using a public footpath to the east of the A37 to rejoin the line (183 ST 628510).

After some lunch at the point where the public footpath crossed the line amidst some old brick ruins that looked vaguely military, we followed the trackbed through the trees to a minor road where the bridge was missing and the trackbed indistinct. Beyond the minor road (183 ST 630511) the trackbed disappeared into some cropped fields, forcing us to follow some hedgerows to the B3139 (183 ST 632512) at the western edge of Chilcompton. To the north of the B3139 the trackbed was inaccessible due to farm buildings and housing development. We shadowed the line as much as possible on the road through Chilcompton, but it was impossible to access any of the remaining (short) sections of trackbed, and the site of Chilcompton Station (183 ST 645514) had completely disappeared under new development. After a circuitous route through Chilcompton we eventually regained the trackbed via a public footpath that joined and utilised the trackbed at the site of an overbridge (183 ST 649515). The footpath followed the trackbed to the cutting of the south portal of Chilcompton Tunnel (183 ST 652522). The 64-yard long tunnel had twin single bores, similar to Winsor Hill Tunnel. The 'Up' portal was bricked up with a steel door and the 'Down' portal was open but the tunnel had been blocked at the northern end. A footpath led out of the cutting to cross an open field that was obviously an infilled cutting that eventually dipped down to the re-emerging trackbed (183 ST 654525), with no sign of the buried north portal of Chilcompton Tunnel.

A well walked section of line gave fine views across the surrounding countryside and was a fine walk to the cutting that marked the southern end of Midsomer Norton South Station (183 ST 664536). We were greeted by quite a sight as some track had been relaid, with plenty more track stacked in a pile by the new formation. After walking round the curve of the cutting the full extent of the work revealed itself. A large restoration project, by The Somerset & Dorset Heritage Trust (www.sdjr. co.uk) was well underway with a substantial amount of track relaid and extensive renovation of the station buildings having been undertaken. There was also a significant amount of rolling stock of mixed vintage at the station site in various states of repair.

Midsomer Norton Bridge (183 ST 664537) that once stood at the northern end of the station was completely demolished, with only a steep embankment on the northern side of the B3139 remaining. The trackbed north had been developed for housing, so we decided to set off down the hill into the town. Midsomer Norton is one of those places that sounds better that it actually is. After a depressing pint in a depressing pub and a fruitless search for a B&B we took the bus to Bath for an overnight stop, which proved much more agreeable.

### Bath to Midsomer Norton (12 ½ miles)

Due to the vagaries of bus times we decided to walk the last leg back to front, starting at Bath Green Park Station (172 ST 746648). The spectacular façade of the station remains largely intact and is now home to 'The Green Park Brasserie'. The magnificent train shed canopy also remained and is used as a market with a large banner in the shape of an old station totem advertising bars, shops and restaurant. The once substantial area of sidings, goods and engine sheds had been replaced by a Sainsbury's supermarket and associated car park.

After a wander through the streets we picked up the first trace of the trackbed at an overgrown redundant blue-brick bridge (172 ST 733646) still in-situ across the existing Bath to Bristol Line. Following the curve from the bridge the trackbed emerged as 'Bath Linear Park', a pleasant green oasis used by joggers and dog walkers, with the stiff 1:50 gradient still very obvious. The linear park ended at an infilled cutting that once ran to the north portal of the 447 yard Devonshire Tunnel (172 ST 744635), now completely obscured by the infilling. It was possible to scramble up the bank to the road and pick our way through the streets to regain the line close to the southern portal (172 ST 748634) of Devonshire Tunnel. A shaded, grassy trackbed left the bricked up southern portal to run along Lyncombe Vale across a couple of short viaducts and under a small overbridge to the northern portal of the 1,829 yard Combe Down Tunnel (172 ST 753653). The stone portal was blocked by massive, heavily graffitied, steel doors that meant we had to climb up the steep slope from the cutting to take a circuitous route and eventually emerge onto the A3062. A footpath starting on a bend in the A3062 (172 ST 761627) heading south, descended the slope of Combe Down. At the base of the hill the trackbed was easily accessible and could be walked back along a heavily buttressed cutting to the brick south portal of Combe Down Tunnel (172 ST 763619). The south portal had equally formidable steel doors barring access, courtesy of Wessex Water who now own the tunnel. A local group is currently in negotiations with various parties, including Wessex Water, to create a cycle path along this section of line, including plans to re-open Devonshire and Combe Down Tunnels (www.twotunnels.org.uk/index.html), that would make a through cycle route from Bath to Midford.

A good trackbed continued south from Combe Down Tunnel into the picturesque Horscombe Vale. The line was conveyed across the watercourse via the 8-arched Tucking Mill Viaduct (172 ST 763617) that had a 2-metre wall at each end, which needed to be climbed to gain access and egress. The trackbed became a surfaced public footpath a short distance south of Tucking Mill Viaduct, passing under a fine elongated bridge (172 ST 761610) that carries a minor road over the line where the trackbed becomes part of the National Cycle Network Route 24. We made good progress to Midford Station (172 ST 761607) where the single platform remained in reasonable condition. Just south of Midford Station stood the 8-arched 168 yard long Midford Viaduct (172 ST 761605), that once took the S&DJR high across Cam Brook and the dismantled Camerton to Limpley Stoke Line. A curious feature at this point was the fact that the Camerton to Limpley Stoke Line was also on a lower viaduct, passing directly under Midford Viaduct, making a very unusual 'X' formation. The lower viaduct was badly overgrown and partially obscured by surrounding trees.

The cycle route continued along the trackbed through pleasant countryside until the eastern edge of the village of Wellow, where it joined a minor road (172 ST 746583) at a pony trekking centre. The minor road passed under a high bridge of the S&DJR just west of the pony trekking centre, but we opted to take a public footpath along Wellow Brook to join another minor road that climbed the hill into the village. We walked through the 'chocolate-box' village and down a track to the site of Wellow Station (172 ST 738581), now a private dwelling. The owner of the station saw me wandering about and came out for a chat. She very kindly allowed me round the back to the trackbed, now filled in and grassed over, to take a photo of the wonderfully preserved station. I did not get the owners name, but she was a local cycling officer for the area and was very interested in the S&DJR and its fate since closure.

The line west of Wellow Station disappeared into the surrounding fields of Wellow Valley, with the only remaining visible artefact being an infilled bridge (172 ST 734576) that once took a minor road across the line. We eventually accessed the embanked trackbed (172 ST 732573) via a farm track that led to a large shed (172 ST 732575). An overgrown but largely walkable trackbed continued along the valley, passing under a notable twin arched overbridge (172 ST 725565), before becoming impenetrable with brambles and nettles. Fortunately a public footpath ran parallel to the line to the site of Shoscombe & Single Hill Halt (172 ST 719561), with all trace of the halt having long vanished under grassy fields. The trackbed continued as public footpath from the site of the halt for a few hundred metres where the path veered north (172 ST 716559) It was possible to stay on the trackbed to a minor road where a now truncated, low viaduct (five brick arches remaining) (172 ST 714559) once crossed. From this minor road the S&DJR once again became a cycle route for the rest of the way into Radstock.

Radstock was once a major hub of Somerset coal mining, with considerable railway sidings and yards, being served by the S&DJR and the Bristol & North Somerset Railway. The S&DJR Radstock North Station (172 ST 689550) was demolished and was now a car park. The level crossing at the A367 was also completely gone, but the line continued south westwards as a foot/cycleway to Midsomer Norton.

At the time of our walk, the S&DJR appeared to be in a period of great change, with many diverse groups undertaking projects relating to their particular area of interest. The reader will no doubt be witness to more change if they decide to venture out onto this wonderful part of our railway heritage.

*A fine example of a crossing gate has been lovingly restored and remains in-situ at Corfe Mullen Crossing (195 SY 976983).*

*Early morning light emphasises the features of Charlton Marshall Halt (195 ST 898040). The trackbed is today in use as part of the North Dorset Trailway.*

*This gradient marker close to Charlton Marshall reminds passers-by of the history of the trackbed that they now enjoy.*

*The ramshakle remains of Stourpaine & Durweston Halt (194 ST 861091) make a forlorn sight.*

*Restoration work is well underway at Shillingstone Station (194 ST 825116). The ultimate aim is for the station to be used as a heritage centre and museum.*

*Although the trackbed and station at Sturminster Newton are long gone, it is good to see these memorials to the S&DJR and the men who worked on the line.*

*The missing iron mid-section of the bridge across The River Stour (194 ST 783144) makes an awkward obstacle.*

*This gate (183 ST 721211) marks the southern end of 2ft gauge Gartell Light Railway.*

*A bewildering array of signals on The Gartell Light Railway.*

*An atmospheric pub sign in Templecombe.*

*A splendid 'doubled' overbridge (183 ST 709243) over a clear trackbed north of Templecombe.*

*Road wins over rail: a missing bridge over the A371 (183 ST 639375) can be easily bypassed by the walker.*

*Charlton Road Viaduct (183 ST 628435), bordering the town of Shepton Mallet is the undisputed crown of the S&DJR. Note how one half of the structure is constructed in brick, and one half in stone. This was a result of the doubling of the line.*

*Bath Road Viaduct (183 ST 620442) was also doubled, and had to be re-built in 1946 after storm damage, as noted in this water-stained plaque.*

*Winsor Hill Tunnel (183 ST 615450) is in fact two separate tunnels, with the second bore being added during the doubling of the line. These views are of the longer 'down' tunnel. The picture above is of the south portal, and below is the north portal.*

*The twin-bores of Chilcompton Tunnel (183 ST 652522) make a fine study. This view is the southern end of the tunnels. The northern end has been completely infilled.*

*Midsomer Norton South Station (183 ST 664536) is another station on the S&DJR undergoing restoration.*

*The viaduct at Shoscombe (172 ST 714559) has been chopped off at both ends with the arches being used as storage areas.*

*Although the trackbed is now a lawn, Wellow Station (172 ST 738581) is a wonderfully preserved building that has been sympathetically maintained.*

*Combe Down Tunnel (south portal above, north portal below) was the longest tunnel on the S&DJR.  It is now owned by Wessex Water, and the portals are barred by massive steel doors.  There are plans however, to reopen both Combe Down and Devonshire Tunnels as part of a cycleway that would eventually join up with the path at Midford.*

*The beautiful canopy of Bath Green Park Station now covers a retail area and car park, where locomotives have been replaced by shopping trolleys....*

# WALK XXX
# The Symington, Biggar & Broughton Railway
# (Peebles to Symington)

| Walk Summary | |
|---|---|
| Date walked | April 2006 |
| Line mileage | 19 |
| OSLR Maps | 72, 73 |
| Opened to Passengers | [1]05 11 1860, [2]01 02 1864 |
| Closed to Passengers | 05 06 1950 |
| PGAG Reference | 30 |
| Pre-grouping Company | Caledonian Railway |

[1]Symington to Broughton, [2]Broughton to Peebles

## Walk Highlights

Neidpath Tunnel, Neidpath Viaduct, Lyne Station Viaduct, Biggar Station. A generally excellent trackbed and the picturesque scenery of the upper Tweed valley.

## Public Transport

Peebles is served by First Bus service 62 from Edinburgh Bus Station. Edinburgh is on the ECML. Symington is linked to Lanark (for trains to Glasgow) by Stuart's Coaches service 30.

## Background

The Symington, Biggar & Broughton Railway was a cross country route running along the Tweed Valley from Peebles West Station to Symington Station. The route joined the Peebles Loop (Walk XXIII) with the WCML, making journeys from Peebles to Glasgow possible.

336

We had decided to do an ambitious 40 mile circle in two days by starting at Peebles, walking west to Symington, and then returning on the old line from Carstairs (Walk XXXI) to rejoin the Peebles Loop (Walk XXIII) at Leadburn.

## Walk Description

### Peebles to Symington (19 miles)
The ulterior motive for a start at Peebles was to sample the atmosphere and fine ales of The Bridge Inn. The landlord, Tam, was very obliging in helping us sample his collection of real ales, that were all served to perfection. With a 19-mile hike ahead in the morning, however, a late night in The Bridge was not the best of ideas.

A beautiful spring morning helped clear our heads as we set off in search of Peebles West Station (73 NT 247403). The station site was now unrecognisable and was a housing estate on the south bank of the River Tweed. After following the riverside path we joined the trackbed close to the eastern portal of Neidpath Tunnel (596 yards) (73 NT 234402), that was named after the nearby Neidpath Castle. The single-track stone portal was partially bricked up to allow the placement of large doors that were missing, making access easy. The tunnel was slightly curved and was in good condition throughout with only the odd damp section underfoot. The western portal was similar to the eastern portal in design but it had additional moss-covered stone buttressing extending from the portal into the cutting. Neidpath Tunnel cuts through a steep spur in a sharp bend in the Tweed, and as the line emerged from the tunnel it immediately crossed a gently flowing Tweed via Neidpath Viaduct (73 NT 233402). Neidpath Viaduct was a splendid 8-arched stone viaduct in a beautiful setting, and the elegant structure still sported the original iron railings of an intricate and ornate design.

At the western end of Neidpath Viaduct the trackbed became the 'Tweed Walk', and continued as an easy and very scenic walk to a viaduct (73 NT 209400) just east of Lyne Station (73 NT 208399), that was now a private house. This viaduct was shorter than Neidpath Viaduct, but it also sported the same design of ornate railings and even had large cruciform shapes recessed into the buttresses. As the trackbed west was

337

now part of Lyne Station's garden we detoured round on a minor road that paralleled the line to the north, before cutting across a field to rejoin the line at a small wooded cutting (73 NT 205399).

A marvellous grassy trackbed continued along the north bank of the Tweed giving splendid views of the surrounding hills, with the Tweed glistening like a iridescent snake basking in the sun, to Stobo Station (72 NT 173362). The only remnant of Stobo Station was the stone goods shed that sat in a landscaped garden complete with daffodils adding a splash of colour. The owner of Stobo goods shed was working in his garden, and seeing us taking an interest in the shed, he kindly invited us in to have a look inside whereupon we observed its new function as a garden store and workshop.

A short distance beyond Stobo Station the trackbed became a private track to a house built on the line, so we followed the B712 to a point just beyond the house (72 NT 170359) before regaining a wooded trackbed. After only a few hundred metres we were presented with a similar situation with another house (72 NT 166356) built on the trackbed, forcing another short detour on the B712 before we could regain the line in a shallow cutting where the road bridge (72 NT 165356) was infilled. An excellent trackbed continued along the north bank of the Tweed on a low embankment that had an avenue of trees, before ending abruptly in a boggy mess close to some farm buildings (72 NT 157356). It was a simple enough task to first drop down the bank round the buildings, and then climb back up to the farm track that now occupied the trackbed for a few hundred metres before veering off towards the river. An occasionally overgrown trackbed was a delight to walk as it hugged the north bank of the Tweed, before veering sharply out of the Tweed Valley into the broad swathe of the valley of less substantial Biggar Water.

The line now in use as a farm track emerged through a short rocky cutting (72 NT 124349) at the site of the junction with the 8 ½ mile Talla Reservoir Railway. During planning I had overlooked this obscure branch line so we vowed to come back and walk it another day.

Another mile or so of easy walking across the floodplain of Biggar Water took us to Broughton, where the line passed under the A701 (72 NT 113360). A curious feature of this bridge was that it was two bridges in a 'V' shape, with one carrying the road and one seemingly being a footway/pipeline bridge. Broughton Station (72 NT 110361) now cleared, was home to a works yard where only small traces of a platform remained.

Beyond Broughton the trackbed was a wonderful grassy track with an unusually long dead-straight section of about 2 ¾ miles, that gave excellent views both of the line and the surrounding countryside. On the approach to Biggar the trackbed skirted the edge of a caravan park and golf course, before ending abruptly at a high chain link fence (72 NT 043372) surrounding some kind of yard and Biggar Station site. We followed a footpath into the village of Biggar and took a minor road south for a look at the remains of Biggar Station (72 NT 039372). Although a close inspection was impossible, the substantial stone station buildings and signal box could be clearly seen when looking east from the road.

The trackbed west of Biggar Station had disappeared under some new houses, but the estate was bounded by a large playing field that made it easy walking to a point where an indistinct trackbed emerged close to the A72. To the west of the A72 (72 NT 033369) the trackbed once more became clear and walkable to Coulter Station (72 NT 019364). The single-storey stone station house was in use as a private dwelling with part of the platform remaining. Just across the road from Coulter Station was a tiny remnant of trackbed that once ran onto Coulter Viaduct; an iron structure on stone pillars that once took the line over the River Clyde (72 NT 018363). Only the stone supports of the viaduct remained which meant a short detour to cross the Clyde on the A72 road bridge. A good trackbed, occasionally overgrown, continued west to the northern edge of Symington, where we left the line at the site of a rubbish strewn overbridge (72 NS 997357) as the line disappeared into the gardens behind some houses. A short walk took us to the site of Symington Station (72 NS 991361) that was now just some wasteland next to the WCML.

As we waited for the bus to Carstairs, we reflected on what was an excellent walk. Although it was a long walk, the lack of major obstacles had made it seem easy. In terms of 'walkability' one could not find a better example of than The Symington, Biggar & Broughton Railway.

*Almost immediately after emerging from the wetsern portal of Neidpath Tunnel the line crosses the Tweed on the ornate Neidpath Viaduct (73 NT 233402) (above).*

*The easily accessible eastern portal of Neidpath Tunnel (73 NT 234402) (right) sits quietly in the woods.*

*Nearing the end of the line, the walker is forced on a detour to avoid the missing structure of Coulter Viaduct (72 NT 018363), where only the pillars remain.*

# WALK XXXI
## The Dolphinton Branch (Carstairs to Dolphinton) and The Leadburn, Linton & Dolphinton Railway (Dolphinton to Leadburn)

| Walk Summary | |
|---|---|
| Date walked | April 2006 |
| Line mileage | 21 |
| OSLR Maps | 72, 73 |
| Opened to Passengers | [1]01 03 1867, [2]04 07 1864 |
| Closed to Passengers | [1]04 06 1945, [2]01 04 1933 |
| PGAG Reference | 30 |
| Pre-grouping Company | [1]Caledonian Railway, [2]North British Railway |

[1]The Dolphinton Branch, [2]The Leadburn, Linton & Dolphinton Railway

## Walk Highlights

Bridge over the North Medwin, an excellent trackbed and the wide open scenery.

## Public Transport

Carstairs Junction is on the WCML. Leadburn is connected to Edinburgh by First bus service 62.

## Walk Description

### Carstairs to Leadburn (21 miles)

The Carstairs Arms Hotel, located in the tired looking village of Carstairs, was essentially a bar with a couple of cheap rooms to let. The guests of the hotel were usually railway workers, and consequently it perplexed the landlord no end as to why two *walkers* would want to stay in Carstairs, as is definitely not renowned for its outdoor leisure potential.

It was a crisp clear morning as we walked down the minor road to Carstairs Junction. A track running alongside Carstairs Junction Station yard (72 NS 952455) allowed us to skirt round the station into a field. After a wet few hundred metres along a fence line, we crossed under the existing railway via a small bridge (72 NS 957454) used for farm access. It was a simple job to take a sharp left from under the bridge and climb up a grassy embankment to join the line a few metres east of Dolphinton Junction (72 NS 958454). Dolphinton Junction was just one part of a once complex junction arrangement centred on Carstairs. A grassy trackbed with a few trees ended abruptly at a minor road (72 NS 964454) and disappeared into a field to the east of the road. We took a course across the field heading for a point just north of some substantial farm buildings. When we emerged onto the farm track (72 NS 966454) we were spotted by the farmer, who challenged us in an unfriendly way, so we politely and firmly pointed out that we had a legal right to walk across non-cultivated fields according to 'The Scottish Outdoor Access Code'. That stopped him in his tracks, and he retreated muttering something about "bloody walkers having no respect for the countryside".

Leaving the grumpy farmer behind, we climbed a sloping field to regain a good trackbed at the end of a clear cutting (72 NS 967452). An excellent trackbed continued east, running close to some large meanders of the River Clyde and into the valley of Medwin Water, before stopping at the B7016 where the bridge (72 NS 980446) was demolished. Just to the east of the B road was the site of Bankhead Station (72 NS 981446) that was now private houses and sheds. We skirted the site of Bankhead Station in a field on the south side to respect the privacy of the owners, and rejoined the line in the cutting to the east. The glorious morning was matched by the excellent condition of the trackbed, and we made quick progress crossing a notable three-arched stone bridge across the North Medwin (72 NS 992449), and under a fine stone overbridge (72 NT 016447) before arriving at the site of Newbigging Station (72 NT 021450). Newbigging Station house sat on the embankment of the line hidden by trees, so we took a farm track that led down to the A721

342

where the rail bridge had been demolished.

It was possible to immediately rejoin the embanked line on the other side of the A721. The trackbed, still wonderfully clear and walkable, now gently curved along the broad valley of the South Medwin. The views of the countryside were excellent, and we passed under a couple of redundant overbridges before the church at Dunseyre, sitting on a knoll just north of the line came into view. Only the stone abutments of the bridge (72 NT 074481) at Dunsyre village remained, but it was easy to descend from the embankment to the minor road. The platform at Dunsyre Station (72 NT 075481) was still extant with a wooden fence on top that now marked the boundary of a private garden, with the trackbed being used for access. Due to the vegetation and fence on the platform, it was impossible to see if the house was the original station house or otherwise.

We skirted Dunseyre Station in a field south of the site before rejoining the trackbed in thick woods a little further east. The bridge across West Water (72 NT 092486); probably an iron structure judging by the remaining stone abutments, was missing. Fortunately the water was very low, enabling us to ford the stream close to the site of the former bridge. The excellent trackbed continued to an infilled overbridge (72 NT 102483), before paralleling a minor road to Dolphinton Station (Caledonian Railway) (72 NT 112478). With little time to linger it was difficult to see if much of the original station structure remained as the trackbed went behind some trees and houses. There was also no trace of the former level crossing across the A702. Dolphinton was the location where the Caledonian Railway met The North British Railway at Dolphinton Junction (72 NT 114478), to eventually become a through route. The junction site was now occupied by new houses. We did not see the North British Station (72 NT 113477) but subsequent research suggests that the original building remains, and is in use as a private house.

From Dolphinton the line swung northeast with the trackbed becoming flat and vague across some grazing fields for about 1 ¾ miles before becoming an obvious farm track at Medwyn Mains (72 NT 131490). After a similar distance, we left the line at a minor road (72 NT 149498), as the trackbed disappeared in a field used for grazing horses. From the map it was obvious that the rail bridge (72 NT 154509) across Lyne Water was missing, so to avoid a lengthy detour we took a track that crossed the river (72 NT 156503) on a pipe bridge close to an outward bound facility called Broomlee Centre. Skirting Broomlee Centre we emerged on the B7059 next to Broomlee Station (72 NT 154510), a single storey house that was now a private residence. Opposite Broomlee Station the trackbed was occupied by a private road to some new houses so we skirted round in a field and regained the steeply climbing trackbed just beyond the houses (71 NT 158512). The trackbed was once again remarkably clear apart from the occasional fence, and we passed under a pair of lonely looking stone bridges (72 NT 167520 and 175526) as the line climbed to another bridge and Macbie Hill Station (72 NT 186527), where only the faintest hint of a platform remained.

With the line now a farm track that levelled out, we crossed a very wide open landscape towards the intriguingly Spanish-sounding station of Lamancha (73 NT 207528). The station house was in use as a private dwelling and the remains of the platform were visible as we approached from the west. We skirted the station site to the south and crossed the A701 at the site of the former crossing, before climbing the fence into a field where the only clue to the alignment of the line was an overbridge (73 NT 209528). The bridge heralded the start of a good trackbed that ran to a minor road where the bridge (73 NT 216531) was demolished. Running above, and parallel to, the A701 we passed some animal sheds and a large poultry shed before the ground became more moor-like as we approached the pine plantation close to Leadburn Junction (73 NT 235549). This was the point where The Leadburn, Linton & Dolphinton Railway joined the Peebles Loop (see Walk XXIII). Retracing the short section of the Peebles Loop, we headed for The Leadburn Inn, only to find a huge pile of charred rubble, the place having recently burnt to the ground.

Therefore we had to catch the bus into Edinburgh for our traditional post-walk pint. With over an hour to wait in Edinburgh for the train home we settled in at a splendid Victorian pub, The Guildford Arms, which has an exceptional selection of ales, and is very close to Waverley Station.

*The substantial overbridge (72 NS 992449) across the North Medwin has stood the test of time very well.*

*The bridge across West Water (72 NT 092486) has not fared so well. Is it possibly because this bridge may have had an iron mid-section?*

*A fine embankment (72 NT 070480) to the west of Dunseyre Village of-fers a good view of the village church.*

*A bare trackbed, an isolated and redundant overbridge (72 NT 167520) symbolise the fate of so much of our railway heritage.*

# WALK XXXII
## The Cairn Valley Railway (Moniaive to Dumfries) and The Dumfries, Lochmaben & Lockerbie Railway (Dumfries to Lockerbie)

| Walk Summary | |
|---|---|
| Date walked | June 2006 |
| Line mileage | *18, ⁺14 ¾ |
| OSLR Maps | 78, 84 |
| Opened to Passengers | *01 03 1905, ⁺01 09 1863 |
| Closed to Passengers | *03 05 1943, ⁺19 05 1952 |
| PGAG Reference | 26 |
| Pre-grouping Company | *Glasgow & South Western Railway, ⁺Caledonian Railway |

*The Cairn Valley Railway, ⁺The Dumfries, Lochmaben & Lockerbie Railway


**Walk Highlights**

*The Cairn Valley Railway:* Moniaive Station, Cairn Water Viaduct, the generally excellent condition of the trackbed and the wonderful open scenery of the Cairn Valley.
*The Dumfries, Lochmaben & Lockerbie Railway:* The generally very good trackbed, and the scenery.


**Public Transport**

Dumfries is served by trains from Carlisle and Glasgow. Carlisle and Glasgow are on the WCML. Moniaive is connected to Dumfries by Stagecoach bus service 202. Lockerbie is on the WCML, between Carlisle and Glasgow.

## Background

The Cairn Valley railway was a country branch line that once connected Dumfries with the picturesque village of Moniaive. The line ran along the very scenic Cairn Valley and, sadly, but unsurprisingly survived for less than 40 years in its passenger transporting role.

### The Cairn Valley Railway; Moniaive to Dumfries (18 miles)

After getting off the bus in Moniaive into the glare of a hot morning, we ambled through the pretty village and stopped outside the chapel where a local group were undertaking a footpath survey for the surrounding countryside. The survey was for walkers to detail their preferences for paths on copies of a local map, for the authorities to establish 'core' public paths in the area sometime in the future. It was whilst enthusiastically pencilling over the route of The Cairn Valley Railway that I fell into discussion with a jolly, bearded chap. The beard belonged to Hugh Taylor, a well established writer of walking and historical guides for areas across the British Isles. We told him of our plan to walk the line back to Dumfries, of which he greatly approved. He even had the decency not to ask why I had a metre or so of aluminium stanchion sticking rather awkwardly out of my rucksack.

A track led directly from the A702 to the site of Moniaive Station (78 NX 779907), now in use as a farm yard. A solitary goods shed and an obviously once elegant but now sadly dilapidated wooden station building remained, with its painted shiplap timbers looking weathered and the clay roof tiles set at odd angles. We left the quietly decaying station heading east through a gate into a grazing field. The trackbed was not discernible, so we took a straight line to Dalwhat Water (78 NX 784904) where only remnants of the bridge abutments remained. The water was low and stepping stones were present, just as Hugh Taylor had described earlier. An excellent grassy trackbed continued before becoming a farm track close to some farm buildings at Cairn Water where another bridge (78 NX 792902) was missing. The water was low, which was fortunate, as it would have been very tricky, if not impossible to cross, and a significant detour would have been required. A vague trackbed continued across fields with tall grass shimmering in the summer sun, before appearing more clearly as a low embankment

348

in some trees (78 NX 797901) before entering a shallow cutting (78 NX 803900). After crossing a minor road we quickly arrived at another minor road (78 NX 811896) that was the site of Kirkland Station, which was now a single-story private house. Beyond Kirkland Station the trackbed disappeared into a ploughed field, leaving us no alternative but to detour along a minor road running down the valley parallel to the line.

The trackbed re-appeared adjacent to the minor road (78 NX 817890) where it was easily accessed a short distance further along. A reasonable trackbed continued, becoming a farm track just west of Crossford Station (78 NX 834883), where a single-storey cottage remained in use as a private dwelling. Apart from a small grassy mound of what was probably the platform, the level crossing and other features at Crossford Station had vanished. The line continued across the road to become a low embankment with an avenue of trees offering some welcome shade on a blisteringly hot afternoon. With the line following the course of Cairn Water closely, the trackbed was a delight to walk as it became a well used farm track on a dead straight section on a low embankment (78 NX 852855) heading towards Dunscore Station (78 NX 858842). Dunscore Station once sat in a deep cutting. The northern end of the cutting was very overgrown with what was probably the station house being well concealed by the trees. The cutting had a sharp curve, swinging the line to the southwest with the original overbridge (78 NX 858840) having been infilled. The once deep cutting to the south of road had also been partially infilled to a point (78 NX 858838) where an enormous, steep wall of debris including tree trunks, rubble and soil had to be negotiated to rejoin the trackbed in the bottom of the impressive cutting.

Upon exiting the cutting a splendid grassy trackbed swung due south before coming to a sharp bend in Cairn Water where the line was carried across on a splendid three-arched, blue-brick viaduct (78 NX 856836), that still sported original iron railings. The rather tame nature of the Cairn Valley Railway thus far had suddenly got more dramatic as the valley narrowed a little. A good trackbed continued, curving back round to the southeast, still running close to Cairn Water before entering an overgrown, but still navigable cutting that had the skeletal remains of an old footbridge (78 NX 861822) close to the cutting's southern end. A few hundred metres from the cutting, the trackbed became sandwiched between Cairn Water and the minor road. With the trackbed either vague or overgrown it was easier to walk along the road, past Stepford Station (78 NX 864816) where the station house remained, and was now a private house.

We continued along the minor road and rejoined the trackbed at the site of an unusual overbridge (78 NX 878801) at the site of Newtonairds Station. We found no sign of the station, but the bridge had ornate solid iron plates forming a wall between the stone pillars. From the bridge a very overgrown trackbed ran close to Cairn Water along the edge of a field before ending abruptly at the site of a demolished bridge (78 NX 880800). After cutting across the field we rejoined the minor road with some difficulty as our way was blocked by a fiendish wall/electric fence barrier (78 NX 883800). After studying the map it was obvious that a further two bridges were missing across Old Water (84 NX 886799) and Cluden Water (84 NX 897799), so we were left with no alternative but to continue along the minor road for a further 1 ½ miles. From the road it was possible to see some remains of the line, notably an isolated embankment (78 NX 902801), but it was obvious that significant sections had been lost to the plough. At a convenient point along the road we scaled the fence and headed directly across fields to regain a vague trackbed (78 NX 905802), using a truncated low embankment as our point of reference in an otherwise flat landscape. From the low embankment a good trackbed soon entered a shallow cutting (78 NX 910803) that petered out just west of Irongray Station (78 NX 918803), where a hint of platform remained with the station house, that was now in private use.

To the east of Irongray Station the line was obliterated where it once crossed two minor roads in a sharp kink. We had no alternative other than to take the minor road and look for where the line re-emerged. A tell-tale tree line marked the end of an overgrown cutting (78 NX 925804), where we were able to follow a field edge and regain the overgrown trackbed. About halfway along the cutting a now clear trackbed passed under a fine stone overbridge (78 NX 928803) before rising to the B729 where the cutting and overbridge had been infilled. A good clear trackbed continued east from the B729 before ending abruptly in a ploughed field at about 78 NX 938941. After a dog-legged route around the fields, we emerged at a minor road (78 NX 943800) where a tree covered trackbed continued east, with a clear dog walker's path meandering in between, to the A76(T). Across the main road a nicely wooded trackbed ended abruptly at a minor road (84 NX 958797), before disappearing into the open fields, to the site of Cairn Valley Junction (84 NX 967791) on the existing Dumfries to Glasgow line.

Retracing our steps to the A76 we decided to get the bus into Dumfries, as 18 miles in the heat had taken its toll. The bus timetable indicated that we would have to wait a long time for the next bus, so I stuck my thumb out to the southbound traffic on the A76. There were no offers from the main road traffic and we were losing hope when we heard a toot from a car emerging from the Moniaive turn off just down the road. The driver had seen me hitching and the kindly old chap offered us a lift into town. Although he had stopped to pick us up our driver was in a hurry, as he wanted to get to the bookies to place a bet before it closed.

## The Dumfries, Lochmaben & Lockerbie Railway; Dumfries to Lockerbie (14¾ miles)

This route was to be a historic day for Chris and I, as we were about to walk our 1000th mile of dismantled railway line, and fortunately an overcast and cooler morning greeted us as we left our B&B to set off towards Dumfries Station. We joined the line at the site of the former goods yard (84 NX 977764) that was occupied by an industrial estate access road just east of Dumfries Station. It was possible to walk along the access road to the end of the industrial estate to a point where the line becomes 'The Caledonian Cycle Route' (84 NX 977769) close to a breakers yard. The tarmac surfaced cycle route then continued northeast towards Lochabriggs, passing under an unusual iron-spanned overbridge (84 NX 984778) that was adorned with tufts of bright yellow broom. The Caledonian Cycle Route ended in Lochabriggs (78 NX 993803), just south of Lochabriggs Station site (78 NX 993804). With new houses surrounding the site of the station, we could not see any remains of the station buildings. The line was either built on or obliterated until we reached a minor road that marked the southern boundary of Lochabriggs sandstone quarry. Some of the stone used in the grand 'Station Hotel' in Dumfries was excavated from this quarry.

At the point where the line crossed the minor road (78 NX 993810) the bridge was missing with only the abutments remaining. After clambering up the steep embankment and getting over the fence we discovered that the trackbed had been removed by the extensive quarry workings. All was quiet, so we skirted the edge of the quarry and headed off to a bend in an access road (78 NX 992813) that lead to a property named Cullivait. We found the trackbed at a point where it was shielded in a small wood (78 NX 993814). After only a hundred metres or so, the wooded trackbed suddenly ended at a point where a massive section of embankment had been removed to accommodate an access road and conveyor belt in the quarry workings, with the continuing embankment clearly visible across the broad gap. It was a relatively simple scramble down one side, across the conveyor and up the slope of the severed embankment to regain the overgrown trackbed. A well defined but occasionally overgrown trackbed continued to the site of Amisfield Station (78 NX 998828). We saw no obvious trace of the station but the site was occupied by houses and gardens, which forced us to join the minor road that paralleled the trackbed heading northeast. It was a simple task to rejoin the line in a good, clear cutting (78 NY 001830) by walking across a paddock and dropping down the slope. Although the sun was obscured by cloud, it was warm and very humid as we had some lunch, enjoying the tranquillity of the cutting.

The trackbed at the northern end of the cutting became vague as it traversed some open grazing land with several tricky fences (some electric) to cross before ending at a minor road (78 NY 004834), that also required the negotiation of another awkward fence and hedgerow. After about a hundred metres across an open field, where the line appeared to run an infilled cutting we arrived at the A701(T), where no sign of the bridge remained. It was not until we pushed through the trees by the side of the road that we found the trackbed, running in a boggy, overgrown cutting, complete with a fine redundant overbridge (78 NY 007836). The shady and very wet cutting continued north before opening out into flat and drier grazing land before petering out altogether (78 NY 012843). The original alignment closely followed Amisfield Burn curving due east, and we could see a stout stone overbridge (78 NY 022844) still conveying a minor road over the absent trackbed that made an excellent marker. From the bridge a reasonable trackbed continued across open fields to the small settlement of Shieldhill where we left the line to join the minor road as houses and gardens occupied the trackbed and station site (78 NY 029851).

We rejoined the line in a cutting (78 NY 034853) at the point where the minor road from Shieldhill crossed the line. A walkable trackbed continued running close to the road for about ¾ mile before ending abruptly in a field (78 NY 043850) where a section of embankment had been removed. The continuing overgrown embankment, adorned with hawthorn in blossom, was clearly visible on the other side of the field. This embankment was in turn truncated at the point where the line crossed an access track (78 NY 048848) to a property marked on the map as 'Trailflat'. After another short section across an open field the embankment re-appeared for another 500 metres before ending at a stream (78 NY 053846). The best crossing point over the stream was over the access track to Belzies Farm, and we found the line a few hundred metres east (78 NY 055844) on a clear trackbed.

Prior to the walk I had calculated that we would have walked 1000 miles of dismantled railway line at Lochmaben. We were now less than 2 miles from the point where we would pass that 1000 mile point, and the trackbed was excellent and easily walked to the shores of Mill Loch, and to the minor road overbridge (78 NY 078833) on the edge of the village of Lochmaben. As we approached the unremarkable overbridge, I remember thinking that it was just another overbridge in a field somewhere, like hundreds that we had seen over the last six years. On the approach to the bridge, I had that odd feeling that one gets when nearing the end of a good book; you are desperate to know how things end but at the same time don't want it to end as you have enjoyed the story so much.

We scaled the tatty barbed wire fence that guarded the bridge and shook hands as we stood on what felt like sacred ground. With some relief Chris emptied the half bag of concrete that he had been carrying over the last couple of days and set off to Mill Loch to get some water for the mix. Meanwhile, using my folding spade, I dug a small hole for the 1.5m length of angle iron that I had carried for the last two days; also glad to be rid of the thing that had been intent on trying my patience by getting snagged on so many branches. After bashing the angle iron into the whole we poured in the concrete and tamped it down. Also contained in my rucksack was a commemorative plaque to mark this very special occasion, which was duly stuck onto the angle iron post that was now firmly embedded in the ground. As I write, I wonder if the plaque remains, and whether any reader of this book has seen it, or will go and see it? I would like to know if it is still there. After a few photographs we followed the line into the village of Lochmaben for a marvellous post-1000 mile pint, at 'The Railway Inn' which seemed very appropriate. Although it was gone 4 o'clock on a quiet Sunday afternoon and the kitchen was closed, the landlord very kindly made some delicious club sandwiches for us, which when washed down with a couple of cold lagers that seemed to make all the aches, pains and scars obtained over the last 1000 miles worthwhile.

Feeling rather chuffed with ourselves we left the comfort of The Railway Inn, but we could find no trace of Lochmaben Station (78 NY 082833) as the site was now occupied by houses. From the station site the line was obliterated, and we negotiated the streets of Lochmaben heading for the village's eastern edge where the trackbed had also been built on. The trackbed re-appeared along a field edge just south of Lochmaben (78 NY 086824). We crossed a farm track at the site of an infilled bridge that heralded the start of a badly overgrown cutting (78 NY 087823), that forced us to walk along the top edge. At the end of the cutting the trackbed improved and was walkable to the access road (78 NY 102814) of a large dairy. The line disappeared at the dairy site across the access road, but it was an easy walk round the perimeter fence of the site to the remains of the River Annan Viaduct (78 NY 106815). All that remained of the viaduct were the four sandstone main span supporting pillars and a couple of pillars on the eastern floodplain of the river. It was impossible to ford the river so a lengthy detour via the A709 road bridge was required. Getting from the A709 back to the line was also difficult as a substantial ditch barred the way along the eastern bank of the River Annan. We crossed this obstacle on a bridge at just north of Shillahill Farm (78 NY 111810) to access the embanked line about 500m further north. The embankment was clear and provided good walking to a point where the line disappeared into a field (78 NY 123816) just west of Lockerbie. From this point the line was infilled and obliterated by the A74(M) and other developments in Lockerbie itself. After crossing the motorway on the minor road bridge we took the streets of Lockbie to the station for the train back to Carlisle.

*The neglected station building at Moniaive (78 NX 779907) is now just part of a farm yard.*

*The Cairn Valley Railway offers some superb walking on a clear track-bed.*

*Cairn Water Viaduct (78 NX 856836) is the most substantial structure on The Cairn Valley Railway, and although overgrown remains in good condition.*

*The remains of the River Annan Viaduct (78 NY 106815) on The Dumfries, Lochmaben & Lockerbie Railway.*

*Chris Harrison and The Author celebrate walking 1000 miles of dismantled railway. The commemorative plaque was placed under an overbridge (78 NY 078833) on the edge of the village of Lochmaben, Dumfries & Galloway.* (photo by Chris Harrison)

# SECTION 3

# FURTHER READING AND REFERENCES

**Books About Walking Dismantled Railways:**

A Walk Along The Tracks, Hunter Davies, ISBN 0-297-78042-5
Border Railway Rambles, Alasdair Wham, ISBN 1 84033 289 1
Discovering Britain's Lost Railways, Paul Atterbury,
ISBN 0-7495-1045-5
Discovering Lost Railways, F.G. Cockman, ISBN 0-85263-325-4
Edinburgh And Lothians, Exploring The Lost Railways, Alasdair Wham,
ISBN 978-1-872350141
Lost Railway Lines South of Glasgow, Alasdair Wham,
ISBN 1 872350 089
Railway Paths in County Durham (set of leaflets), Durham County
Council Tel. (0131) 383 4144
Railway Walks: Exploring Disused Railways, Gareth Lovett Jones,
ISBN 0-7153-8543-7
Railway Walks GWR & SR, Jeff Vinter, ISBN 0-86299-578-7
Railway Walks LMS, Jeff Vinter, ISBN 0-86299-734-8
Railway Walks LNER, Jeff Vinter, ISBN 0-86299-732-1
Railway Walks Wales, Jeff Vinter, ISBN 0-7509-0141-1
Scottish Railway Walks, M.H. Ellison, ISBN 1-85284-007-2
The Lost Railway Lines of Ayrshire, Alasdair Wham,
ISBN 1 872350 27 5
The Lost Railway Lines of Galloway, Alasdair Wham,
ISBN 1 872350 96 8
Walking The Disused Railways of Sussex, David Bathhurst,
ISBN 1-85770-292-1
Walking Northern Railways, Volume One: East, Charlie Emett,
ISBN 0902-363-76-X
Walking Northern Railways, Volume Two: West, Charlie Emett,
ISBN 1-85284-006-4
Walking Old Railways, Christopher Somerville, ISBN 0-7153-7681-0
Walking West Country Railways, Christopher Somerville,
ISBN 0-7153-8143-1
Walking The Line, Anthony Burton, ISBN 0-7137-1554-5

**Books About Dismantled Railways:**

Lost Lines, Birmingham & The Black Country, Nigel Welbourn, ISBN 0711028443
Lost Lines, Eastern, Nigel Welbourn, ISBN 0-7110-2383-2
Lost Lines, LMR, Nigel Welbourn, ISBN 0-7110-2277-1
Lost Lines, London, Nigel Welbourn, ISBN 0-7110-2623-8
Lost Lines, North Eastern, Nigel Welbourn, ISBN 0-7110-2522-3
Lost Lines, Southern, Nigel Welbourn, ISBN 0-7110-2458-8
Lost Lines, Scotland, Nigel Welbourn, ISBN 0-7110-2276-3
Lost Lines, Wales, Nigel Welbourn, ISBN 0-7110-2921-0
Lost Lines, Western, Nigel Welbourn, ISBN 0-7110-2278-X
Lost Lines, Muriel V. Searle, ISBN 0 904568 41 5
The Great Central, Then and Now, Mac Hawkins,
No ISBN (David & Charles)
LSWR, Then and Now, Mac Hawkins, ISBN 1-84013-322-8
The Somerset & Dorset, Then and Now, Mac Hawkins,
ISBN 0-85059-797-8
LNER Branch Lines, C. J. Gammell, ISBN 0-86093-509-4
Scottish Branch Lines 1955-1965, C. J. Gammell,
ISBN 0-86093-005-X
Waverley, Portrait of a Famous Route, Roger Siviter,
ISBN 1-870875-38-7
On The Waverley Route, Robert Robotham, ISBN 0-7110-2414-6
The Waverley Route, The Postwar Years, Robert Robotham,
ISBN 0-7110-2674-2
Border Country Branch Line Album, Neil Caplan,
ISBN 0-7110-1086-2
On Somerset & Dorset Lines, Robert Robotham, ISBN 0-7110-2413-8
The Somerset & Dorset Railway, Robin Atthill, ISBN 330-02478-7
The Somerset & Dorset Railway, D. S. Barrie and C. R. Clinker, No ISBN (The Oakwood Press)
The Wick and Lybster Light Railway, Iain Sutherland,
No ISBN (Iain Sutherland 18 Smith Terrace, Wick, KW1 5HD)
Dumfries & Galloway's Lost Railways, Gordon Stansfield,
ISBN 1-84033-057-0
Lost railways of The Lothians, Gordon Stansfield,
ISBN 1-84033-270-0
Lanarkshire's Lost Railways, Gordon Stansfield, ISBN 1-872074-96-0

The Lost Railways of The Scottish Borders, Gordon Stansfield,
ISBN 1-84033-084-8

Lost Railways of North & East Yorkshire, Gordon Suggett,
ISBN 1-85306-918-3

Forgotten Railways, H.P.White, ISBN 0-946537-13-5 (Parent volume
to the Forgotten Railways series)

Forgotten Railways Volume 1: North-East England, K.Hoole,
ISBN 0-7153-5894-4

Forgotten Railways Volume 2: East Midlands, P. Howard Anderson,
ISBN 0-7153-0694-9

Forgotten Railways Volume 3: Chilterns and Cotswolds, R. Davies &
M.D. Grant, ISBN 0-946537-07-0

Forgotten Railways Volume 4: North and Mid Wales, Rex Christiansen,
ISBN 0-7153-7059-6

Forgotten Railways Volume 5: Scotland, John Thomas,
ISBN 0-7153-8193-8

Forgotten Railways Volume 6: South East England, H. P. White,
ISBN 0-946537-37-2

Forgotten Railways Volume 7: East Anglia, R. S. Joby,
ISBN 0-946537-26-7

Forgotten Railways Volume 8: South Wales, J. H. R. Page,
ISBN 0-7153-7734-5

Forgotten Railways Volume 9: North West England, John Marshall,
ISBN 0-7153-8003-6

Forgotten Railways Volume 10: West Midlands, Rex Christiansen,
ISBN 0-946537-01-1

Forgotten Railways Volume 11: Severn Valley and Welsh Borders,
ISBN 0-946537-43-7

Riccarton Junction; Just a Few Lines by Christopher 'Kit' Milligan,
No ISBN (Avaliable from The Waverley Route Heritage Association,
see internet resources)

## Atlases and Other Reference Books:

British Railways Pre-Grouping Atlas and Gazetteer, Ian Allan Publishing, ISBN 0-7110-0320-3 *(See PGAG references in the Walks Summary section of each walk)*
The Railways of Great Britain, A Historical Atlas Volume 1, Col. M. H. Cobb, ISBN 07110-3002-2
The Railways of Great Britain, A Historical Atlas Volume 2, Col. M. H. Cobb, ISBN 07110-3003-0
Passenger No More, Gerald Daniels & L. A. Dench, ISBN 0-7110-0438-2
Sectional Maps of The British Railways as at December 1947, ISBN 0-7110-1156-7
Railways in the British Isles, Landscape, land use and society, David Turnock, ISBN 0-7136-2281-4
The Reshaping of British Railways, Part 1: report, Part 2: Maps, HMSO, S. O. Code No. 88-832
The Great Railway Conspiracy, David Henshaw, ISBN 0-948135-30-1
Bradshaw's 1922 Railway Guide, No ISBN (Reprints from Guild Publishing/David & Charles)

## Dismantled Railway Websites:

The Railway Ramblers: www.railwayramblers.org.uk
Disused Railways: www.disused-rlys.fotopic.net/
Forgotten Relics of an Enterprising Age: www.forgottenrelics.co.uk/index.html
Railscot: www.railscot.co.uk/
Railway Junction Diagrams: http://web.ukonline.co.uk/Members/cj.tolley/rjd/rjd-intro.htm
Railway Station database: http://www.mulehouse.demon.co.uk/stations/links.htm
Railway Walks: http://www.railwaywalks.co.uk/
The Somerset & Dorset Railway Trust: http://www.sdrt.org.uk/
The Somerset & Dorset After Closure: http://www.nevard.com/sdjr/
The Two Tunnels Greenway (S&DJR campaign group): http://www.twotunnels.org.uk/
The Waverley Route Heritage Association: http://www.wrha.org.uk/

Disused Stations: http://www.disused-stations.org.uk/
Photographs of Pre-Grouping Railways:
http://pre-grouping.fotopic.net/
Northumbrian Railways: http://www.northumbrian-railways.co.uk/
The Northern Viaduct Trust: http://www.nvt.org.uk/
The Great Northern Rail Trail: http://www.thegreatnortherntrail.co.uk/
Britains Lost Railways Group:
http://finance.groups.yahoo.com/group/Britains_Lost_Railways/
British Railways Board: http://www.brb.gov.uk/home
The Railways Archive: http://www.railwaysarchive.co.uk/
The Scottish Outdoor Access Code: www.outdooraccess-scotland.com
The UK Railway & Canal Tunnel Database and Bridges & Viaducts
Database: www.pullman-publications.co.uk
A few pictures from our walks:
http://www.industrialghosts.co.uk/index.html


**Public Transport Websites:**

National Rail Enquiries: http://www.nationalrail.co.uk/
Chester-le-Track: http://www.nationalrail.com/
Transport Direct:
http://www.transportdirect.info/TransportDirect/en/Home.aspx
Traveline Scotland: http://www.travelinescotland.com/default.jsp
Traveline: http://www.traveline.org.uk/index.htm


**Miscellaneous Websites:**

Campaign for Real Ale: http://www.camra.org.uk/
The Ordnance Survey: http://www.ordnancesurvey.co.uk/oswebsite/
The Meteorological Office: http://www.metoffice.gov.uk/
Old Ordnance Maps: http://www.ponies.me.uk/maps/osmap.html
Old Ordnance Maps: http://www.npemap.org.uk/
The Mountain Bothies Association: http://www.mountainbothies.org.uk/index.php
The League Against Cruel Sports: http://www.league.org.uk/index.asp